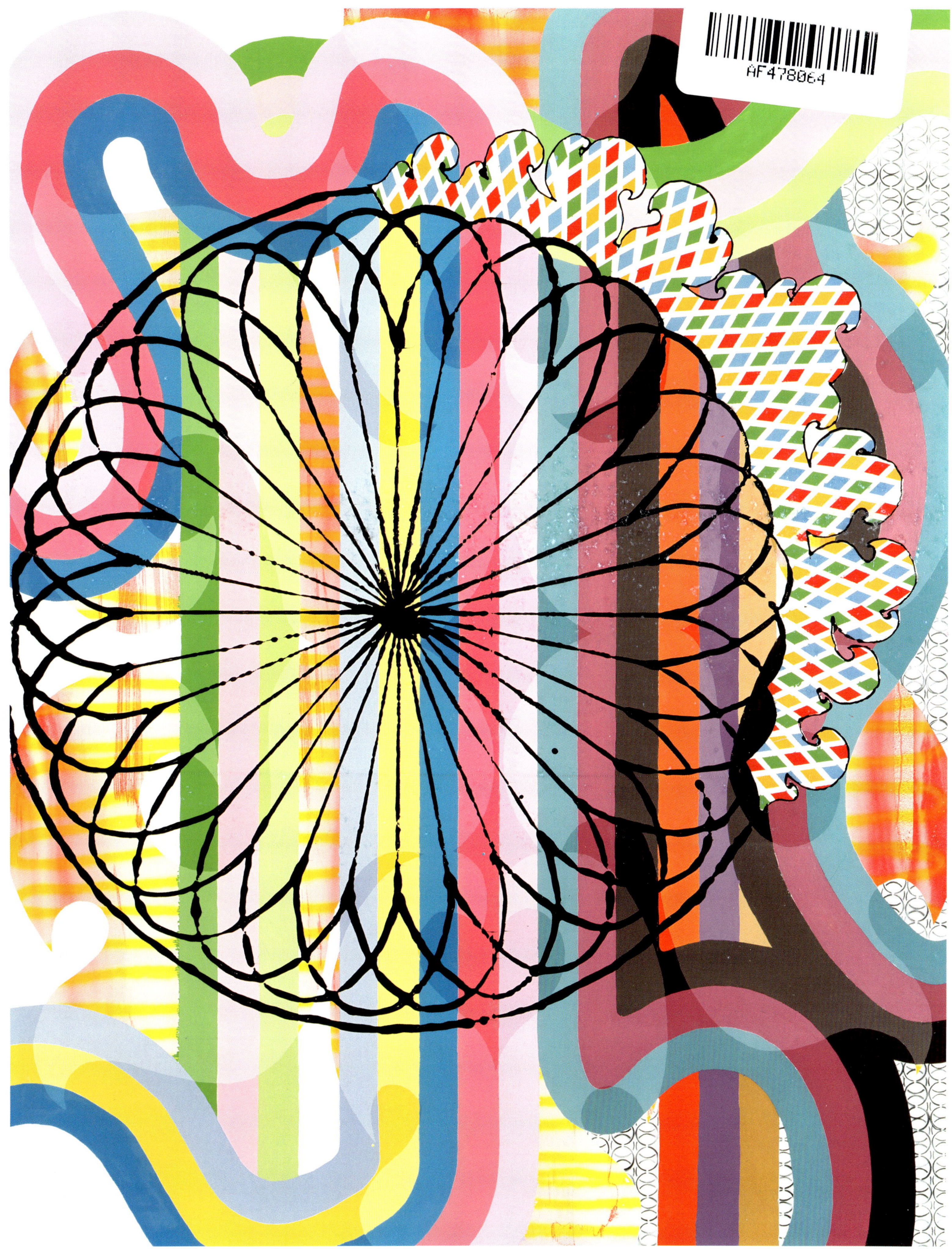

Feuerrad

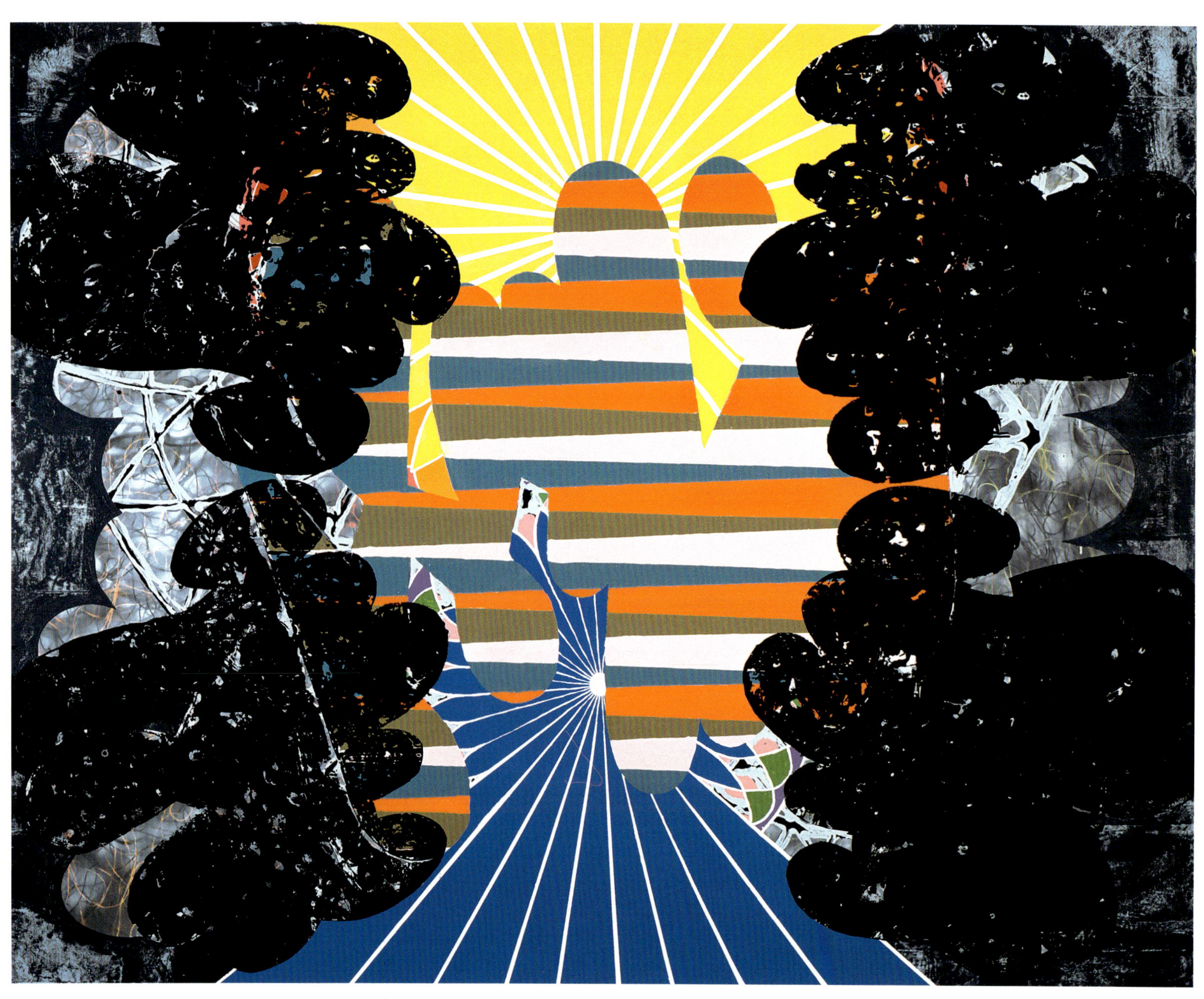

Radar

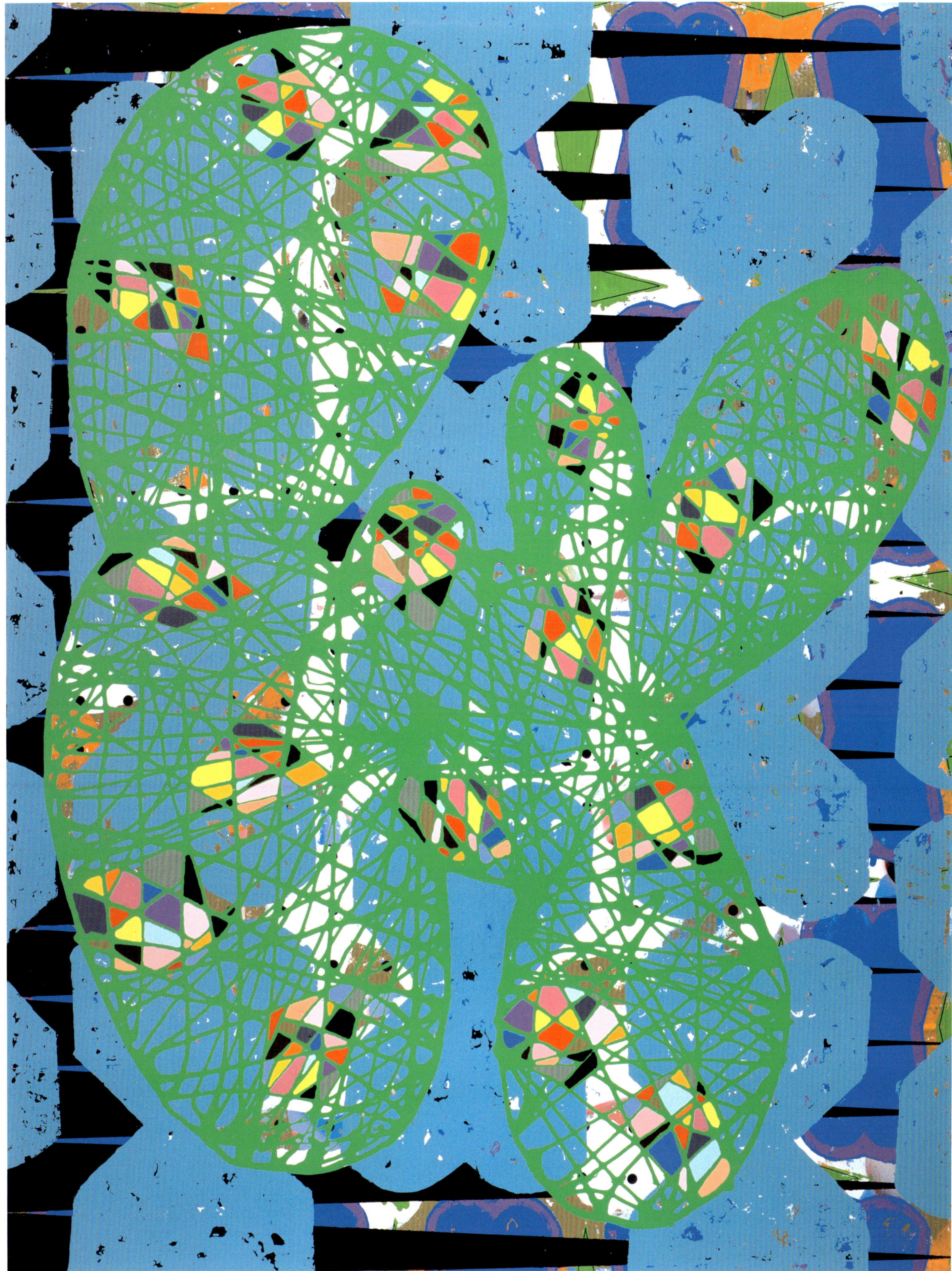

Matrix

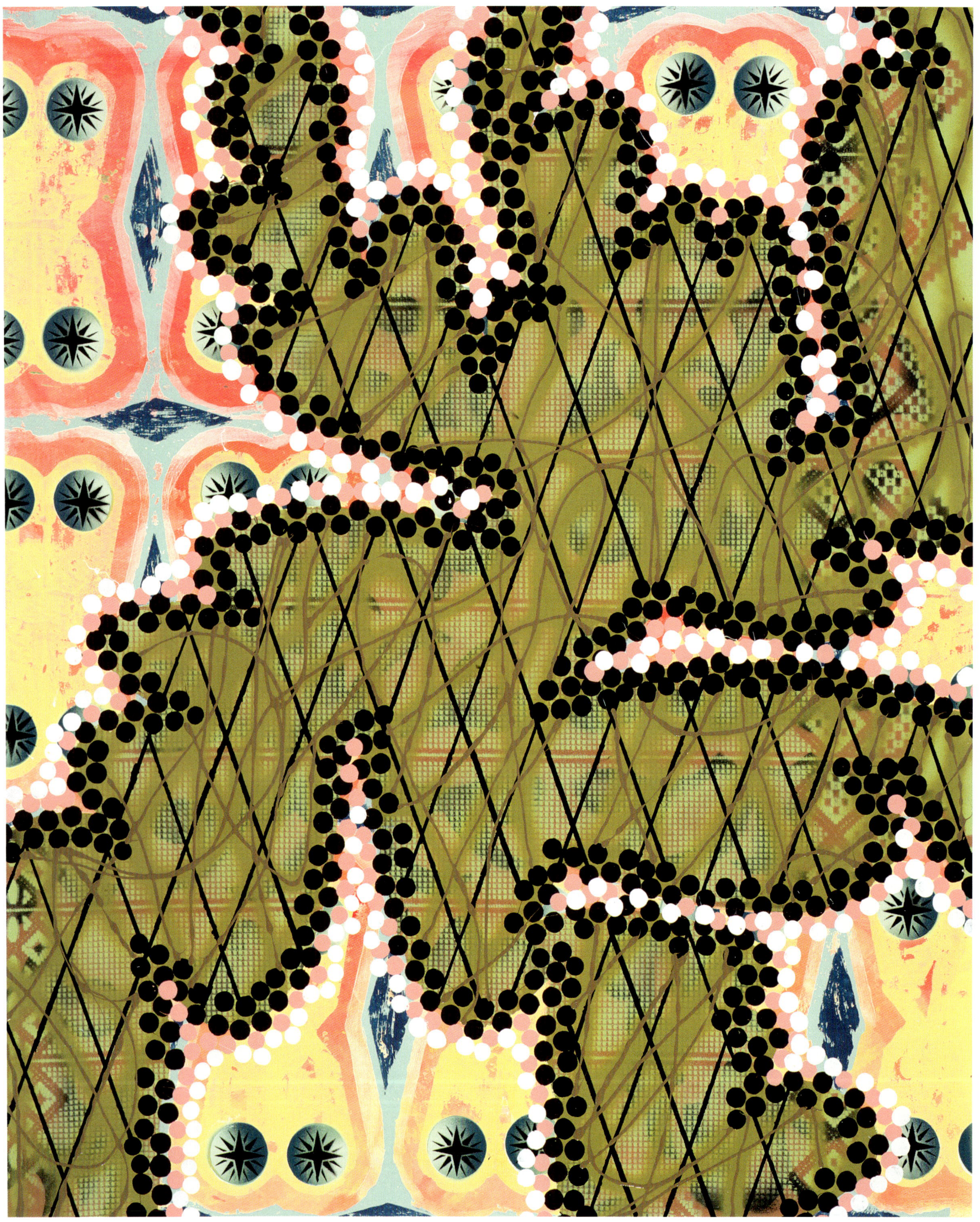

snoop

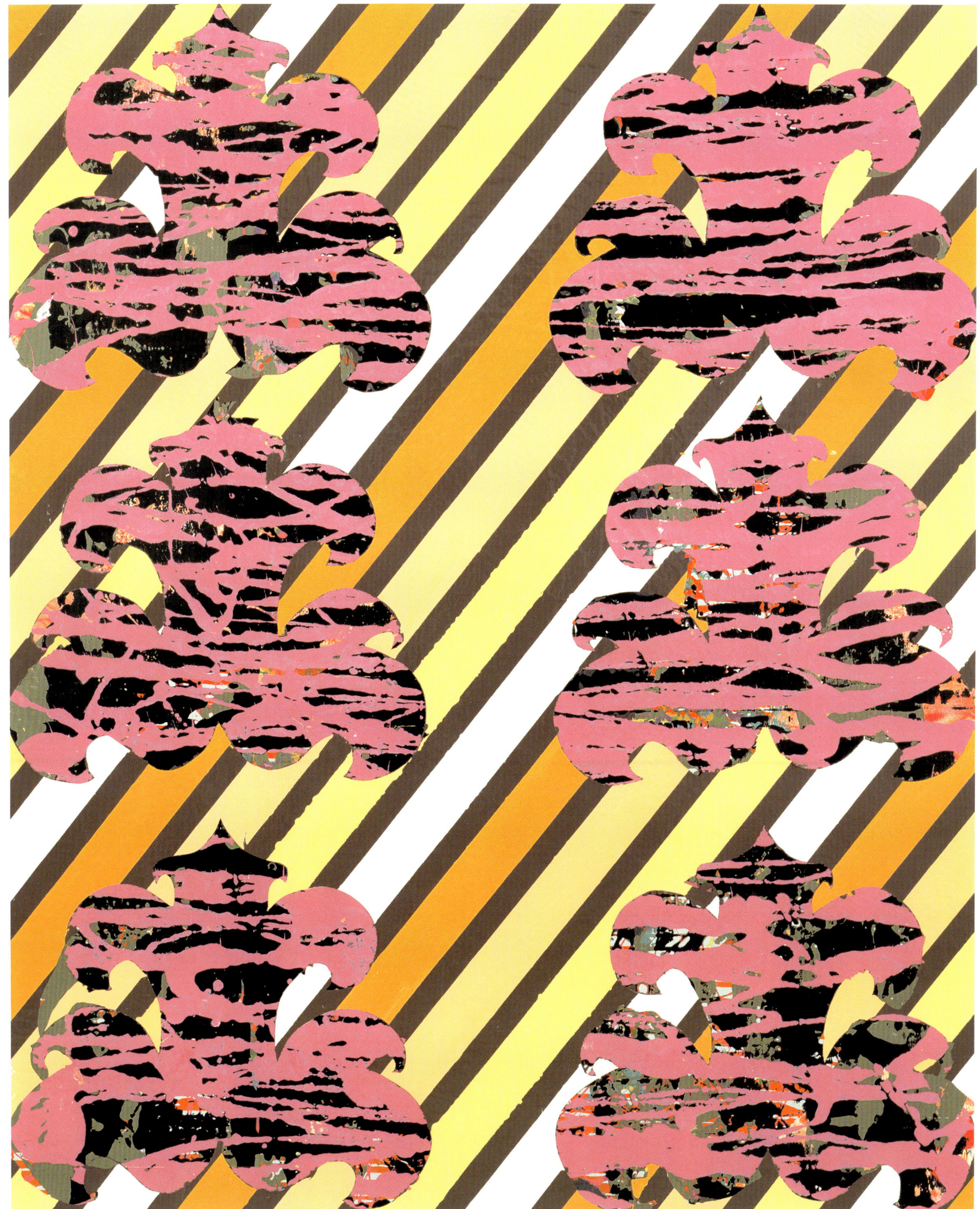

Triumph

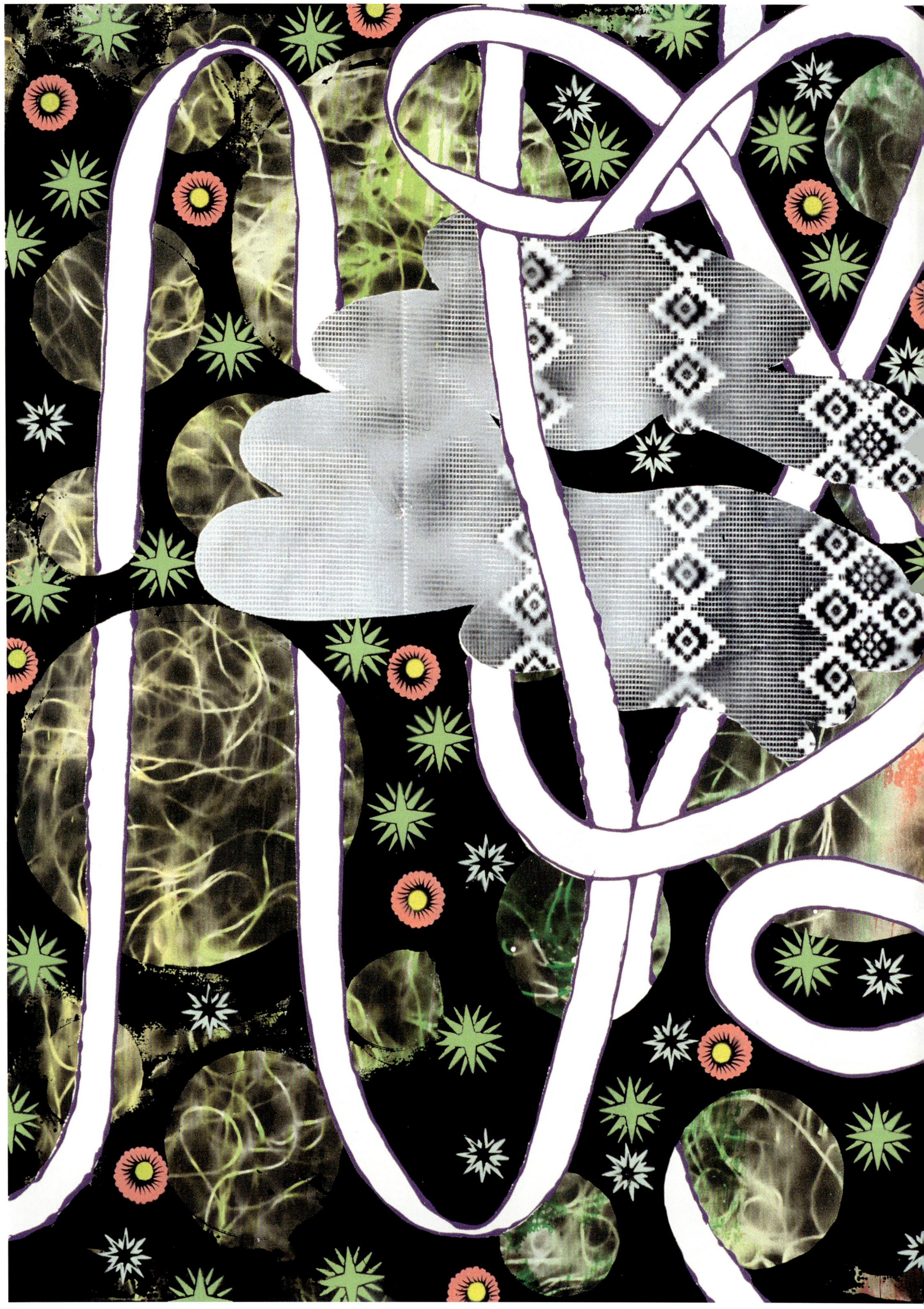

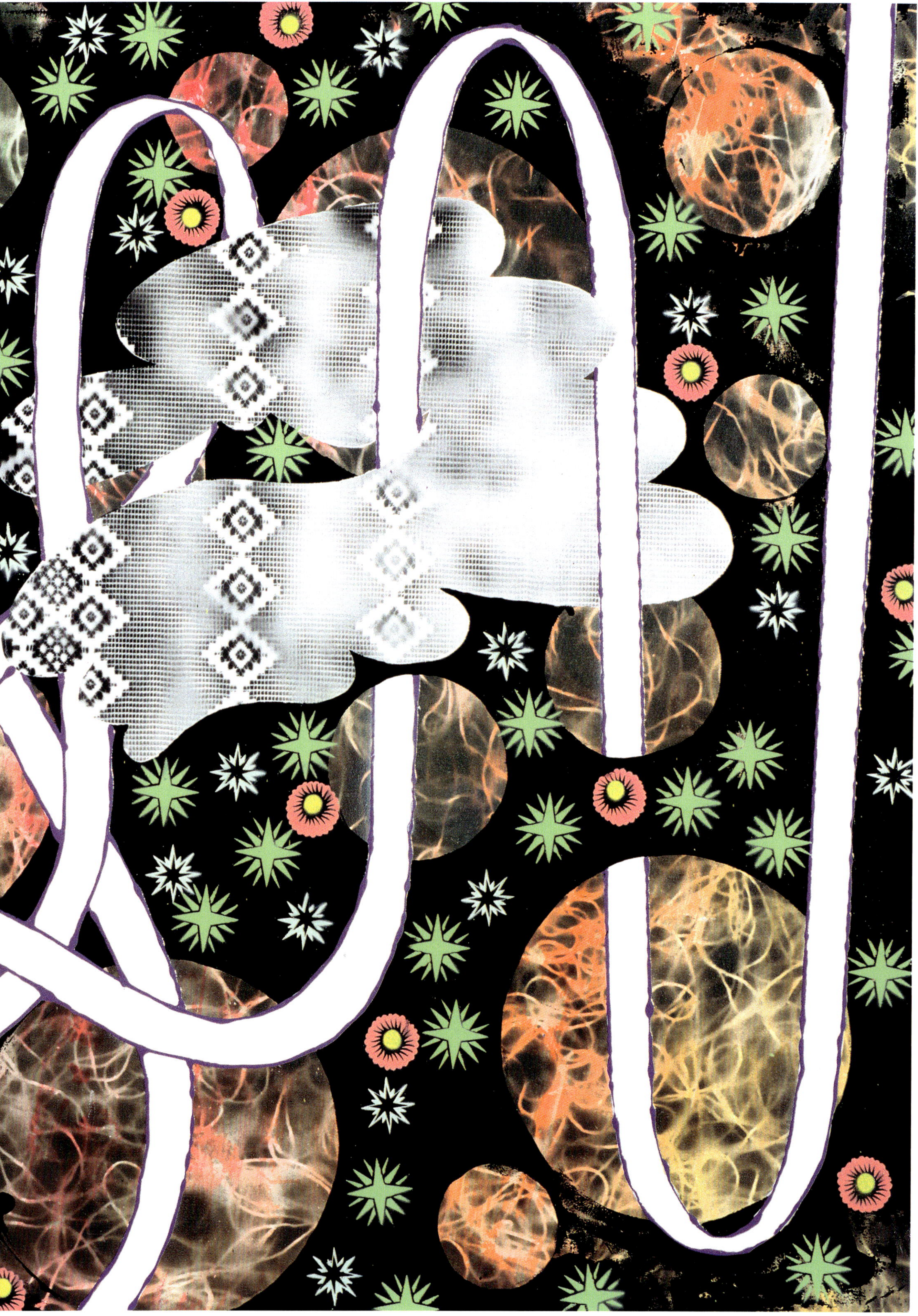

Vergissmeinnicht

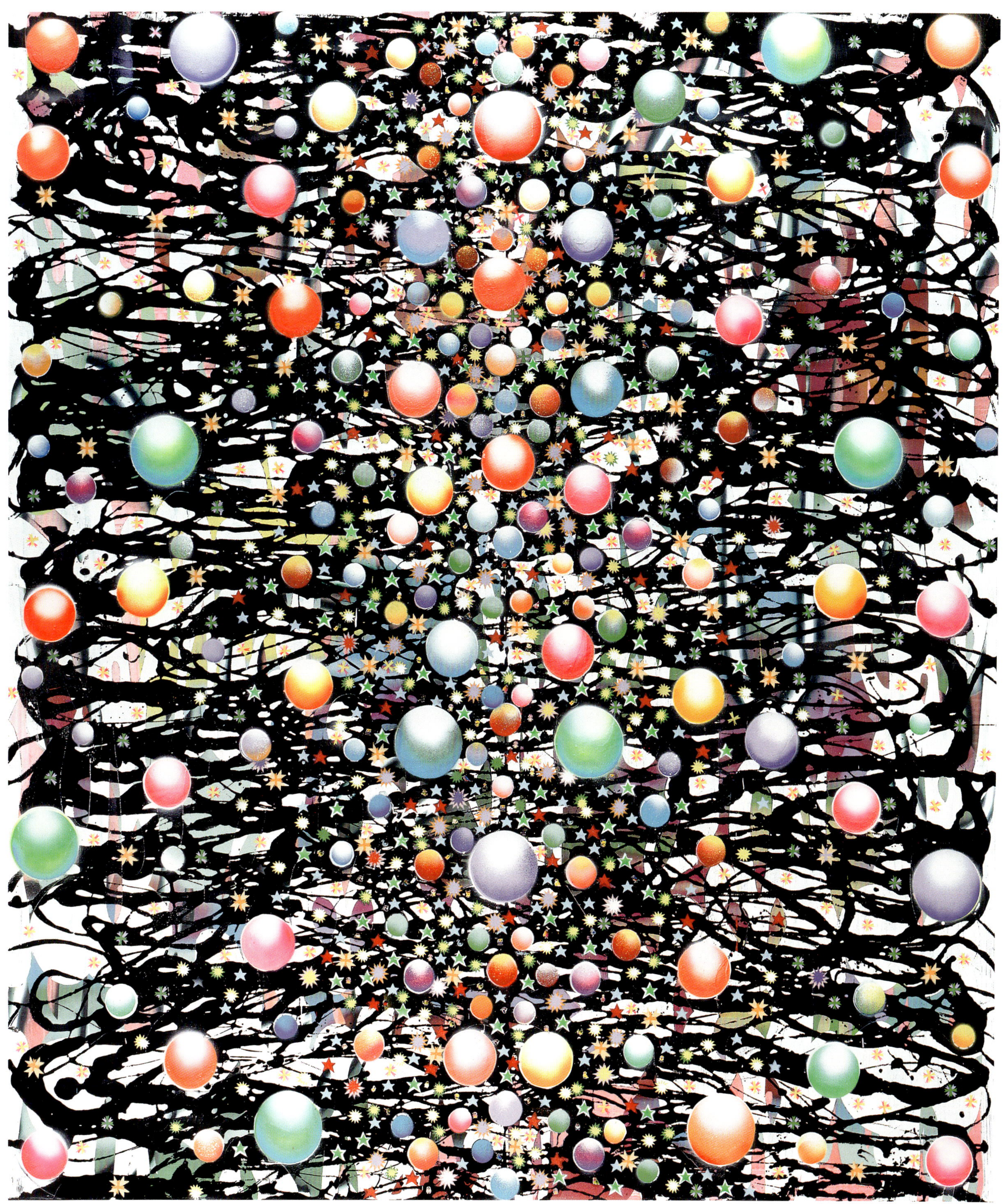

100 aspects of the moon

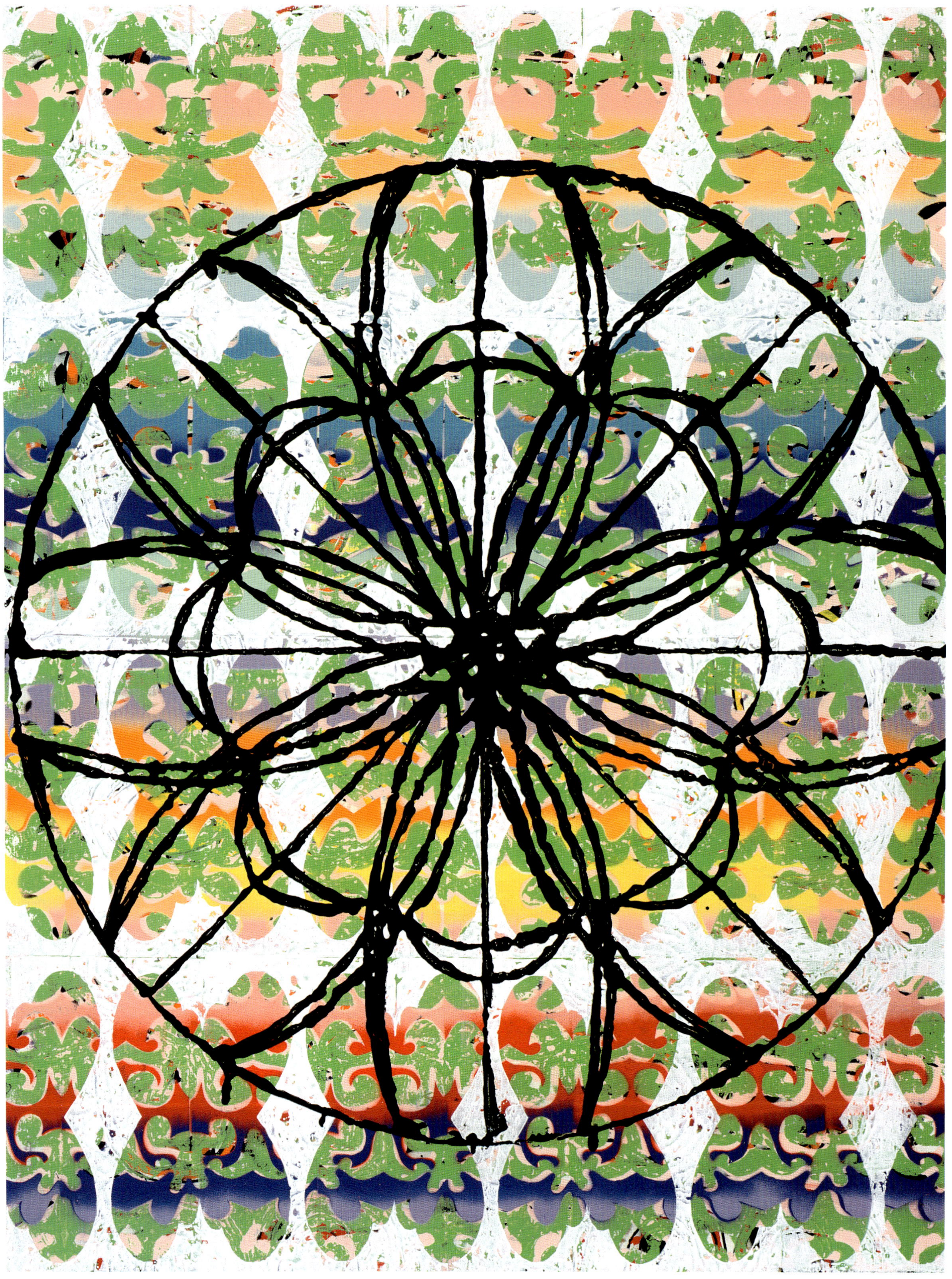

Mandala

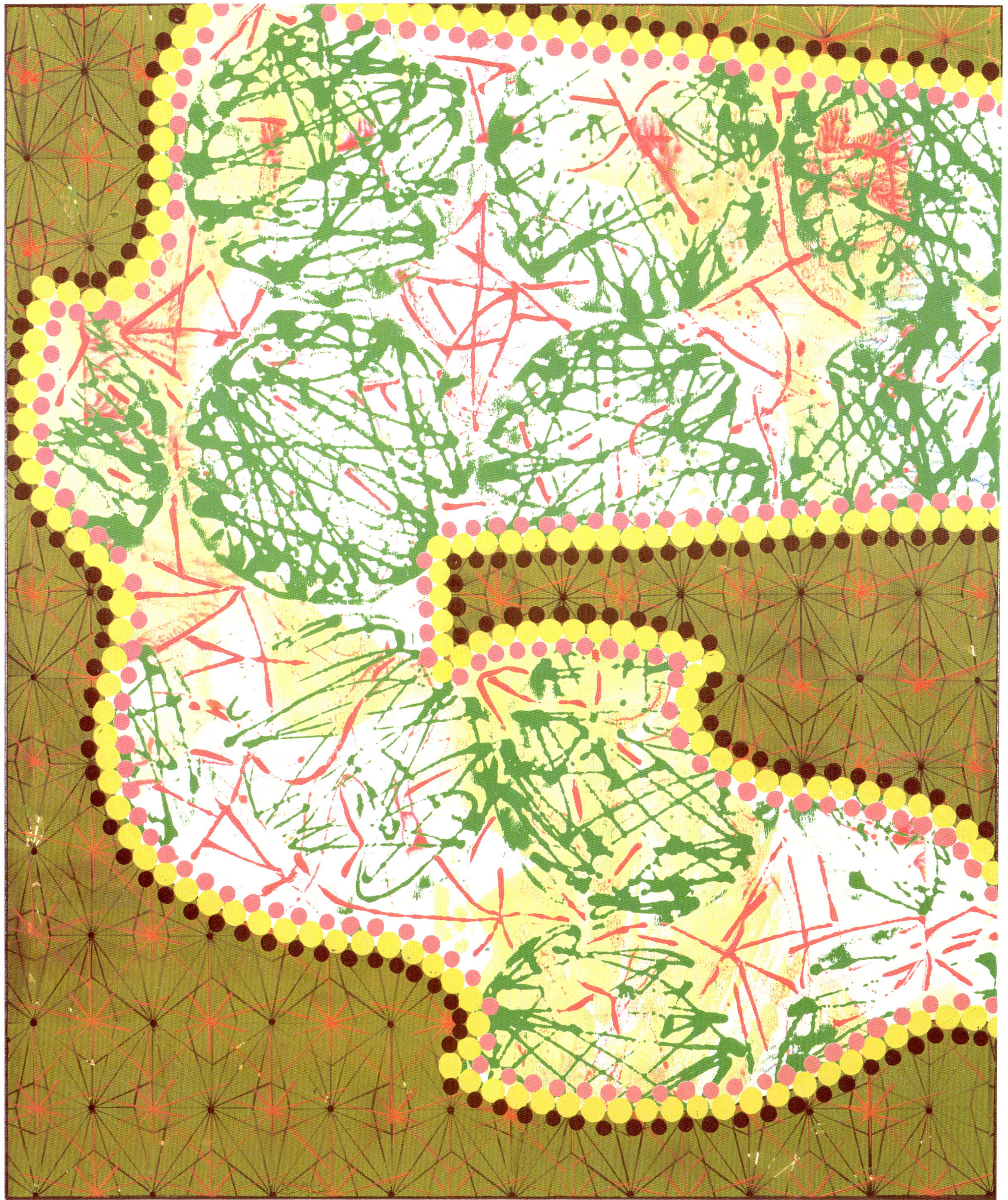

heaveninside

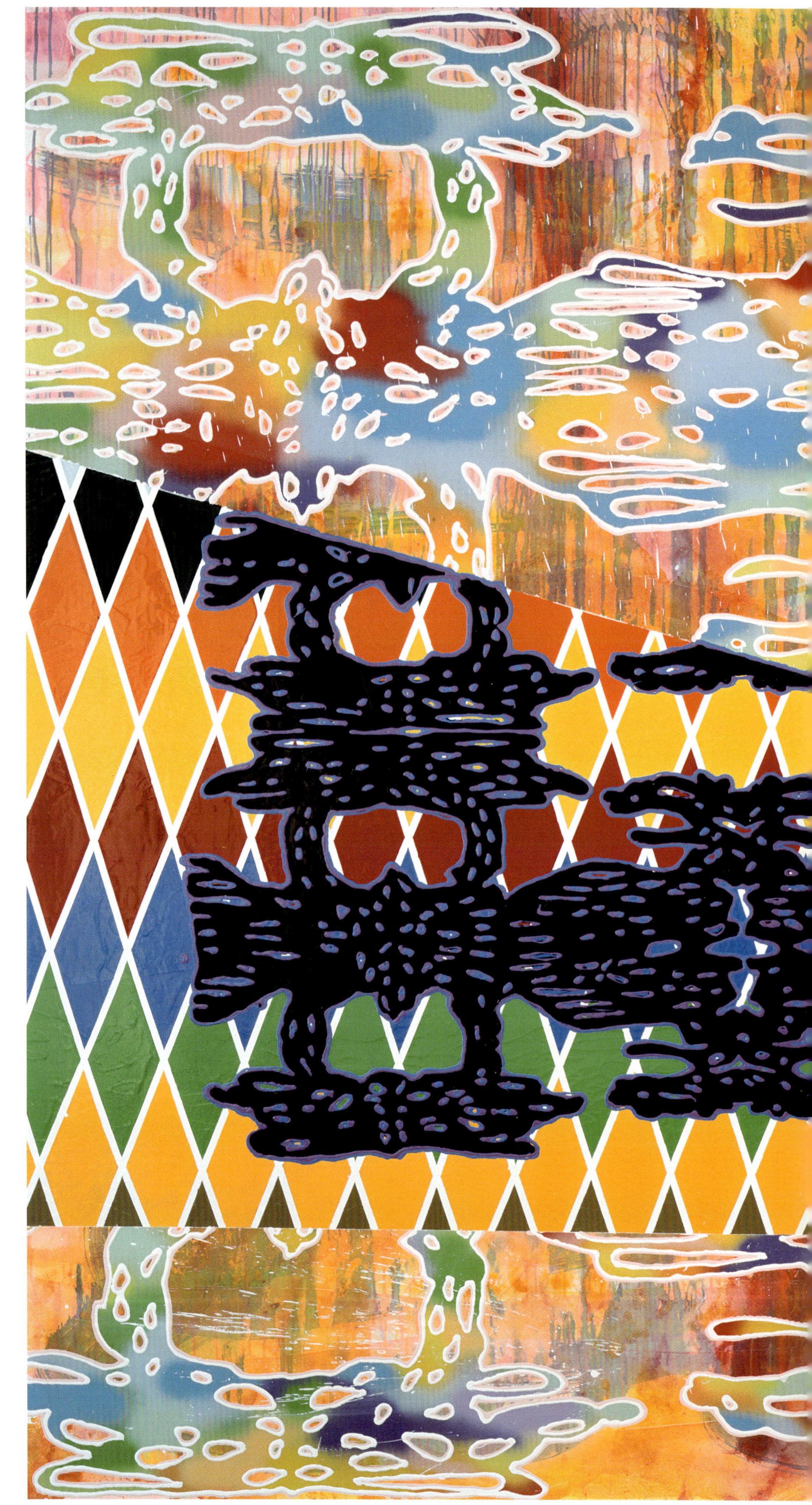

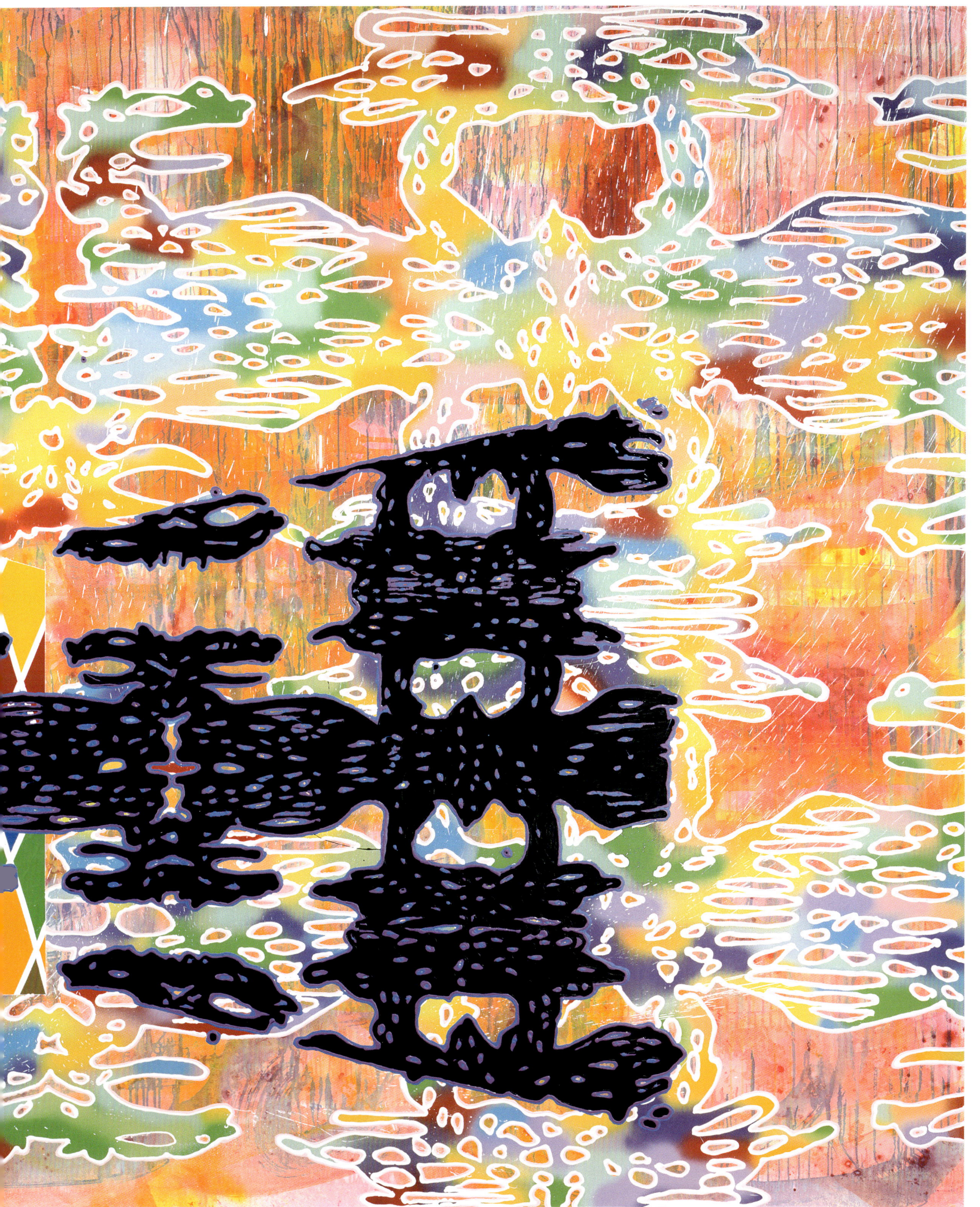

Sumo

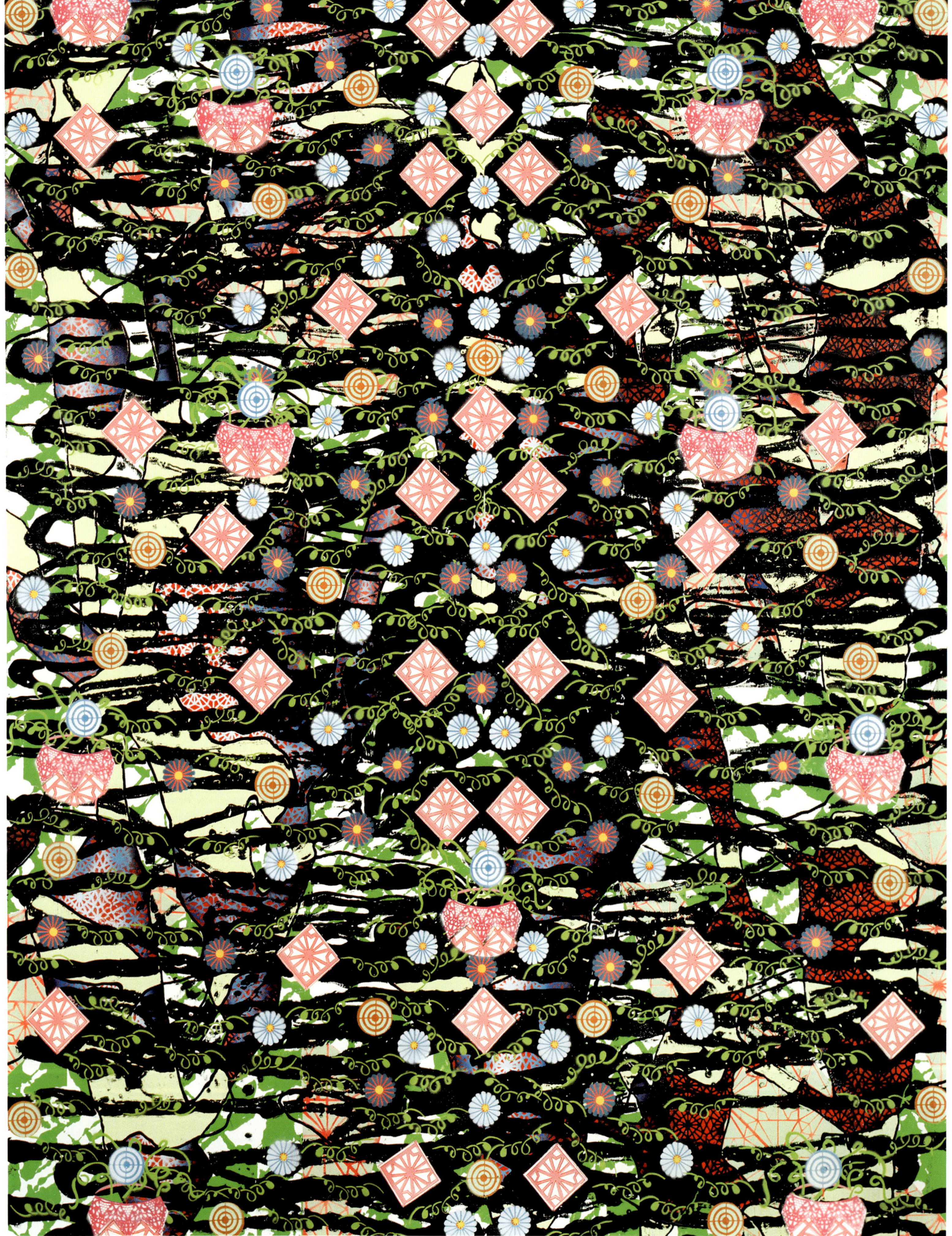

Wucher

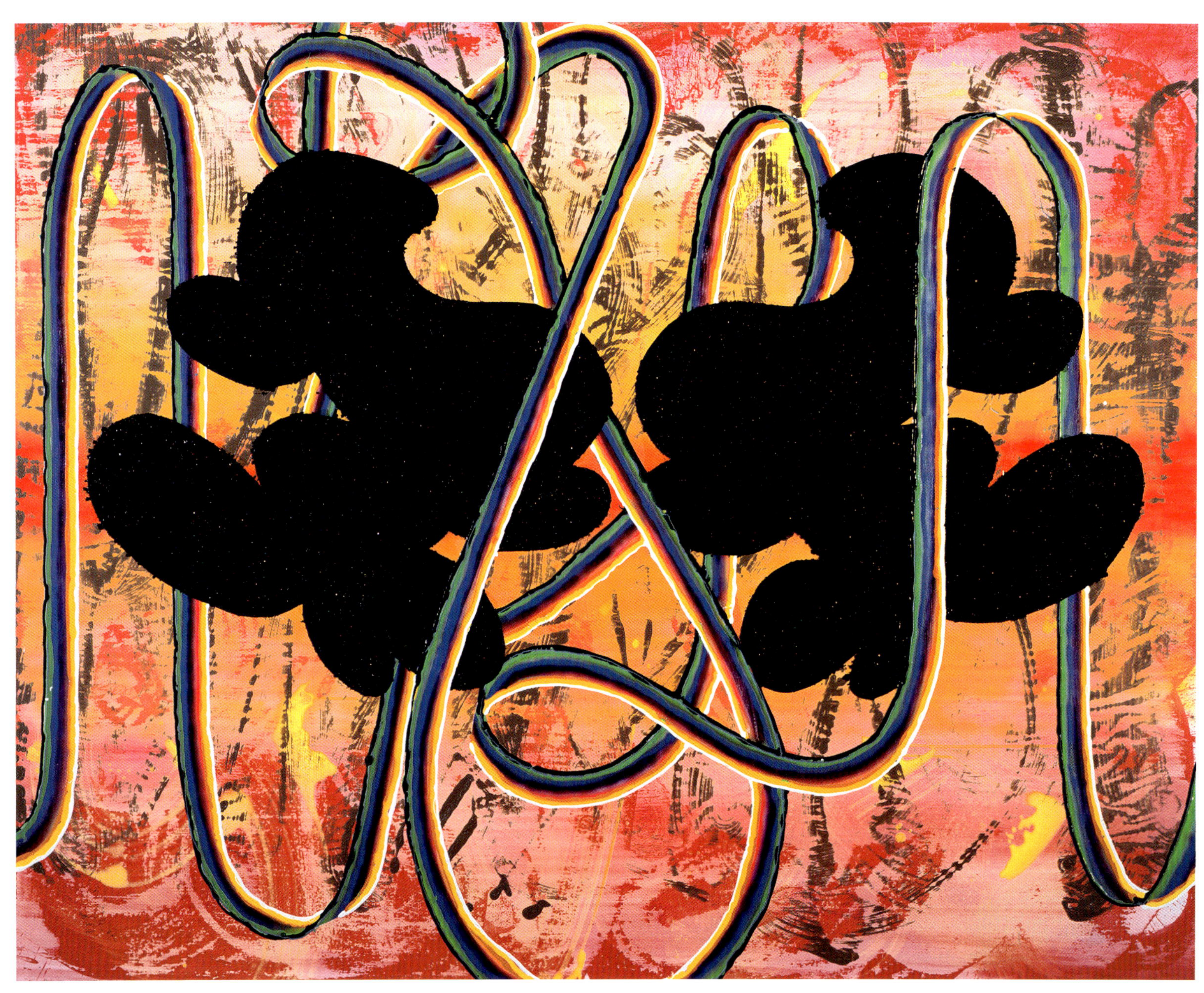

toptop

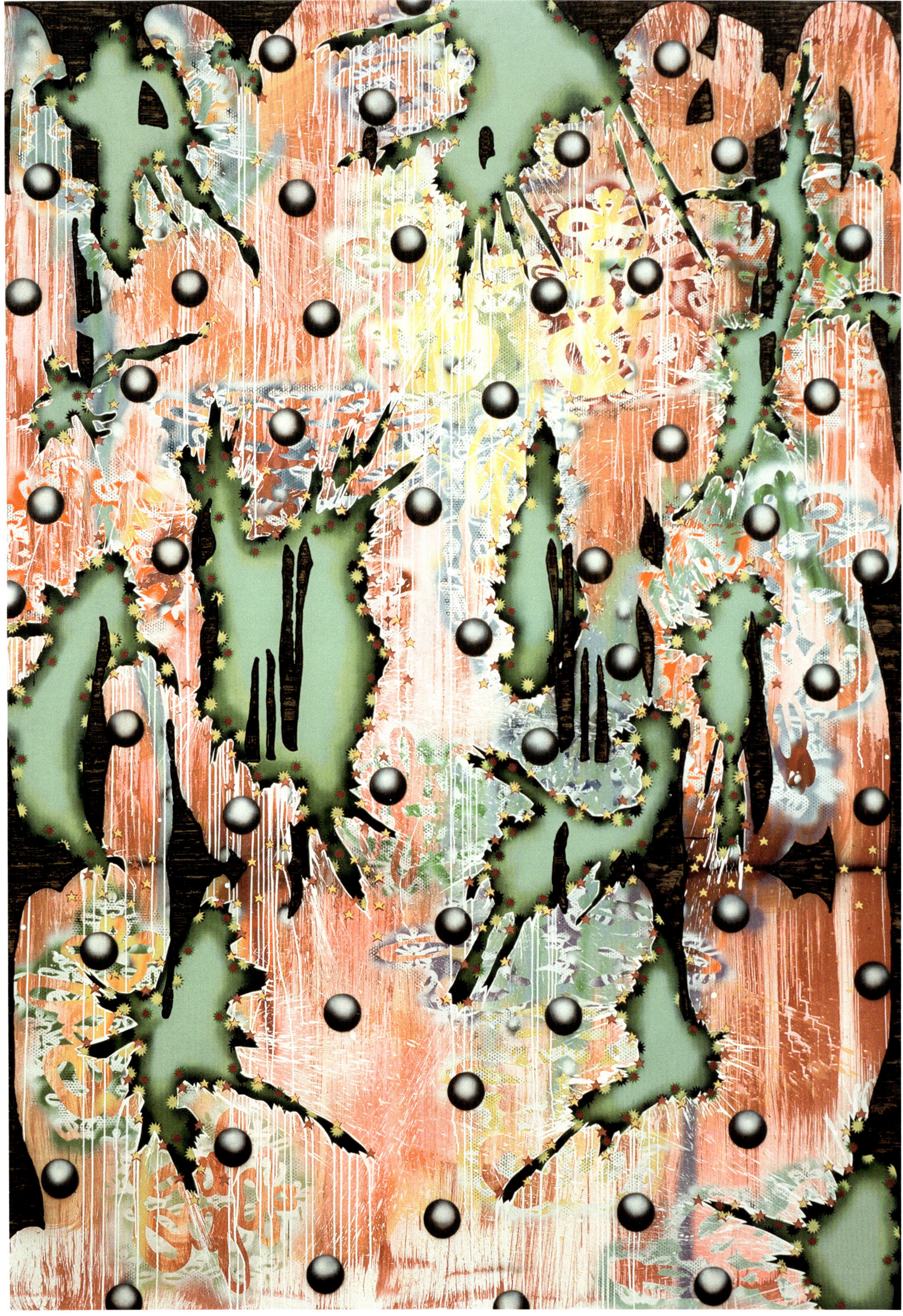

Jackpot

Christine Streuli
bumblebeee

Verlag für moderne Kunst Nürnberg

Isabel Zürcher

Wer hat Angst vor der Malerei?

Malerei ist Spektakel, ist Sensation. Bunt und vielschichtig, experimentierfreudig und in grossen Formaten pocht Christine Streuli auf die »Power« ihres Mediums. Ihre Arbeit beruht auf der Verfügbarkeit von Bildern in einer Gegenwart, die visuelle Anregung in grosser Beschleunigung zu verschiedensten Zwecken und mit verschiedensten Mitteln in die Welt stülpt. Unaufhaltsam treibt die Künstlerin die Überflutung der Augenreize auf die Spitze. Sie sucht die extreme Künstlichkeit und lässt Formen und Farben unvermittelt aufeinandertreffen. Sie meidet besänftigende Übergänge und erzeugt gerade darin eine verblüffende Opulenz: Der Erlebnisraum der Malerei entsteht in einem Neben- und Übereinander, ohne dass die einzelnen Ebenen unter sich eine Verständigung suchen. Ebenso in Zeichnung, im Gross- und im Kleinformat beheimatet, setzte Christine Streuli anlässlich ihrer Ausstellung im Kunstraum Kreuzlingen 2005 zu einer raumfüllenden Inszenierung an: Malerische Sensationen nehmen kein Ende mehr an der Grenze mittelformatiger Leinwände. Folgerichtig greifen sie aus in den Raum, denn Malerei ist nicht aufzuhalten: Unersättlich nimmt sie Muster, Raster, Kugeln, Kleckse und deren Spiegelungen in sich auf, mutet denselben Oberflächen händische Pinselspuren wie synthetische Glanzeffekte zu, um sich gleich wieder dem harmlosen Spiel hinzugeben. *Ich lieb Dich, ich lieb Dich nicht…* ist nur einer von vielen Titeln, die die visuelle Herausforderung mit einem beiläufigen Hinweis auf eine ausserbildliche Wirklichkeit beantworten.

New York, Kairo, Beinwil (CH), zuletzt San Francisco waren nebst Zürich Stationen von Christine Streulis Werdegang. Sesshaftigkeit ist nicht ihre Sache. Mehrere Auslandsaufenthalte trugen ihr in den letzten Jahren neue Perspektiven zu. Ihre Arbeit speist sich aus dem Zustand des Unterwegsseins und aus der Erfahrung, dass überall gleichzeitig Bilder oder deren Teile zitierbar sind. Die Energie, die jeder Neubeginn freisetzt, führt Streuli kompromisslos ihrer Arbeit zu, wobei das Atelier zur jeweils temporären Heimat wird. Jeder Ort könne für sie Atelier sein, überall biete sich dieses an, um die grosse Welt auf die kleine treffen zu lassen und beide modellhaft miteinander zu vermengen. Ob dunkle Kammer, Garage, Wohnzimmer oder Fabrikhalle, immer stelle das Atelier Material bereit, das bewegt und eingesetzt werden will: »So empfinde ich jedenfalls, wenn ich Farbtuben, Papier, Karton, Spraydosen, Holz oder Sonstiges um mich herumstehen sehe: Alles schreit nach Einsatz, nach Aktion oder Reaktion, nach Bewegung.«

In Anlehnung an die Ikonografie barocker Stillleben oder an historische Arabesken in Grafik und Architektur bedient sich Streuli eines Vokabulars, das ihr die Überlieferung zuspielt. Ohne Berührungsangst orchestriert sie es neu. Die eindringliche Präsenz von Gegenständen im Stillleben des 17. Jahrhunderts wird in künstlicher Farbigkeit mit Lack frisch aufgemischt, geht auf in unverfrorener Lust an der Sinnlichkeit fliessender Farbe. Die Kombinatorik von Mustern und ihrer Spiegelung, von ornamentalen Details und ihrer Vervielfachung kokettiert mit Teppich und Tapete oder sucht die Nähe zum Rapport im Stoffdruck: Aus der Erinnerung und in einem Abdruck-Verfahren gelangte zum Beispiel in *Falter* (2005) die Struktur eines Afro-Stoffs auf die Leinwand, ein oval umrissenes Blumenmotiv gerinnt in *wing* (2004) zum sperrigen Muster. »Ich mag die totale Klarheit, die Unübersichtlichkeit und Aufgeregtheit evoziert.« Klarheit als Stimulator von Unruhe, Übersicht als Erzeuger von Irritation? – Es ist der Widerspruch, an dem sich Streulis Malerei immer wieder neu entzündet, ihr vielleicht wichtigstes Prinzip. Laufend sind Erwartungen infrage gestellt, das Wissen um Gesetzmässigkeiten einer Figur, eines Gegenstands wird konkurrenziert durch die Autonomie des Mediums. So widersetzen sich die manuell aufgetragenen Farbschichten der Ästhetik digitaler Gleichförmigkeit. Indirekt oder beiläufig hinterlässt auch das nüchterne Zitat auf Bildoberflächen die Spuren von handschriftlicher Bewegung. *Hinterlässt Spuren*, so ein Titel von 2005, scheint einer solchen Beobachtung recht zu geben, doch gerade da nimmt sich dann die Malerei als »écriture« wieder ganz zurück. Regelmässig erweist sich auch das Vertrauen in die Konsistenz eines Details als haltlos: Spiegelung oder Abdruck stellen es als Zeugnis indirekter Wirklichkeit bloss, eine nächste Schicht bindet die räumlich gelesenen Indizien an die Fläche zurück. Auch das ist Malerei: Alles Fake, alles Täuschung und Trompe-l'Œil, alles Glamour pur.

Warum hält Streuli an der Kunst der Verführung fest? – »Mich interessiert der Moment, wo bei uns allen ein Stern oder auch nur ein farbiger Punkt eine riesige Geschichte zu erzählen beginnt. Die Schnittstelle, wo zum Beispiel Rot als Farbe zum Inhalt wird, wo unsere Assoziationen herkommen oder erwachen.«[1] Streulis Arbeit ist ein Zeugnis eher dafür, wie stark Malerei mit Assoziationen rechnen kann. Der Abdruck einer schwarzen Rosette ebnet den Weg zur Kathedrale des Mittelalters, zum Mandala auch, matt schimmernde Bälle in synthetischer Farbigkeit rufen Modelle aus Chemielehrbüchern in Erinnerung, ein kleinteiliges Sternen- oder Blumenmuster Buchillustrationen aus Kinderzeit. Verführung hier ist Ablenkung, ist ein bewusstes Spiel mit dem Zuviel an Möglichkeiten: Immer wieder den Vorhang ziehen und kein Geheimnis lüften, Indizien kundtun, doch die Geschichte im Zusammenhang nicht erzählen. Verführung ist auch Ergebnis einer schier unmöglichen Zusammenfassung: In der Kombinatorik von bildlichen Zitaten und ihrer Rhythmisierung erhärtet sich der Eindruck von Räumen, die keine Kontinuität der Zeit anerkennen. Umso mehr mutieren sie zum feinmaschigen Fangnetz subjektiver Assoziationen.

Methoden der Popindustrie vergleichbar, jongliert Streuli mit Elementen, zu denen sich punktuell und individuell Bezüge herstellen lassen. Ihr Vorgehen kann sich keinem Stil verpflichten, greift doch die Arbeit auf verschiedenste bildnerische Quellen zu, um das »Konstrukt« der Malerei zu testen und zu erweitern. In der Folge spontaner Entscheidungen setzt sich die Künstlerin selbst immer wieder neugierig ihren eigenen »Rorschach-Tests« aus. Einen Teil des Bildaufbaus delegiert sie mit Vorliebe an Verfahren, die Überraschungen bereithalten. Spiegelungen etwa bergen ein Mass an Unberechenbarem und bieten sich in einem zweiten Schritt für Verfremdungen an. Die Umkehrung im Abdruck oder das Negativ beim Einsatz von Schablonen legen eine Basis für das malerische Experiment. »Unbesorgt«, wie sie selber sagt, geht sie über die möglichen Konsequenzen einer Entscheidung auf der Bildfläche hinweg, konfrontiert sich vor der Leinwand mit dem Ergebnis rasch getroffener Massnahmen. »Ich versuche, den wichtigen und schwerwiegenden Akt des Sich-Entscheiden-Müssens schnell und leicht, unbeeindruckt zu nehmen. Ich denke, dass die Leichtfüssigkeit und meine unbeeindruckte Haltung gegenüber endgültigen Entscheidungen meine Arbeit ausmachen. Ich will handeln und reagieren, auf alles, was sich mir entgegenstellt. Diese Haltung ruft Vorkommnisse hervor, die ich nicht planen kann. Das interessiert mich am meisten an der Malerei, es hält mich wach und aufgeregt.«

Tempo ist ein Faktor hier. Und während die Künstlerin ihre Zugehörigkeit zur langen Tradition der Malerei voll anerkennt, hält sie sich nicht zurück mit Zeichen, die der Last der Überlieferung etwas Leichtes entgegenhalten. In der raschen Handschrift, im Spray oder Abklatsch sitzt bei allem Ernst ein erfrischender Rest an Rebellion gegen das gewichtige, das Massstäbe setzende Bild. Ergebnis von Streulis konzentrierter Wachsamkeit ist ein Werk, das die dogmatische Unterscheidung zwischen Figuration und Abstraktion ebenso hinter sich lässt wie die im aktuellen Diskurs gelegentlich behauptete Polarität zwischen einer selbstreflexiven künstlerischen Praxis und dem Bezug zur gesellschaftlichen Gegenwart. Als Kennerin der zeitgenössischen Tendenzen wie der Geschichte der Malerei korrigiert sie dezidiert voreilig formulierte Vereinfachungen: »Die zeitgenössische Malerei interessiert mich darum sehr, weil seit einigen Jahren nun schon wieder unglaublich viele unterschiedliche Wege gegangen werden. Ich glaube nicht an die Vorstellung, dass ›autonome‹, ›selbstreflexive‹ Malerei nichts mit Gesellschaft und nichts mit Politik oder Kulturbezug im umfassenden Sinn zu tun hat. Oder umgekehrt, dass figurative Malerei zwingend und automatisch einen Bezug zur Wirklichkeit ›ausserhalb‹ der Leinwand herstellt. So interessiert mich an dieser Debatte eigentlich nur immer die spezifische Arbeit an der Malerei.«

Wie bereits angedeutet, nimmt diese Malerei auch die Sprache für sich in Anspruch und erweitert mit den oft nachträglich formulierten Titeln den visuellen Raum um eine gedankliche Assoziation. *Sumo* (2005) legt unerwartet einem vervielfachten, mehrfach gespiegelten Farbfleck eine asiatische Herkunft zugrunde. *Ich lieb Dich, ich lieb Dich nicht…* (2004) ergänzt drei leuchtende Farbschlaufen um ein harmlos anmutendes Spiel emotionaler Entscheidung. Bei *Radar* mag man an Wettervorhersagen und Flugkontrollen denken. Während die Worte individuelle Bilder evozieren, fordert die Dichte visueller Zitate einen Blick, der sich in Sprache übersetzt. »Und dort, wo sich dann beide Vorstellungen treffen, die Sprache und das Bild, dort befindet sich meine Arbeit.« – Dort bewegt sich die Arbeit, möchte man hinzufügen, denn von einer in sich ruhenden Befindlichkeit kann nicht die Rede sein. Es ist, wie wenn das Bild, während es sein Gemacht-Sein ganz zur Schau trägt, seine eigene Auflösung mit inszeniere. Gemaltes ist der Übermalung ausgesetzt, Ornamentales beschnitten. Die »Selbstzersörung« oder mindestens sichtbare Gefährdung einzelner Bildebenen spiegelt den Verzicht auf eine einzig mögliche Form.

Das Risiko, dass sich die Malerei zu viel zumutet und im Zuviel sich selbst gefährdet, ist gleichzeitig ihr Antrieb, Lebensnerv und Stimulator. »Who is afraid of the big bad wolf?« – Die zunächst ans Kind gewandte Frage liess offen, ob sich dieses möglichst vor Risiken hüten oder der Gefahr ins Auge blicken soll: Es gibt weder richtig noch falsch, bloss die Offenheit, die einer individuellen Antwort Raum lässt. Deswegen konnte Barnett Newman den Satz auf sein Bild übertragen: *Who is afraid of Red, Yellow and Blue* von 1967 fasst die Radikalität seiner Malerei zusammen und entzieht sich klug dem Vorwurf des Banalen. Wer sich der Gefahr nicht aussetzt, hält den Risiken zeitgemässer, konsequenter bildnerischer Forschung nicht Stand. Christine Streuli hat keine Angst vor der Malerei. Ihre Äusserung macht es deutlich: »Ich will handeln und reagieren auf alles, was sich mir entgegenstellt.« – Das heisst heute und in ihrem Fall: Reagieren auf die grosse Flut bildnerischer Möglichkeiten. Der üppig bebilderten Welt und der Geschichte der Bilder wieder mit Bildern begegnen. Wachsam, aufgeregt, handelnd.

1 Dieses wie die nachfolgenden Zitate von Christine Streuli entstammen einem Diaolg per E-Mail mit der Autorin vom 17. März 2006.
Der Text erschien in einer ersten kurzen Fassung in *artist Kunstmagazin* Nr. 67, 2006.

Isabel Zürcher

Who is afraid of painting?

Painting is a spectacle, a sensation. Christine Streuli plays up the "power" of her medium with work that is bright and has many layers, taking pleasure in experimentation, and using large formats. Her work relies on the availability of pictures in a present that churns out visual stimulation at a high speed, for all kinds of different purposes and using all kinds of different means. The artist goes to extremes, producing an unstoppable flood of visual stimulation. She looks for extreme artificiality and allows shapes and colors to collide head on. She avoids soft transitions and this very fact makes for a surprising opulence. The viewer experiences her painting as a series of spaces next to and on top of one another without the individual levels ever trying to come to an understanding amongst themselves. Equally at home with drawing, in both large and small formats, when she exhibited at Kunstraum Kreuzlingen in 2005, Christine Streuli came up with a show that filled out the entire space available: her painting sensations are not limited by the boundaries of medium-format canvasses. They consistently reach out into the room, because painting cannot be stopped: she voraciously absorbs patterns, grids, spheres, splotches and their reflections, is happy to use both traces of manual brushstrokes and gleaming synthetic effects on the same surface only to return to the harmless game immediately afterwards. *Ich lieb Dich, ich lieb Dich nicht…* is only one of many titles that answer the visual challenge with an incidental reference to a reality outside the picture.

Alongside Zurich, New York, Cairo, Beinwil (Switzerland), and, most recently, San Francisco have all been stopping-off points along the way for Christine Streuli. Settling down has never been one of her strong points. In recent years, several stays abroad have provided her with new perspectives. Her work thrives on her nomadic existence and on the knowledge that images or sections of such images can be quoted anywhere, simultaneously. Streuli uncompromisingly invests the energy generated by each new beginning in her work and each time her studio becomes her temporary home. For her, anywhere could be a studio; she sees possibilities of the kind everywhere, possibilities for allowing the big wide world to come into contact with the smaller one, and for amalgamating the two in exemplary fashion. Whether it be a dark room, a garage, a living room or a factory hall, as she sees it, the studio always provides material that is just asking to be handled and used: "At least, that's the way I feel when I see tubes of paint, paper, cardboard, aerosol cans or the like lying about around me. Everything is crying out for use, for action or reaction, for movement."

Taking her inspiration from the iconography of Baroque still lifes or historical arabesques in graphics and architecture, Streuli avails herself of a vocabulary handed to her by tradition. And she is quite happy to re-orchestrate this vocabulary, preparing the insistent presence of 17th-century still life objects in a new way, using the artificial colors of fresh paint, taking unabashed pleasure in the sensuality of flowing paint and getting lost in it. Her way of combining patterns and their reflections, ornamental details and their duplication echoes those of carpets and wallpaper or even the repeat pattern of printed fabrics. For example, in *Falter* (2005), working from memory and using an impressing process she commits the structure of an Afro print to canvas. In *wing* (2004), a flower motif with an oval outline coagulates into an awkwardly shaped pattern. "I like that total clarity that evokes excitement and a lack of overview." Clarity to stimulate agitation, an overview to induce confusion? – It is contradiction that repeatedly reignites Streuli's painting, contradiction that is conceivably its most important principle. Our expectations are permanently questioned, our knowledge of the conformity of a figure to natural laws made to compete with the autonomy of the medium. Accordingly, her manually applied layers of paint stand in opposition to the aesthetics of digital uniformity. Indirectly or incidentally, the sober quotation on the surface of her pictures leaves traces of the artist's handwriting. *Hinterlässt Spuren*, a work dating from 2005, appears to support observations of this nature, but, at this very point, she completely retracts the notion of painting as "écriture". And it regularly turns out that our trust in the consistency of a detail is unfounded: a reflection or an imprint exposes it as a testimony to an indirect reality, a subsequent layer once again binds the signs that we have interpreted spatially to the surface. This too is painting: everything is a fake, deception and trompe-l'œil, everything pure glamour.

Why does Streuli cling so tightly to the art of seduction? "What interests me is the moment when, for us all, a star or perhaps even only a colorful dot starts to tell a great story. The point of interface where, for example, red as a color becomes content, the point where our associations come from or awaken."[1] Streuli's work is rather more a testimony to the extent to which painting can count on associations. The imprint of a black rosette paves the way to the cathedral of the Middle Ages, to the mandala too, shimmering matte balls in bright, synthetic colors call to mind those models from the chemistry textbooks, an intricate star or flower pattern, book illustrations from our childhood. Here, seduction is distraction, a conscious act of playing with the plethora of possibilities: drawing back the curtains over and over again without revealing any secrets, dropping all kinds of hints but not telling a coherent story. Seduction is also the result of a practically impossible summary: the way she combines pictorial quotations and orchestrates them reinforces the impression of places that do not recognize a continuity of time. All the more reason for them to mutate into a fine-meshed net for trapping subjective associations.

Using methods similar to those of the pop industry, Streuli juggles with elements for which it is possible to create selective, individual references. Her modus operandi cannot be associated with any particular style since her work makes use of all kinds of pictorial sources, testing and expanding upon the "construct" of painting. The artist comes to spontaneous decisions and then, consumed by curiosity, submits herself to her own, repeated "Rorschach tests". She has a predilection for delegating a section of the pictorial composition to processes that hold surprises. Reflections, for example, boast a host of unpredictable elements and are ideal for alienation purposes as a second step. Reverse prints on negatives when using templates form the basis for her painting experiments. "Carefree" is how she herself describes her dismissive attitude to the possible consequences of a decision on the surface of a picture, confronted with the results of rapidly adopted measures in front of the canvas. "I try to perform the important and far-reaching act of coming to the inevitable decision quickly and lightly, unfazed. I believe that my fleet-footed, undaunted approach to irreversible decisions makes my work what it is. I want to act and react to everything I am faced with. This attitude provokes occurrences that I am unable to plan. This is what interests me most of all in painting, it keeps me alert and excited."

Pace is a factor here. And although the artist does fully recognize her place in the long tradition of painting, she does not hold back with symbols that counter the burden of tradition with something light. However serious things may be, her quick handwriting, something sprayed on or copied, demonstrates a refreshing hint of rebellion against the deadly serious, standard-setting picture. The outcome of Streuli's concentrated alertness is a body of work that leaves behind it not only the dogmatic differentiation between figuration and abstraction but also that polarity occasionally highlighted in current discourse between a self-referential artistic practice and one that relates to the social present. A connoisseur both of present-day tendencies and of the history of painting, she emphatically corrects hastily formulated simplifications: "The reason why contemporary painting interests me so very much is that for some years now people have been going in an unbelievably large number of different directions. I don't believe the idea that 'autonomous', 'self-referential' painting has got nothing to do with society and nothing to do with politics or interest in culture in a wider sense. Or vice versa, that figurative painting necessarily and automatically references the reality 'outside' the canvas. So actually, all that really interests me about this debate is a specific piece of work, of painting."

As already suggested, this painting also makes demands on language, combining mental associations with the visual aspect in the form of the titles, which Streuli often formulates retrospectively.

Sumo (2005) unexpectedly furnishes a multiple, repeatedly reflected splotch of paint with a Far Eastern background. *Ich lieb Dich, ich lieb Dich nicht ...* (2004) adds the dimension of a seemingly harmless game that helps with emotional decisions to three bright loops of paint. In the case of *Radar* (2005), viewers might be reminded of weather forecasts and flight checks. But whereas the words evoke individual images, the profusion of visual quotations demands a way of looking at things that translates itself into language. "And where the two notions, language and image, meet each other is where my work is located." – Or, as one would like to add, this is the area where the work moves, because there is no question of its just, quiet existence. It is as if, by completely showing off its fabricated state, the picture is playing its part in staging its own disintegration. The painted is exposed to over-painting, the ornamental cut back. The "self-destruction" or at least visible endangerment of individual pictorial levels reflects her unwillingness to restrict herself to a single possible form.

The risk that her painting demands too much of itself and by doing so endangers itself is simultaneously what stimulates her, is her lifeblood and raison d'être. "Who's afraid of the big bad wolf?" – This question, originally posed to children, never made it clear whether the latter should do their best to avoid risks or should be looking danger in the eye: there is no right or wrong, only that openness that leaves room for individual answers. And this is why Barnett Newman was able to transfer the sentence to his 1967 picture. Who is afraid of Red, Yellow and Blue summarizes the radical nature of his painting and cleverly avoids the reproach of banality. Anyone who does not expose him- or herself to danger cannot withstand the risks of contemporary pictorial research. Christine Streuli is not afraid of painting. The abovementioned remark makes this clear: "I want to act and react to everything I'm faced with." – What this means today and in her case is reacting to the great flood of pictorial opportunities. Meeting the lavishly illustrated world and the history of images with images of her own. Alert, excited, active.

1 This and the following Christine Streuli quotations are taken from an e-mail dialogue she conducted with the author on March 17, 2006. Translation: Jeremy Gaines

The text has been published in a shorter version in *artist Kunstmagazin* Nr. 67, 2006.

Madeleine Schuppli

Symmetrien

Für Christine Streuli ist die Symmetrie ein kompositorisches Prinzip, auf das sie seit den Anfängen ihrer malerischen Arbeit immer wieder zurückgreift. Ihr Werk ist von enormer Vielfältigkeit, energetischer Dichte und Spannung. In dieser malerischen Erlebniswelt, in dieser Vielschichtigkeit an Farben und Formen und in den überraschenden Variationen des Duktus innerhalb ein und desselben Bildes, in dieser visuellen Abenteuerreise bringen die symmetrischen Bildelemente ein wohltuendes strukturierendes Element in die kompositorische Aufgewühltheit.

Christine Streuli gelangt über zwei unterschiedliche Wege zu symmetrischen Kompositionen: durch den Einsatz von Schablonen und durch den Farbabklatsch. Der malerische Prozess, der zu den Abklatschbildern führt, beginnt mit einer Folie, die mit Farbe bearbeitetet wird. Das Plastikstück wird zusammengeklappt und die Farbverteilung damit symmetrisch. Die Folie wird anschliessend auf die Leinwand gedrückt und die Farbe so auf die Bildfläche übertragen. Ein frühes Beispiel für diese Technik ist das Bild *Rorschach* (2002). Auf einem hellen Grund zeichnet sich entlang der Bildachse eine schmale elliptische Form ab, die links und rechts von Farbtupfen begleitet wird: eine Figur aus symmetrisch angeordneten Farbflecken, eingefasst von einem hellgelben Pinselstrich zur Festigung der polymorphen, flüchtigen Figuren. Selbst in Unkenntnis des Titels liegt die Assoziation zum berühmten Rorschachtest auf der Hand. Der Schweizer Psychiater Hermann Rorschach (1884–1922) hatte sein weltbekanntes Verfahren 1921 erstmals publiziert. In diesem psychoanalytischen Test deutet ein Analytiker die Assoziationen von Patienten zu abstrakten, symmetrischen Tintenklecksbildern. Die Art der Wahrnehmung eines Bildes soll Rückschlüsse auf die psychische Verfassung des Betrachters liefern.

Das Verfahren des Rorschachtests eignet sich als Metapher für die Betrachtung von Kunst ganz allgemein. Jedes Kunstwerk – und in besonderem Masse das nicht figurative Malen – ist für die Betrachtenden eine Art Test. Der Unterschied liegt nur darin, dass kein Psychiater zugegen ist, der die Rezeption beurteilen würde. Als beflissene Kunstbetrachter sind wir bemüht, die Wirkung des Seherlebnisses in uns abzufragen. Wir fühlen uns aufgefordert, ein Bild zu lesen, und wir sind uns bewusst, dass unsere Lesart weder unschuldig noch »gottgegeben«, d.h. »objektiv«, ist, sondern von uns selber, bewusst oder unbewusst, verantwortet wird. Sigmund Freuds zum Allgemeingut gewordene Theorie des freien und unzensurierten Assoziierens haben wir längst kollektiv verinnerlicht. Gerade Bilder, wie diejenigen von Christine Streuli, fordern uns in diesem Sinne.

Neben den Abklatschbildern hat Christine Streuli auch eine andere Gruppe von Werken mit symmetrischen Elementen geschaffen, die sie mit Hilfe von Schablonen herstellt. Der malerische Prozess und das Resultat unterscheiden sich aber stark vom Abklatsch. Während dieser psychologisch aufgeladen zu sein scheint und bei der Herstellung ein unkontrollierbares Element enthält, hat die Schablonentechnik eher etwas Stereotypisierendes, denn es geht zuerst um reine Verdoppelung. Die vorgefertigte Schablone ermöglicht eine genaue Wiederholung. Ein- oder mehrfach an einer Achse gespiegelt, werden Bildelemente seitenverkehrt vervielfacht. Diese Multiplizierung von bildlichen Elementen ist im Werk von Christine Streuli ein Mittel, um vom Einfachen zum Komplexen zu gelangen. Diese Wiederholung kann eine einfache Spiegelung an der Bildachse sein: In *Tollkirschen* (2004), einer kleinen Malerei auf Holz, klappt die Künstlerin die schwarze Silhouette von Vögeln auf einem Zweig zuerst auf die rechte und anschliessend auf die untere Bildhälfte. In anderen Arbeiten, wie etwa *Wucher* (2006), wird eine Vielzahl von Motiven mittels Schablonen an einer Mittelachse gespiegelt und multipliziert. Blüten, Rosetten, Rhomben, Kreise oder mondförmige Spitzenelemente verteilen sich beidseits einer imaginären Bildmittelachse. Eine Überfülle entsteht, die an mittelalterliche Millefleur-Teppiche erinnert. Das Malen solcher Bilder ist vergleichbar mit der ritualisierten Arbeit an Mandalas, wo in vielen Stunden gleichförmigen Arbeitens vielteilige, komplexe Kompositionen geschaffen werden. Es ist eine penible und arbeitsintensive Malweise, ein fast obsessives Aneinanderreihen und mehrfaches Spiegeln ein und desselben Elementes. Dabei geht es Christine Streuli nicht ums Ornamentale, das Wiederholen kommt vielmehr einem Insistieren gleich: Sie besteht auf ihrer malerischen Aussage, behauptet diese, indem sie ihr ästhetisches Statement viele Male wiederholt.

Die Symmetrie ist eine der kompositorischen Strategien, die sich durch Christine Streulis Werk ziehen. Im Schaffen der Künstlerin stehen die Bilder in einer engen Beziehung zueinander, und ein Werk baut auf dem nächsten auf, ein Gedanke wird von einer Arbeit in die nächste weitergetragen. Ein malerischer Versuch erhält im nächsten Bild nochmals eine Chance. So lotet sie die Möglichkeiten der Spieglung aus, und der Prozess nimmt immer wieder einen anderen Ausgang. Interessant ist dabei, dass die symmetrischen Bildelemente jeweils Reminiszenzen an verschiedene gestalterische und handwerkliche Techniken, die wir in unterschiedlichen Kulturkreisen verorten, beinhalten. So entstehen Verweise auf mittelalterliche Teppichmuster, auf das heimatliche Scherenschnitthandwerk, auf ornamental durchbrochene Fensterabdeckungen aus dem asiatischen Raum, auf traditionelle Stoffmusterungen oder auf barocke Gitterstrukturen. Dieses vielfältige Repertoire an gestalterischen Verfahren und Materialien, auf welche die symmetrischen Bildelemente in Christine Streulis Arbeit zu verweisen scheinen, haben ihre Entsprechung in der Vielfalt der von der Künstlerin angewandten malerischen Verfahren. Die Malerei weist damit über ihre schlichte Essenz aus Farbe und Trägermaterial hinaus und öffnet sich auf einen Illusionsraum hin, der weniger narrativ geprägt ist, als vielmehr von den Möglichkeiten und Herausforderungen einer ästhetischen Sprachvielfalt zeugt.

Madeleine Schuppli

Symmetries

For Christine Streuli, symmetry is a compositional principle to which she has repeatedly had recourse ever since she began to paint. Her work is extremely varied and possesses a vigorous denseness and tension. In this particular painterly world, in these multilayered colours and forms and in the surprising variations in the brushwork within one and the same painting, on this visual magical mystery tour, the symmetrical pictorial elements introduce a pleasing structuring element into the compositional turbulence.

Streuli arrived at her symmetrical compositions by two different routes: the use of stencils and decalcomania. The painterly process leading to the decalcomanias begins with paint being applied to a transparency. The piece of plastic is then folded so that the paint is distributed symmetrically. Then the foil is pressed onto the canvas and the paint transferred to the surface. An early example of this technique is Streuli's *Rorschach* (2002). On a bright ground, a narrow elliptical shape emerges along the picture axis accompanied to the left and right by spots of paint: a figure made up of symmetrically ordered spots, its polymorph fleetingness enclosed by a bright yellow brush outline. Even without knowing the title, the association with the famous Rorschach test is obvious. The Swiss psychiatrist Hermann Rorschach (1884–1922) publicised his famous procedure in 1921. In this psychological test an analyst interprets the patient's associations on seeing abstract symmetrical ink blot images; the way the viewer perceives these is thought to provide conclusions about his or her psychological state.

The Rorschach test procedure is an appropriate metaphor for the observation of art in general. Each work of art – particularly of non-figurative painting – is a kind of test for the viewer, the only difference being that there is no psychiatrist present to judge the reception. As dedicated viewers of art, we endeavour to query the impact which the visual experience has on us. We feel challenged to read a painting and we are aware of the fact that our reading is neither innocent nor "God-given", i.e., is not "objective", but that we ourselves are consciously or unconsciously responsible for it. We have collectively internalised Sigmund Freud's theory of free and uncensored association. It is in this sense that paintings such as those by Christine Streuli present us with a challenge.

In addition to the decalcomanias or blot print paintings, Streuli has produced another group of works containing symmetrical elements which she created by using stencils. Here, however, both the painterly process and the result differ greatly from the blot print. While the latter seems to be psychologically charged and its production determined by an uncontrollable element, the stencil technique stereo-typifies, given that it is initially about pure duplication. The prefabricated stencils enable exact repetition. Mirrored one or more times on an axis, pictorial elements are duplicated in reverse. This multiplication of the pictorial elements in Streuli's works is a means of advancing from the simple to the complex. The repetition can be a simple mirroring on the pictorial axis: in *Tollkirschen* (2004), a small painting on wood, the artist folds the black silhouette of birds on a branch first onto the right part and then onto the lower part of the painting. In other works, such as *Wucher* (2006), a number of different motifs are mirrored on the central axis using stencils. Blossoms, rosettes, lozenges, circles or jagged moon-shaped elements are distributed on both sides of an imaginary middle axis so that the resulting abundance is reminiscent of medieval mille fleurs tapestries. The work of painting such images is comparable to the ritualised work on a mandala, for which hours of monotonous work are required to produce a complicated multi-part composition. This is a meticulous and demanding way of painting, an almost obsessive arranging and repeated mirroring of one and the same element; yet Streuli's concern is not the ornamental, but instead her repetition resembles an insistence: she insists on her painterly statement and asserts this by repeating her aesthetic statement many times.

Symmetry is one of the compositional strategies that run through Streuli's works. Her paintings are closely related to one another; one work builds upon the next; an idea is carried along from one work to the next; an artistic experiment is given another chance in the next painting. In this way the artist explores the possibilities of mirroring, and each time the process ends differently. What is interesting here is that the symmetrical pictorial elements each contain reminiscences of various graphic and craft techniques which can be found in different cultures. There are references to medieval tapestries, to the local craft of the silhouette, to ornamental open-work window guards in Asia, to traditional fabric patterns or to Baroque grille structures. This varied repertoire of processes and materials, to which Streuli's symmetrical pictorial elements would seem to allude, has a correspondence in the diversity of the painterly processes she uses. This way of painting points beyond its simple essence, the paint and the carrier, opening out into a space of illusion that is not narrative, but instead testifies to the possibilities and challenges of a varied aesthetic idiom.

Translation: Pauline Cumbers

C.F. Schröer

Der La Streuli Code

Nichts nervt mich mehr als Sätze wie »... Streulis Werke sind nicht zu entschlüsseln.« – Das trifft meine Eitelkeit als Kritiker und Kunstliebhaber zentral. Oder, wie der verehrte Wiener Kollege Alfred Polgar so beneidenswert elegant zu sagen verstand: »Das trifft den Nagel an der empfindlichsten Stelle des Kopfes.« Den derartige Ohnmachtsbezeugungen angesichts Streuli'scher Werke insinuieren eine Weisheit, die sich aber gleich als doppelte Dummheit herausstellt. 1. Streuli verschlüssele überhaupt irgendwas, irgendeine geheime (?) Botschaft. 2. Der Schreiber, Kritiker oder Kunstgelehrte scheitere von Mal zu Mal daran, diese innere Botschaft zu entschlüsseln, den *La Streuli Code* zu knacken, den sie geschickt etwa unter allerhand bunten Zeichen, Linien und Kreisen, ornamentalem Gedröhne und farbenfrohem Getöse hieroglyphengleich verberge. Überdies will mir sein Eingeständnis vom eigenen Scheitern, ach wie eine kavaliersmäßige Verbeugung alter Schule erscheinen. Eine tiefe Verbeugung vor dem jungen Kunstgenie.

Überhaupt bin ich naturgemäß gegen eine solche Arbeitsteilung: Der Künstler verschlüsselt, damit der Kritiker anschließend sich der Mühe der Entschlüsselung unterziehen kann. Der Verschlüsselungskünstler brauche erst recht den Entschlüsselungsfachmann. Blinkt da nicht der alte Anspruch durch die falsche Bescheidenheit, wonach Künstler ihre Werke schaffen, damit die Kunsthistoriker in Lohn und Brot kommen?

Überhaupt gefällt mir diese Nachbetrachtungs- und Aufarbeitungspflicht wenig. So viel Selbstverleugnung erregt mein Misstrauen gegen die eigen en Zunft. Dieses ewige Hinterherhinken und Nachbuchstabieren. Viel lieber wollte ich doch selbst etwas schaffen, was andere meinetwegen entschlüsseln und zu Ende decodieren, selbst wenn ich gar keine geheimen Botschaften senden wollte. Meinetwegen. (Ich verstehe ja schon, selbst die Vermutung auf einen Code macht manches Werk interessanter. Oder machtes für manche überhaupt erst interessant.)

Was mich an Streulis Werken freut, mich geradezu begeistert und hochauf beglückt, ist die radikale Abwesenheit von Zeichen, Symbolen, Bezügen, Botschaften und deren flachere oder tiefere Bedeutung. Welch eine Befreiung. Ein Aufatmen und tief Lufthohlen! Keine Verschlüsselung, keine Verständnisfallen, kein unterdrücktes, verbotenes oder verloren gegangenes Wissen, auch kein vermeintliches Tabu wird malerisch bearbeitet, keine Weltinnensicht und kein Psychogramm wird mitgemalt. Ein Wiener Kollege von mir und Polgar, Karl Kraus, hat dazu die prägnanteste Formel gefunden: »Nichts ist tiefer als die Oberfläche.« Streulis Bilder bieten galaktische Weite und abgründige Tiefe. Darin herumzuschweifen, kometengleich zu kreisen, die Weite auszukosten, aus der Umlaufbahn zu geraten, gefährlich zu trudeln, mich in die Hängematte zwischen die bunten Sterne zu legen, die Tiefe fürchten zu lernen oder in ihr zu versinken. Das reicht mir.

C.F. Schröer

The La Streuli Code

There is nothing more annoying than statements like "Streuli's works cannot be decoded." – They are anathema to my vanity as a critic and art lover. Or as Alfred Polgar, my venerable Viennese colleague, put it with such enviable elegance, "that hits the nail on the most sensitive part of the head." The more so as such confessions of impotence – when faced with Streulian works – insinuate a sagacity that instantly proves to be stupidity twice over. Namely that 1. Streuli even encodes anything at all, any secret (?) message, and 2. the writer, critic or art scholar fails, from one time to the next, to decipher the inner message, to crack the *La Streuli Code* that the artist has cleverly concealed in a motley, hieroglyphic array of signs, lines and circles, in an ornamental uproar and a colourful clamour. Moreover I can't help reading his self-confessed failure as an oh so oldschool cavalier obeisance to the young artist-genius.

I am by nature opposed to such a division of labour: the artist encoding so that the critic can subject himself to the travail of decoding. In fact, the encoding artist cannot do without the services of the expert decoder. But then, doesn't that dependency smack of a false modesty, whereby artists create their works in order to fill the coffers of the art historians?

Besides, the obligation to review work a posteriori does not appeal to me. All that self-denial makes me slightly suspicious about my own trade. Eternally limping along behind and spelling things out. I'd much prefer doing my own creating; others can do the decoding – for all I care – even though I have no intention of sending any secret messages. (Of course, I'm fully aware that even the suspicion of a code makes many an œuvre more interesting. Or, for that matter, interesting to begin with.)

What I like about Streuli's works, what absolutely thrills and delights me, is the radical absence of signs, symbols, references, messages and their shallow word-deep significance. What liberation, what a sense of relief! No encoding, no obstacles to understanding, no suppressed knowledge, no supposed taboo is being subjected to painterly scrutiny; no innerworldview and no psychogram is oozing out of the paintbrush. Karl Kraus, a Viennese colleague of mine and Polgar's as well, has expressed it in the most incisive terms: "Nothing is deeper than the surface." Streuli's pictures offer galactic expanses and unfathomable depths. Roving about in them, circling like a comet, savouring the vastness, spinning out of orbit, heading into a dangerous tailspin, lying down in a hammock amongst the colourful stars, discovering the fear of depth or sinking into it – that'll do for me.

Translation: Catherine Schelbert

Roman Kurzmeyer

Poetische Reflexion

Das ästhetische Bild ist nach einem Wort der Kunstkritikerin Juliane Rebentisch im Unterschied zum dokumentarischen Bild »kontextoffen«. Es lenkt unseren Blick nicht auf die Welt, um diese zu zeigen, damit wir sie verstehen, sondern thematisiert seine eigene Sichtbarkeit. Da es die Welt nicht übersetzt, sondern selbst eine Form von erfahrener Welt ist, wird die Antwort auf die Frage, was ein bestimmtes Werk darstelle, nicht einfach ausfallen. Ästhetische Bilder vermögen uns anzusprechen, zu verführen, zu begeistern, aber auch vor den Kopf zu stossen, ohne dass wir sie deswegen auch unmittelbar verstehen müssen. Das dokumentarische Bild dagegen steht immer im Dienste eines meist engagierten politischen Inhalts, den man genau benennen kann. Anlass visueller Erfahrung und zugleich ihr Zweck ist beim ästhetischen Bild die Sichtbarkeit selbst. Ambivalenter Wirklichkeitsbezug und reflexive Wahrnehmung bedingen sich gegenseitig.

Christine Streuli malt Bilder, welche die Bedingungen für ihre Wahrnehmung selbst herstellen. Es gibt kleine und sehr grossflächige Gemälde, gemeinsam ist ihnen der mehrschichtige malerische Aufbau. Streuli arbeitet mit Symmetrie, Spiegelung und Wiederholung. Sie verwendet handwerkliche Vervielfältigungsverfahren wie den Handdruck, den Abklatsch oder die Schablone. Vereinzelt greift die Künstlerin dabei auf technisch hergestellte Schablonen und Matrizen zurück, doch meistens stellt sie diese selbst her. Die auf der Leinwand abzubildende Figur wird dabei auf Papier, Karton oder Holz übertragen, ausgeschnitten, und die dabei entstandene Schablone für die Applizierung der Farbe auf den Bildträger eingesetzt. Pinsel verwendet sie selten. Diese indirekte Malweise führt zu stark formalisierten Bildern von einer eigenen distanzierten Bildhaftigkeit. Denn die Herstellung der Matrize ist ein Transformationsprozess, in dem die vorgefundene oder durch Abklatsch erzeugte Figur vereinfacht und so weit formalisiert wird, dass sie leicht zu vervielfältigen ist. Ungenauigkeiten, Fehler und Verschiebungen, die sich bei der impulsiven Anwendung von Reproduktionsverfahren einstellen, interessieren Streuli nicht nur deshalb besonders, weil diese visuell überraschende, neue Elemente bilden und das Bedeutungsspektrum ihrer Arbeiten vergrössern können, sondern auch aus dem einfachen Grunde, dass sie vor Augen führen, wie unter Verwendung einer Reproduktionstechnik Originale entstehen. Das einzelne Bild zeigt seine Herstellung. Die Künstlerin bekräftigt die Autonomie des gemalten Bildes und verweist zugleich mit jeder ihrer Arbeiten auf die künstlerische Praxis im Atelier.

In den vergangenen Jahren sind neben Gemälden vereinzelt auch installative Arbeiten entstanden. So beispielsweise *eksam-nedma* (2004) für die Ausstellung im Dachstock einer isoliert in den Bergen gelegenen Scheune in Amden am Walensee. Die mit Lackfarben bemalte und mit der Säge beschnittene und konturierte Holztafel in der Form eines Farbkleckses ermöglichte dem Auge wegen den an verschiedenen Stellen im Bild vorhandenen Fenstern und Einschnitten, das Licht wahrzunehmen, das zwischen den rohen Brettern der unregelmässigen Holzverplankung in den grossen fensterlosen Ausstellungsraum hinter der als Raumteiler ausgestellten Arbeit einfiel. Dieses Licht aktivierte die Malerei, die wie eine Maske das imitiert, was sie verdeckt: Bretter, Lichtschlitze, Raum.

Die Installation *ensemble ensemble* (2005), die Streuli für den Kunstraum Kreuzlingen geschaffen hatte, war Werk und Ausstellung in einem. Die ausgestellten Arbeiten waren anders als *eksam-nedma* vor Ort entstanden. Die Künstlerin nutzte diesmal den Ausstellungsraum als Atelier. Zunächst belegte sie den Fussboden mit einem grossen Papier und stempelte darauf ein einfaches, regelmässiges zweifarbiges Muster in kräftigen Farben. Sie markierte einen Raum im Raum. Dieser zweite Boden wirkte wie ein auf dem Hallenboden verrutschter Teppich. Das Bodenmuster übertrug sie durch Abklatsch auf die nun in der Raumdiagonale einander gegenübergestellten Leinwände. Im weiteren Verlauf des bildnerischen Prozesses wurden diese Bilder sowohl einzeln bearbeitet als auch miteinander in Berührung gebracht. An zwei Stellen unterzog Streuli auch die Wand einer künstlerischen Bearbeitung, dort waren horizontal verlaufende gesprühte Linien zu sehen. Im Raum lag ein Druckstock, dessen Abdruck an mehreren Stellen auftauchte. Eines ergab das andere, als ob ein Bild für den Betrachter entfaltet und zugleich an vielen Stellen wieder verdichtet worden wäre. Farbiges Licht setzte Akzente im Raum und entlastete den Boden, aus dem die Arbeit hervorgegangen war und auf den sie bezogen blieb. So war das Publikum in dieser Ausstellung herausgefordert, die Wechselwirkung von Analyse und Synthese nachzuvollziehen und zu erkennen, dass in dieser Ausstellung, die man vielleicht als eine mehrteilige Arbeit auffassen sollte, Präsenz und Repräsentation eine untrennbare Einheit bildeten.

Kunstwerke werden hergestellt und ausgestellt, davon war bislang die Rede; sie sollen beim Betrachter aber auch ein geistiges Bild hervorrufen. Der Bildtheoretiker Lambert Wiesing unterscheidet zwischen Bildobjekt (»die sichtbar werdende Darstellung«) und Bildträger (»das sichtbar machende Bildmaterial«). Das geistige Bild entspricht dabei dem Bildobjekt, das dem Betrachter eines Kunstwerkes erst ermöglicht, ein Werk zu verstehen oder zu lesen, zumindest jedenfalls auf ein Motiv zu beziehen und eine Thematik zu erkennen. Dass bislang, wie man vielleicht meinen könnte, wenig von den Inhalten von Streulis Malerei die Rede gewesen sei, stimmt allerdings nicht, denn das Nachdenken über die technische Verfertigung dieser Werke gehört zum Bild, das wir uns von ihnen machen. Da selbst Pinselstriche und Farbtropfen nicht gemalt, sondern abgebildet und somit als Objekte der Malerei aufgefasst werden, erzeugen Streulis Gemälde beim Betrachter eine gesteigerte Aufmerksamkeit für die Artifizialität des Bildes. Ein Schriftzug etwa ist unverkennbar auch eine Lackspur, und umgekehrt zeigt diese Lackspur, dass sie lesbar ist. Zu erwähnen sind auch die Konturierungen der Figuren, die manchmal an Ornamente erinnern, sich aber auch auf die Sprache von Graffiti oder Tattoo beziehen können. Was der französische Kunsthistoriker Georges Didi-Huberman anhand von steinzeitlichen, farbig umrissenen Handabdrücken feststellt, führt auch in die Gegenwart von Streulis Malerei. Er spricht vom Handabdruck als einer »Berührung der Abwesenheit« und fragt, ob es sich bei diesen Arbeiten der Felsbildkunst um die Präsenz oder die Repräsentation von menschlichen Händen handle? Sie sind keines von beidem, obschon sie die Präsenz einer Hand voraussetzen und die Umrisse von Händen zeigen, die es längst nicht mehr gibt. Der Abdruck ist ein dialektisches Bild, das uns sowohl die sichtbar gemachte Berührung als auch die Abwesenheit des Berührenden vor Augen führt. Berührung und Abbild stellen auch die gemeinsame Referenz der Bilder von Christine Streuli dar. Die Malerei ist direkt und übersetzt in einem, zugleich spontan und distanziert, emotional und reflexiv. Diese doppelte Codierung zeichnet nicht erst das fertige Bild aus, sondern ist eine Eigenschaft jedes einzelnen Bildelementes und daher für das Verständnis ihrer Malerei von entscheidender Bedeutung. Nicht nur, dass die Bilder wegen der Doppelcodierung zwischen Vorstellung und Realisierung oszillieren, sie bringen auch zum Ausdruck, dass vieles schon vorgefertigt vorliegt. Diese Bezugnahme auf die zweite Natur verbindet man heute reflexartig mit dem Namen und dem Werk von Andy Warhol, doch man findet sie bei vielen weiteren Künstlern, bei Johns, Stella, Polke, Sturtevant oder David Reed beispielsweise, die affirmativ mit Zeichensprachen umgehen und in ihrem Werk mit dem Verhältnis von Original und Imitation befasst sind. Ihre Gemälde sind Darstellungen des Darstellens, die den Diskurs über das Malen in Gang halten.

Alles an Streulis Gemälden ist visuell erfahrbar, dennoch übertragen sie sich auf den Betrachter nicht als Bildformeln, sondern als Emotionsträger. Klang, Temperatur, Geschwindigkeit und Raum sind zusammen mit den literarischen Titeln entscheidend für die Qualität der ästhetischen Erfahrung. Obschon Streuli wie viele Künstler in der westlichen Nachkriegskunst seit Rauschenberg die Bildebenen multipliziert, staffelt und verschränkt, finden sich in ihren Gemälden keine Realitätsfragmente. Sie verwendet oder zitiert in ihren Arbeiten weder Siebdrucke noch Fotos, obschon sie ebenfalls mit verschiedenen grafischen Verfahren arbeitet, um ihre Bilder zu entwickeln. Sie sind auf elementaren künstlerischen Darstellungsmitteln wie Linie, Fläche, Punkt, Raster und Ornament, also auf ungegenständlichen Formen aufgebaut, die von Streuli allerdings nicht verwendet, sondern in satten, kräftigen Farben gezeigt werden. Im tendenziell unabschliessbaren Dialog zwischen Künstlerin und entstehendem Bild, den die Gemälde überraschend, verschwenderisch und bewegend sichtbar machen, geht es um die Behauptung von Dauer und die Präsenz des Gemäldes als Bild, die sich beim Betrachten deshalb einstellen, weil das Bild keine instrumentellen Eigenschaften hat, nicht auf eine Wirklichkeit ausserhalb von sich selbst verweisen muss, sondern eine sich selbst entfaltende Welt von Farbformen und Energie ist. Zu situieren ist ihre Malerei innerhalb der neueren Tradition ungegenständlicher Kunst, die Streuli allerdings unter umgekehrten Vorzeichen fortsetzt: Nicht Reduktion der Mittel und Konzentration auf wenige Formen kennzeichnen dieses Werk, sondern im Gegenteil Verfahren der Maximierung. Als ob mit jeder neuen Arbeit getestet würde, wie viel Verschiedenes in einem Bild kombiniert werden kann, ohne es zu überfrachten und in seiner Sichtbarkeit zu überfordern.

Roman Kurzmeyer

Poetic reflexion

In the words of art critic Juliane Rebentisch, unlike the documentary image, the aesthetic image is »open in context«. It does not draw our attention to the world in order to illustrate the latter so that we can understand it. Instead, it centers on its own visibility. Since it does not translate the world but itself represents a kind of perceived world, the answer to the question of what a particular work represents will not be easy to find. Aesthetic images are able to appeal to us, to seduce us, to thrill us, but also to offend our sensibilities without us necessarily understanding them fully because of this. By contrast, documentary images always support some kind of content, usually, an avowedly political one that can be stated exactly. In the case of aesthetic images, the reason for this visual perception and, at the same time, its purpose is visibility itself. An ambivalent attitude to reality and reflective perception condition one another.

Christine Streuli paints pictures that create the conditions of their perception themselves. There are small and very large-format paintings and what is common to them all is a multi-layered painting technique. Streuli works with symmetry, reflection and repetition. She uses manual reproduction techniques such as hand printing, stereotyping and stencils. Occasionally, the artist uses industrially manufactured stencils and matrices, but in most cases she makes them herself. The technique involves transferring the figure to be portrayed onto paper, cardboard or wood, cutting it out and using the resultant stencil for applying the paint to the picture carrier. She rarely uses paintbrushes. This indirect method of painting makes for extremely formalized pictures with their own, distant quality. The reason: making these matrices is a transformation process in which the figure she has happened upon or produced using stereotyping techniques is simplified and formalized to such an extent that it becomes easy to reproduce. The kind of inaccuracies, errors and displacement that occur due to her impulsive approach to reproduction techniques particularly interest Streuli not only because they make for visually surprising, new elements and can enlarge her work‘s spectrum of meanings, but also for the simple reason that they clearly indicate how originals come into being when using reproduction techniques. The individual picture demonstrates its manufacture. The artist affirms the autonomy of the painted picture and, at the same time, uses her work to reference the artistic practices in her studio.

In recent years she has produced not only paintings but also isolated works of installation. One example of this is *eksam-nedma* (2004) for the exhibition in the roof of a barn in an isolated location in the mountains at Amden on Walensee. Because of the windows and incisions located at various points on the picture, this contoured wooden panel, painted with gloss paint and cut with a saw to the shape of a splotch of paint, allowed the eye to perceive the light peeking in through the irregular, untreated planks at the end of the large windowless exhibition room, behind the work itself which had been erected as a room divider. This light activated the painting which, like a mask, imitated what it covered: planks, slits to let in light, the room.

The installation *ensemble ensemble* (2005), created by Streuli for Kunstraum Kreuzlingen, was a work and an exhibition in one. Unlike the case with *eksam-nedma*, Streuli produced the exhibited works on location. This time, the artist used the exhibition room as a studio. To begin with, she laid out a large piece of paper on the floor and stamped a simple, regular pattern onto it in bright colors. She marked out a room within the room. This second floor gave the impression of a rug that had slipped on the floor of the hall. She then transferred the floor pattern to the canvases facing each other across the diagonals of the room, using stereotyping techniques. As a next step in the creative process, these pictures were both treated individually and brought into contact with one another. At two points Streuli also subjected the wall to artistic treatment, spraying on horizontal lines. There was a printing plate lying in the room; its imprint was to be found at several points. The one led to the other, as if a picture were unfolding for the viewer and, at the same time, being condensed again at many points. Colorful light created individual highlights in the room and took the onus off the floor, the original source of the work and still its point of reference. Accordingly, in this exhibition, the public was challenged to understand the interaction between analysis and synthesis and to recognize that in this exhibition, that should perhaps be seen as a work in several parts, presence and representation formed an inseparable entity.

Works of art are created and exhibited; but their aim is also to evoke a mental picture in the viewer. Lambert Wiesing, an expert on the theory of pictures, distinguishes between pictorial object ("a portrayal becoming visible") and picture carrier ("the pictorial material that renders visible"). Here, the mental picture corresponds to the pictorial object without which it would not be possible for the viewer of a piece of art to understand or to read a work, at least, at any rate, to relate it to a motif and to recognize a certain subject-matter. However, the notion that so far there has, as some people might think, been little talk of the content of Streuli's painting, is incorrect, since reflecting on the technical aspects of producing these works belongs to the pictures that we make of them. Since even the brushstrokes and drops of paint are not painted but shown and are thus meant as the objects of painting, Streuli's paintings engender in the viewer a heightened sense of the artificiality of the picture. Writing, for example, is unmistakably also a trail of paint and, vice versa, this trail of paint reveals that it is legible. Also worth mentioning are the contours around the figures, sometimes reminiscent of ornaments, but that could also reference the language of graffiti or tattoos. What French art historian Georges Didi-Huberman notices about Stone-Age imprints of hands with colored outlines also leads us to the present as represented by Streuli's painting. He calls the imprint of the hand the "touch of absence" and asks whether these works of pictorial cave art are examples of the presence or the representation of human hands. They are neither one nor the other, although they presuppose the presence of a hand and so the outlines of hands that ceased to exist a long time ago. The imprint is a dialectic image that clearly shows us both a touch rendered visible and the absence of the touching person. Touch and illustration also represent the common reference in the pictures of Christine Streuli. Her painting is direct and interpreted at the same time, at once spontaneous and distanced, emotional and reflective. This double coding is not only characteristic of the finished picture, it is also true of every individual element of the picture and is thus of fundamental importance to understanding her painting. Not only is it true that the double coding makes her paintings vacillate between impression and realization, they also express the fact that much is already available prefabricated. Today, we automatically associate this reference to second nature with the name and the work of Andy Warhol, but it is to be found in many other artists, such as Stella, Polke, Sturtevant and David Reed, for example, who manifest an affirmative approach to the language of symbols and whose work deals with the relationship between the original and its imitation. Streuli's paintings are portrayals of the act of portraying that keep the discourse on painting alive.

Everything about Streuli's paintings can be perceived visually and yet they do not transfer themselves to the viewer as pictorial formulas but as vehicles for emotion. Together with their literary titles, temperature, speed and space are decisive factors in the quality of the aesthetic experience. Although, like many artists in post-war Western society since Rauschenberg, Streuli multiplies, staggers and mixes up the pictorial levels, her paintings contain no fragments of reality. Her work neither uses nor quotes silk-screens or photographs, although she also works with various graphic techniques in order to produce her pictures. But these works are based on elementary means of artistic portrayal such as lines, surfaces, dots, grids and ornaments, i.e., on non-representational shapes; shapes Streuli does not, however actually use, but demonstrate in luscious, strong colors. In what appears to be an unresolvable dialogue between the artist and the picture, she is producing a dialogue that the paintings render visible in a surprising, extravagant and moving manner; what is under discussion here is the assertion of durability and the presence of the painting as a picture that materializes for the viewer because pictures do not have instrumental qualities, do not have to reference a reality outside themselves, but are a world of colored shapes and energy unfolding for themselves. Streuli's painting belongs within the fairly recent tradition of non-representational art, a tradition which the artist however actually inverts: her work is characterized not by a reduction in media nor by a focus on a small number of shapes, but instead by the use of maximizing techniques. As if, with every new work, she were testing how many different things she can combine in one picture without overloading the latter or overtaxing it in its visibility.

Translation: Jeremy Gaines

Alpha, 2006
Acrylic and enamel on cotton, 230 × 200 cm
Courtesy Mark Müller Gallery, Zürich, *(Ha)*

Aussteiger, 2003
Acrylic and enamel on cotton, 240 × 190 cm
Besitz Zürcher Kantonalbank, *(He)*

automatische Scheibenwischer, 2004
Acrylic and enamel on wood, 16,7 × 24 cm
Privatbesitz, *(Ae)*

bad mood, 2006
Enamel on wood, 31 × 25 cm
Privatbesitz Antonia und Jens Nordmann,
Berlin, *(He)*

banding, 2006
Enamel on wood, 26 × 22 cm
Privatbesitz, *(Ae)*

Bär, 2004
Enamel and oil on cotton, 240 × 190 cm
Eigentum Kunstsammlung Stadt Zürich, *(He)*

Beitrag an das Familienalbum, 2004
Acrylic and enamel on wood, 51 × 41 cm
Privatbesitz, *(Ae)*

Berg, Bäume, Himmel, 2003
Enamel on wood, 20 × 26 cm
Sammlung Cristina und Thomas Bechtler, *(Ae)*

big wave, 2006
Acrylic and enamel on wood, 15 × 24,5 cm
Privatsammlung, Schweiz, *(Ae)*

bin vernetzt, 2005
Enamel on wood, 16 × 25 cm
Privatbesitz, Hamburg, *(Do)*

blacking in my mind, 2005
Enamel on wood, 43 × 51 cm
Courtesy Monica De Cardenas Gallery, Milano, *(Gu/Ri)*

champ, 2005
Enamel on wood, 25,5 × 20 cm
Privatsammlung, Zürich, *(Ae)*

Dämmerung, 2004
Enamel on wood, 14 × 23,5 cm
Sammlung Theresia und Rainer Haarmann,
Neuwittenbek, *(Do)*

Delphi, 2004
Enamel on cotton, 190 × 240 cm
UBS AG, *(He)*

Delta, 2003
Acrylic and enamel on cotton, 174 × 188 cm
Sammlung Ricola, *(He)*

dicht dran, 2005
Acrylic and enamel on cotton, 240 × 190 cm
Courtesy Sfeir-Semler Gallery, Hamburg, *(Bu)*

domestic 1, 2003
Enamel on wood, 20 × 22,5 cm
Sammlung Steinrich Sultier

Egypt Eagle, 2003
Enamel on wood, 18,5 × 19 cm
Privatsammlung, Zürich, *(Ae)*

einsamer Reiter, 2004
Enamel on wood, 40 × 45 cm
Sammlung Steinrich Sultier, *(Ae)*

Erdbeerschale, 2004
Enamel on aluminium, 25 × 31 cm
Kunsthaus Zürich, Vereinigung Zürcher Kunstfreunde,
Gruppe Junge Kunst, *(He)*

Faltblatt, 2005
Acrylic and enamel on wood, 55 × 60 cm
Privatbesitz, *(Ae)*

Falter, 2005
Acrylic and enamel on cotton, 190 × 240 cm
Sammlung Cristina und Thomas Bechtler, *(He)*

fast forward, 2004
Acrylic and enamel on cotton, 240 × 190 cm
Collection De Heus Zomer, *(He)*

Feuerfarbige 2, 2004
Acrylic and enamel on wood, 14,2 × 13 cm
Privatbesitz, Zürich, *(Ae)*

Feuerrad, 2006
Acrylic and enamel on cotton, 240 × 190 cm
Julius Bär Kunstsammlung, *(Ha)*

Flora und Fauna, 2005
Acrylic and oil on wood, 12,5 × 25 cm
Sammlung Cristina und Thomas Bechtler, *(Ae)*

Flusser, 2005
Acrylic and enamel on cotton, 300 × 200 cm, *(Il)*

Fruchtkörbchen, 2006
Enamel on wood, 20,5 × 24 cm
Privatsammlung, Schweiz, *(Gu/Ri)*

frozen for now, 2005
Enamel on cotton, 140 × 120 cm
Courtesy Christopher Grimes Gallery, Los Angeles, *(Bu)*

globe, 2005
Acrylic and enamel on cotton, 150 × 140 cm
Sammlung Ruedi Bechtler, *(Gu/Ri)*

Glutherd, Spechte und Wasserzuber mit Karpfen, 2004
Enamel on aluminium, 25 × 34 cm
Privatsammlung

grotesk, 2004
Enamel on cotton, 240 × 190 cm
Sammlung Steinrich Sultier, *(He)*

Groteskvase mit Blumen 1, 2004
Enamel on aluminium, 34 × 25 cm
Privatbesitz, Zürich, *(He)*

Groteskvase mit Blumen 2, 2004
Enamel on aluminium, 31 × 25 cm
Kunsthaus Zürich, Vereinigung Zürcher Kunstfreunde,
Gruppe Junge Kunst, *(He)*

handmade in Egypt, 2003
Enamel on wood, 16,5 × 21 cm
Privatbesitz Giacomo Santiago Rogado

heartbeat, 2005
Acrylic and enamel on cotton, 200 × 300 cm
Courtesy Christopher Grimes Gallery, Los Angeles, *(Bu)*

heaveninside, 2005
Acrylic and enamel on cotton, 140 × 120 cm
Courtesy Mark Müller Gallery, Zürich, *(Il)*

Hera, 2005
Acrylic and enamel on wood, 30,5 × 45 cm
Privatbesitz Vincent Kriste, *(Ae)*

Herzblut, 2005
Acrylic and enamel on wood, 26 × 20,5 cm
Privatbesitz, *(Ae)*

Herzchen, 2004
Acrylic and enamel on wood, 23 × 34 cm
Courtesy Monica De Cardenas Gallery, Milano, *(Gu/Ri)*

high heels 1, 2006
Acrylic and enamel on wood, 12,5 × 18,5 cm
Sammlung Steinrich Sultier, *(Ae)*

hinterlässt Spuren, 2005
Acrylic and enamel on cotton, 240 × 190 cm
Courtesy Monica De Cardenas Gallery, Milano, *(Gu/Ri)*

horizon takes me 1, 2006
Acrylic and enamel on cotton, 140 × 150 cm
Courtesy Monica De Cardenas Gallery, Milano, *(Il)*

horizon takes me 2, 2006
Acrylic, enamel and stickers on cotton, 240 × 450 cm
Courtesy Mark Müller Gallery, Zürich, *(Il)*

Hummel, 2004
Enamel on wood, 34,5 × 48 cm
Privatbesitz, Bern, *(Ae)*

Humpty, 2005
Acrylic and enamel on cotton, 300 × 200 cm, *(Il)*

Ich lieb Dich, ich lieb Dich nicht…, 2004
Acrylic and enamel on cotton, 255 × 360 cm
Aargauer Kunsthaus Aarau, *(Bu)*

Jackpot, 2004
Acrylic and enamel on cotton, 360 × 255 cm
Privatsammlung, Zürich, *(Bu)*

j'ai besoin de, 2004
Acrylic and enamel on cotton, 240 × 190 cm
UBS AG, *(He)*

Kies, 2005
Acrylic and enamel on cotton, 180 × 140 cm
Sammlung Ricola, *(He)*

Kopfankopfrennen, 2005
Acrylic and enamel on wood, 32 × 34 cm
Courtesy Sfeir-Semler Gallery, Hamburg, *(Do)*

kreisen, 2005
Acrylic and enamel on wood, 28 × 21 cm
Privatbesitz, *(Ae)*

Labor, 2005
Acrylic and enamel on wood, 28 × 45 cm
Privatbesitz Stefanie und Alfredo Häberli, *(Ae)*

La Rondella, 2006
Acrylic and enamel on wood, 23 × 34 cm
Courtesy Monica De Cardenas Gallery, Milano, *(Gu/Ri)*

Leo 1, 2004
Acrylic and enamel on wood, 60 × 35 cm
Sammlung Steinrich Sultier, *(Ae)*

Liebespaar, 2003
Acrylic and enamel on cotton, 180 × 140 cm
Sammlung Theresia und Rainer Haarmann,
Neuwittenbek, *(He)*

magic, 2006
Acrylic and enamel on wood, 46 × 40 cm
Privatbesitz, *(Ae)*

make me change my mind, 2005
Enamel on cotton, 180 × 140 cm
Sammlung Ruedi Bechtler, *(Bu)*

Mandala, 2005
Enamel on cotton, 180 × 140 cm
Courtesy Sfeir-Semler Gallery, Hamburg, *(Bu)*

Moos, 2005
Acrylic and enamel on wood, 22 × 19 cm
Privatbesitz Stefanie und Alfredo Häberli, *(Ae)*

Matrix, 2005
Enamel on cotton, 180 × 140 cm
Courtesy Sfeir-Semler Gallery, Hamburg, *(Be)*

Nachtschattengewächs 1, 2004
Acrylic and enamel on wood, 10 × 20 cm
Sammlung Roderick Hönig, *(Ae)*

nein, nie, 2005
Acrylic and enamel on wood, 28 × 45 cm
Sammlung Steinrich Sultier, *(Ae)*

nonstopraining, 2006
Acrylic and enamel on wood, 20 × 31 cm
Privatbesitz, *(Ae)*

northface, 2005
Acrylic and enamel on wood, 24,5 × 14 cm
Courtesy Sfeir-Semler Gallery, Hamburg, *(Do)*

oasis, 2003
Enamel on wood, 14 × 21 cm
Privatbesitz, Zürich

peeling, 2004
Enamel on cotton, 240 × 190 cm
Sammlung Cristina und Thomas Bechtler, *(He)*

planen, 2005
Acrylic and enamel on cotton, 300 × 200 cm, *(Il)*

Puppe, 2004
Enamel and oil on cotton, 240 × 190 cm
Privatbesitz, Berlin, *(He)*

Radar, 2005
Enamel on cotton, 190 × 240 cm
Courtesy Sfeir-Semler Gallery, Hamburg, *(Be)*

Radar, 2005
Acrylic and enamel on wood, 16 × 25 cm
Privatbesitz Stefanie und Alfredo Häberli, *(Ae)*

Riss, 2005
Acrylic and enamel on cotton, 180 × 140 cm
Privatbesitz, *(He)*

Romanze, 2005
Acrylic, enamel and oil on wood, 60 × 60 cm
Privatbesitz, Köln, *(Bu)*

Rorschach, 2002
Acrylic and enamel on cotton, 183 × 142 cm
Privatsammlung, Zürich, *(He)*

Rotor, 2005
Acrylic and enamel on cotton, 100 × 150 cm
Courtesy Sfeir-Semler Gallery, Hamburg, *(Bu)*

Rotwelk, 2006
Acrylic and enamel on wood, 34 × 23,5 cm
Privatbesitz, *(Ae)*

sandeln, 2006
Acrylic and enamel on cotton, 180 × 140 cm
Privatsammlung, Zürich, *(Il)*

Schlangenfrass, 2004
Acrylic and enamel on wood, 25,5 × 40 cm
Sammlung Steinrich Sultier, *(Ae)*

Schlangenleder, 2002
Acrylic, enamel and oil on cotton, 137 × 137 cm
Aargauer Kunsthaus Aarau, *(He)*

shelter, 2005
Enamel on cotton, 63 × 69 cm
Sammlung Steinrich Sultier, *(Il)*

Skuo, 2005
Enamel on wood, 32 × 34 cm
Courtesy Sfeir-Semler Gallery, Hamburg, *(Do)*

smart bomb, 2003
Enamel on wood, 20,5 × 29,5 cm
Privatbesitz

snoop, 2005
Acrylic and enamel on cotton, 120 × 100 cm
Courtesy Sfeir-Semler Gallery, Hamburg, *(Be)*

Spa, 2004
Enamel on cotton, 190 × 240 cm
UBS AG, *(He)*

Spanschachtel und Nautilus, 2004
Enamel on aluminium, 25 × 26 cm
Kunsthaus Zürich, Vereinigung Zürcher Kunstfreunde, Gruppe Junge Kunst, *(He)*

Spanschachtel mit Römer und Zitrone, 2004
Enamel on aluminium, 25 × 26 cm
Kunsthaus Zürich, Vereinigung Zürcher Kunstfreunde, Gruppe Junge Kunst, *(He)*

stichfest, 2005
Acrylic and enamel on cotton, 140 × 120 cm
Privatsammlung, Zürich, *(Bu)*

stille Wasser, 2005
Acrylic and enamel on wood, 8 × 22 cm
Courtesy Monica De Cardenas Gallery, Milano, *(Gu/Ri)*

Stillleben mit Büchern und Kerze, 2004
Enamel on aluminium, 25 × 42 cm
Privatbesitz, *(Ae)*

Sumo, 2005
Acrylic and enamel on cotton, 255 × 360 cm
Sammlung Ruedi Bechtler, *(He)*

sunset, 2004
Acrylic and enamel on wood, 26 × 20 cm
Courtesy Monica De Cardenas Gallery, Milano, *(Gu/Ri)*

Taucher, 2005
Acrylic and enamel on wood, 51 × 42 cm
Privatsammlung, Schweiz, *(Gu/Ri)*

Teddy, 2002
Acrylic and enamel on wood, 41 × 30,5 cm
Eigentum Kunstsammlung Stadt Zürich

Tollkirschen, 2004
Acrylic and enamel on cotton, 200 × 230 cm
Sammlung Theresia und Rainer Haarmann, Neuwittenbek, *(Ki)*

Tollkirschen, 2004
Enamel on wood, 29 × 23 cm
Sammlung Theresia und Rainer Haarmann, Neuwittenbek, *(Do)*

toptop, 2005
Acrylic and enamel on cotton, 140 × 180 cm
Courtesy Sfeir-Semler Gallery, Hamburg, *(Bu)*

Trauerweide, 2003
Acrylic, enamel and marker on cotton, 240 × 190 cm
Julius Bär Kunstsammlung, *(He)*

Triumph, 2006
Acrylic and enamel on cotton, 120 × 100 cm
Privatsammlung, Schweiz, *(Il)*

trüb, 2005
Acrylic and enamel on wood, 32 × 34,5 cm
Courtesy Monica De Cardenas Gallery, Milano, *(Gu/Ri)*

Unkraut, 2004
Enamel on cotton, 180 × 180 cm
UBS AG, *(He)*

Vergissmeinnicht, 2006
Acrylic and enamel on cotton, 100 × 150 cm
Sammlung Carl Friedrich Schröer, *(Bu)*

von den blauen Bergen, 2003
Enamel on wood, 21 × 23,5 cm
Privatbesitz Christoph Schreiber

Walderdbeeren auf Zinnteller, 2004
Enamel on aluminium, 25 × 31cm
Privatbesitz, Zürich, *(He)*

wasteland, 2002
Acrylic and enamel on cotton 145 × 180 cm
Sammlung BKW/FMB Energie AG, Bern, *(He)*

welken Birnbaum, 2004
Enamel on cotton, 240 × 190 cm
Sammlung Theresia und Rainer Haarmann, Neuwittenbek, *(Bu)*

Wellenschlagen, 2005
Acrylic and enamel on cotton, 300 × 200 cm, *(Il)*

Windhund, 2003
Acrylic, enamel and oil on cotton, 200 × 230 cm
Sammlung Cristina und Thomas Bechtler, *(He)*

wing, 2004
Acrylic and enamel on cotton, 230 × 200 cm
Museum zu Allerheiligen Schaffhausen, *(He)*

Winterschlaf, 2003
Acrylic and enamel on cotton, 230 × 200 cm
Privatbesitz, *(He)*

Woodoo, 2005
Acrylic and enamel on wood, 24,5 × 20 cm
Courtesy Sfeir-Semler Gallery, Hamburg, *(Do)*

Wucher, 2006
Acrylic and enamel on cotton, 240 × 190 cm
Courtesy Monica De Cardenas Gallery, Milano, *(Il)*

Zitrusfrüchte in Porzellanschale, 2004
Enamel on aluminium, 25 × 33 cm
Kunsthaus Zürich, Vereinigung Zürcher Kunstfreunde, Gruppe Junge Kunst, *(He)*

Zitterlein, 2003
Acrylic and enamel on cotton, 190 × 190 cm
Privatsammlung Ursina und Beat Wälchli, *(He)*

1 Mondjahr, 2005
Enamel on wood, 32 × 34 cm
Privatbesitz, Köln, *(Bu)*

2 strukturierte Explosionen, 2005
Acrylic and enamel on wood, 21 × 28 cm
UBS AG, *(Ae)*

100 aspects of the moon, 2005
Acrylic, enamel and stickers on cotton, 230 × 200 cm
Sammlung Cristina und Thomas Bechtler, *(He)*

Photographers:
(Ae) David Aebi, Burgdorf
(Bu) Wolfgang Burat, Köln
(Do) Fred Dott, Hamburg
(Gu/Ri) Annalisa Guidetti/Giovanni Ricci, Milano
(Ha) Peter Hauck, Basel
(He) Heinrich Helfenstein, Zürich
(Il) Andreas Ilg, Zürich
(Ki) Rolf Kissling, Molfsee

Christine Streuli

1975 born in Bern, lives and works in Zürich

1997–2001
Studied at the Hochschule für Gestaltung und Kunst Zürich (HGKZ) and the Hochschule der Künste (HdK), Berlin

2001–2002
International Studio and Curatorial Program (ISCP), New York
Scholarship Yvonne Lang-Chardonnens Stiftung, Zürich

2003
"Artist in Residence", Cairo, Swiss Arts Council Pro Helvetia

2004
"Swiss Art Award 2004", Bundesamt für Kultur, Switzerland

2005
"Swiss Art Award 2005", Bundesamt für Kultur, Switzerland
"Kiefer Hablitzel Preis", Kiefer Hablitzel Stiftung, Switzerland
"Artist in Residence", San Francisco, scholarship City of Zürich

2006
"Swiss Art Award 2006", Bundesamt für Kultur, Switzerland

Bibliografie / Bibliography

2006
Steiger, Bruno, "Ein Bild wie Weihnachten in Las Vegas: Christine Streulis *Jackpot*", in: *Du*, Nr. 5, Juni 2006, p. 20–21.

Zürcher, Isabel, "Christine Streuli", in: *artist Kunstmagazin*, Nr. 67, 2006, p. 4–7.

2005
Kurzmeyer, Roman, "Poetische Reflexion", in: *Unter 30. Junge Schweizer Kunst*, Nr. 3. Exhibition catalogue *Centre PasquArt*, 2005, p. 27–29.

2004
Swiss Arts Council Pro Helvetia (Hg.), "Cahier d'artiste. Christine Streuli", with a text by Beat Wismer, 2004.

Wismer, Beat, "Die Schatten des Hintergrundes, oder: Malerei als latenter Ort, in dem die Bilder aufgehoben sind", in: *Dorothea von Stetten-Kunstpreis 2004*. Exhibition catalogue Kunstmuseum Bonn, 2004, p. 92–111.

Della Casa, Bettina, "Christine Streuli", in: *Sentieri e avvistamenti. Giovane arte contemporanea in Svizzera*. Exhibition catalogue *Centro d'Arte moderna e contemporanea La Spezia*, 2004, p. 58–59.

Steiger, Bruno, "Auf der Suche nach dem gültigen Bild", in: *Tages-Anzeiger*, Zürich, 24.6.04, p. 43.

Einzelausstellungen / Solo exhibitions

2007
Biennale Venedig, Swiss Pavillon (with Yves Netzhammer), Venice
Mark Müller Gallery, Zürich
Kunsthaus Langenthal (with Bruno Jakob), Langenthal (CH)
Monica De Cardenas Gallery, Milano

2005
"double it", Projectroom, Monica De Cardenas Gallery, Milano
"dicht dran", Sfeir-Semler Gallery, Hamburg (D)
"ensemble ensemble", curated by Roman Kurzmeyer, Kunstraum Kreuzlingen, Kreuzlingen (CH)

2004
"eksam-nedma", curated by Roman Kurzmeyer, Amden, (CH)
Projectroom "Enter", Museum of Fine Arts Thun, Thun (CH)
"Tollkirschen", Sfeir-Semler Gallery, Hamburg (D)

2003
"longing/belonging", Mark Müller Gallery, Zürich
"homeland", Mashrabeja Gallery, Cairo

2002
"something in common", (2 person show), Massimo Audiello Gallery, New York
"Hunter", Showroom, Hunter College of Fine Arts, New York

Gruppenausstellungen / Group exhibitions

2006
"Swiss Art Awards 2006", ART Basel, Basel (CH)

2005
"Devil's Punchbowl" curated by Katharina Grosse, Christopher Grimes Gallery, Los Angeles
"rainbow", Sfeir-Semler Gallery, Beirut
"aufgedeckt", Mark Müller Gallery, (3 person show), Zürich
"Swiss Art Awards 2005", ART Basel, Basel (CH)
"Dorothea von Stetten-Kunstpreis", (5 person show) Museum of Fine Arts, Bonn, Bonn (D)

2004
"Forme Originarie", Galica Gallery, Milano
"Reanimation", Museum of Fine Arts Thun, Thun (CH)
"Malerei", Kunstverein Arnsberg, Arnsberg (D)
"Swiss Art Awards 2004", ART Basel, Basel (CH)
"Bilder der Malerei", Mark Müller Gallery, Zürich
"dalla pagina allo spazio", Museo Cantonale d'Arte Lugano, Lugano (CH)

2003
"Neue Räume", Museum of Fine Arts Aarau, Aarau (CH)
"Fragmente des Paradieses", Kunsthalle Palazzo Liestal, Liestal (CH)
"Swiss Art Awards 2003", ART Basel, Basel (CH)

2002
"Spieglein, Spieglein an der Wand, ein Gemälde will schön sein...?", Mark Müller Gallery, Zürich

Autoren / Authors

Claudia Jolles
(*1958), Kunstkritikerin und Chefredaktorin *Kunst-Bulletin*, Zürich.
(*1958), art critic and editor-in-chief of *Kunst-Bulletin*, Zürich.

Roman Kurzmeyer
(*1961), Kunstwissenschafter und Kurator, lebt in Basel. Dozent an der Hochschule für Gestaltung und Kunst Basel und Kurator der Sammlung Ricola. Seit 1999 Ausstellungen und Projekte in der Berggemeinde Amden. Informationen zu diesem Projekt auf www.xcult.org/amden.
(*1961), art theorist and curator, lives in Basel. Lecturer at the Hochschule für Gestaltung und Kunst Basel and curator of the Sammlung Ricola. Exhibitions and projects at the Amden Mountain Community since 1999. For information on this project see www.xcult.org/amden.

Deniz Pekerman
(*1969), lebt in Köln und arbeitet als freier Kunsthistoriker.
(*1969), lives in Cologne and works as a free-lance art historian.

C. F. Schröer
(*1954) arbeitet als Journalist und Publizist im Bereich Kunst und Architektur. Er lebt mit Büchern, Bildern und Garten in Bonn. Aktuelles Motto »Nichts ist tiefer als die Oberfläche«.
(*1954) works as a journalist and publicist in the field of art and architecture. He lives in Bonn with books, paintings and a garden. Current motto: »Nothing is deeper than the surface«.

Madeleine Schuppli
(*1965), Kunsthistorikerin, 1996–2000 Kuratorin an der Kunsthalle Basel, seit 2000 Direktorin Kunstmuseum Thun.
Madeleine Schuppli (*1965), art historian, curator at the Kunsthalle Basel from 1996–2000; Director of the Kunstmuseum Thun since 2000.

Beat Wismer
(*1953), Kunsthistoriker, lebt in Aarau; seit 1985 Direktor des Aargauer Kunsthauses Aarau.
(*1953), art historian, lives in Aarau; Director of the Aargauer Kunsthaus Aarau since 1985.

Isabel Zürcher
(*1970), Kunsthistorikerin, nach mehrjähriger wissenschaftlicher Mitarbeit an der Kunsthalle Basel freischaffend als Kritikerin und Lektorin; Publikationen und Texte vor allem zur zeitgenössischen Kunst und ihrer Vermittlung.
(*1970), art historian, worked for several years as a scientific assistant at the Kunsthalle Basel, free-lance critic and editor; publications and texts mainly on contemporary art and its mediation.

Christine Streuli
bumblebee

Concept: Christine Streuli, Hendrik Schwantes

Texts: Claudia Jolles, Roman Kurzmeyer,
Deniz Pekermann, Carl Friedrich Schröer,
Madeleine Schuppli, Beat Wismer, Isabel Zürcher

Design: Hendrik Schwantes, Berlin
Assistance: Sandra Tebbe

Editorial Assistance: Marina Leuenberger, Zürich
Editing and Proof-Reading: Martina Buder,
Silvia Jaklitsch
English Copy Editing: Angelika Ritter, Zürich
Translations: Pauline Cumbers, Jeremy Gaines,
Catherine Schelbert

Reprographics: Licht & Tiefe, Berlin
Printing: Jütte Messedruck, Leipzig
Silkscreen (Cover): Pawellek, Königs Wusterhausen
Binding: Kunst und Verlagsbuchbinderei, Leipzig

Printed in Germany

ISBN-10: 3-938821-66-3
ISBN-13: 978-3-938821-66-4

Bibliografische Information Der Deutschen Bibliothek:
Die Deutsche Bibliothek verzeichnet diese Publikation in der Deutschen Nationalbibliografie; detaillierte bibliografische Daten sind im Internet über http://dnb.ddb.de abrufbar.

Bibliographic information published by Die Deutsche Bibliothek: Die Deutsche Bibliothek lists this publication in the Deutsche Nationalbibliografie; detailed bibliographic data is available in the Internet at http://dnb.ddb.de.

Distributed in the United Kingdom
Cornerhouse Publications
70 Oxford Street, Manchester M1 5 NH, UK
phone 0044-(0)161-200 15 03,
fax 0044-(0)161-200 15 04

Distributed outside Europe
D.A.P./Distributed Art Publishers, Inc., New York
155 Sixth Avenue, 2nd Floor, New York, NY 10013, USA
phone 001-(0)212-627 19 99
fax 001-(0)212-627 94 84

Ein grosses Dankeschön an / Many thanks to

Monica De Cardenas, Claudia Jolles, Roman Kurzmeyer (Herzblut),
Marina Leuenberger (100 wichtige Fresszettelchen),
Mark Müller (schonsolangsotoll), Deniz Pekerman,
Angelika Ritter, Carl Friedrich Schröer, Madeleine Schuppli,
Hendrik Schwantes (geiles Sofa), Andrée Sfeir-Semler,
Bruno Steiger (Hauptgewinn), Barbara und Rolf Streuli,
Dieter Streuli, Beat Wismer (tief und forever), Franziska Zaugg,
Isabel Zürcher.

Die Publikation wurde ermöglicht durch die grosszügige finanzielle Unterstützung von / The publication was made possible through the great financial support of:

Alfred Richterich Stiftung
Ernst und Olga Gubler-Hablützel Stiftung
Fachstelle Kultur Kanton Zürich
Pro Helvetia, Schweizer Kulturstiftung
Schwyzer-Stiftung
Stadt Zürich, Abteilung Kultur
Steo-Stiftung Zürich

schweizer kulturstiftung
prohelvetia

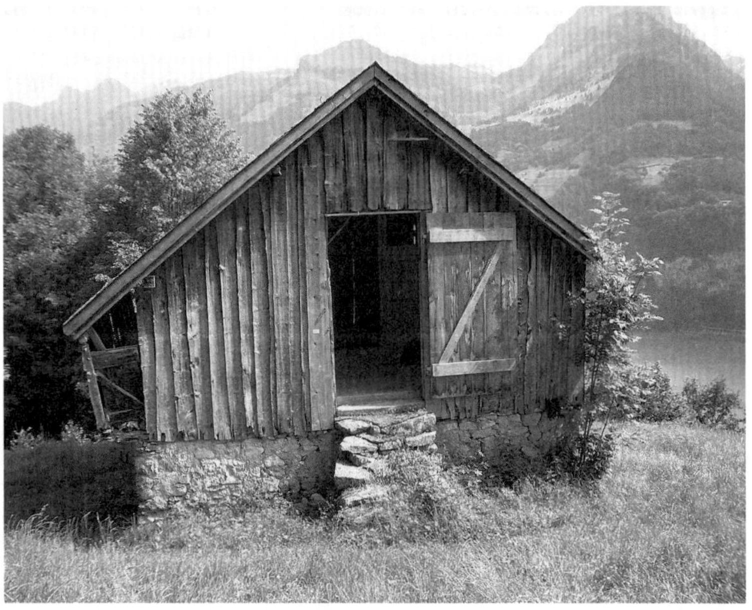

Scheune in Amden am Walensee, Ort der Ausstellung *eksam-nedma* (siehe Text Kurzmeyer).
Barn in Amden on Walensee, location of the exhibition *eksam-nedma* (see text Kurzmeyer).

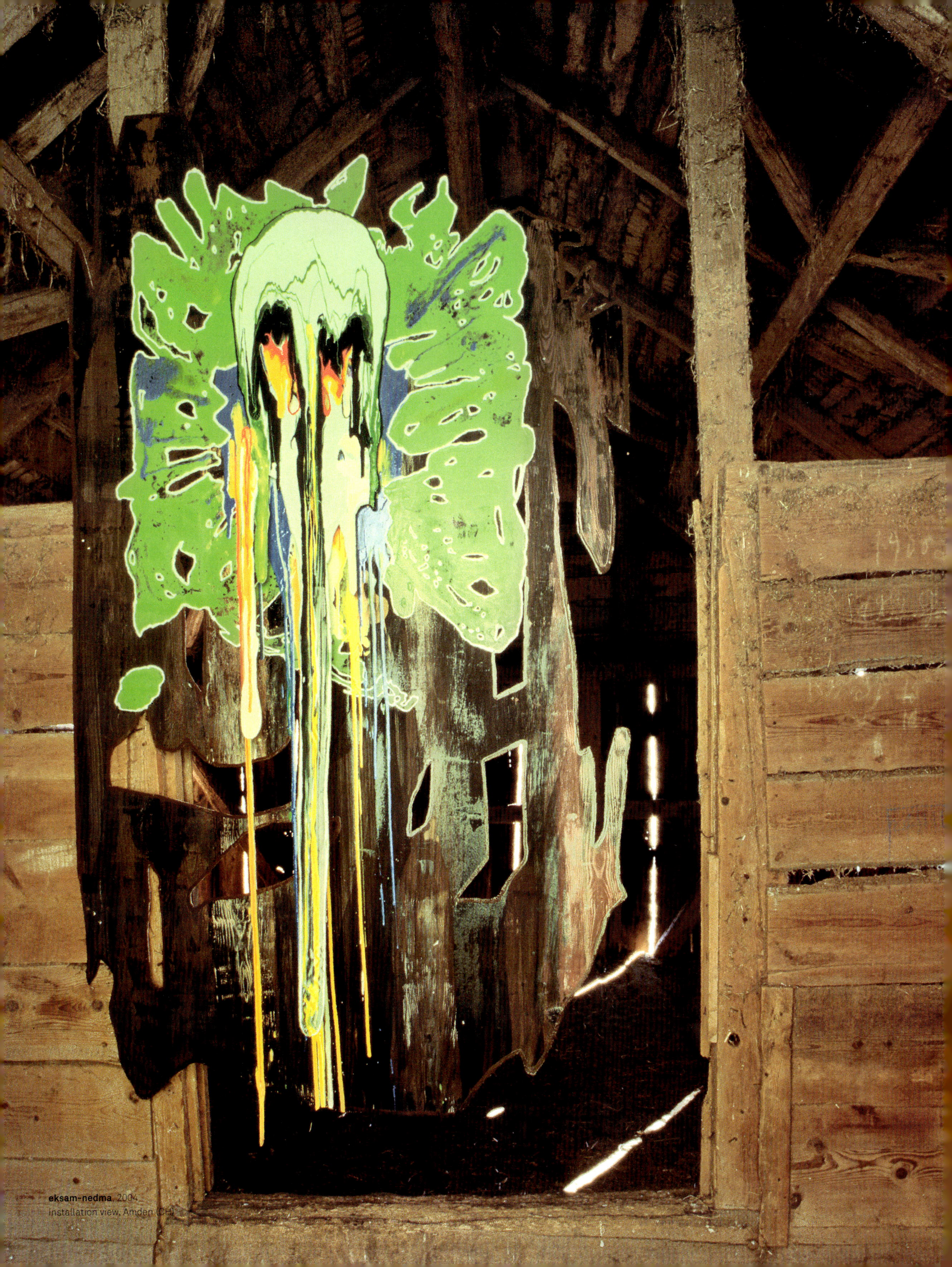

eksam-nedma, 2004
installation view, Amden (CH)

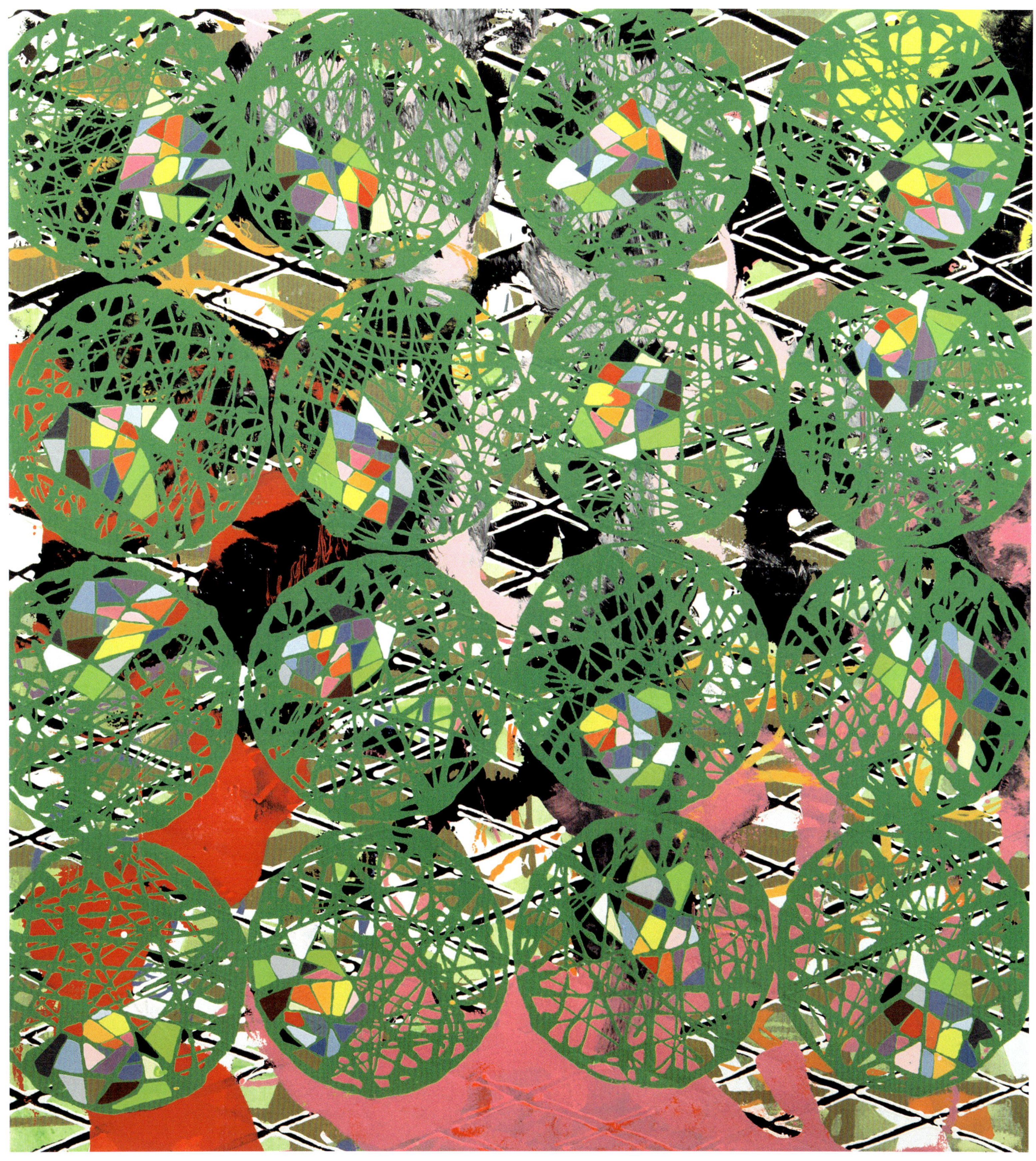

globe

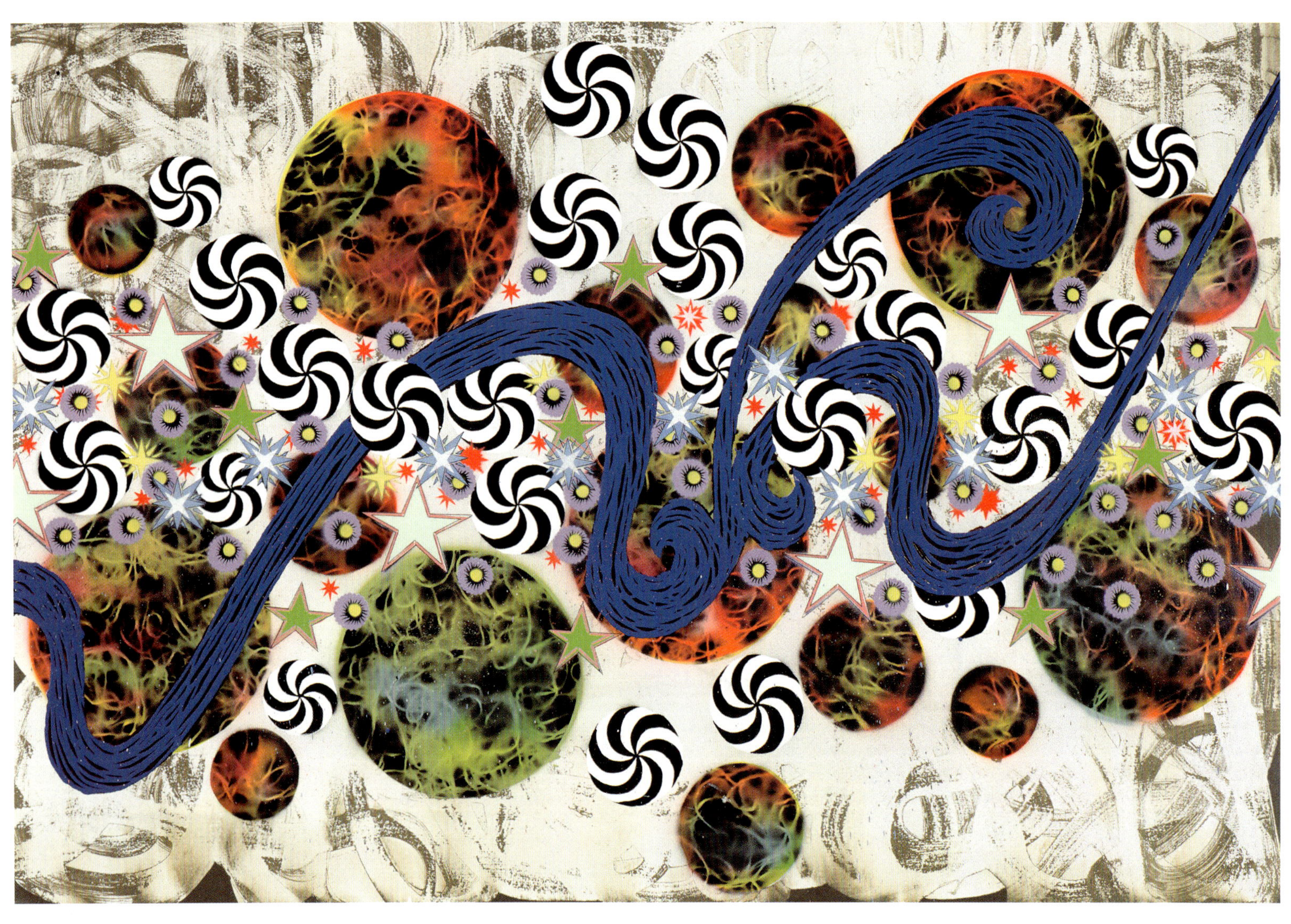

Rotor

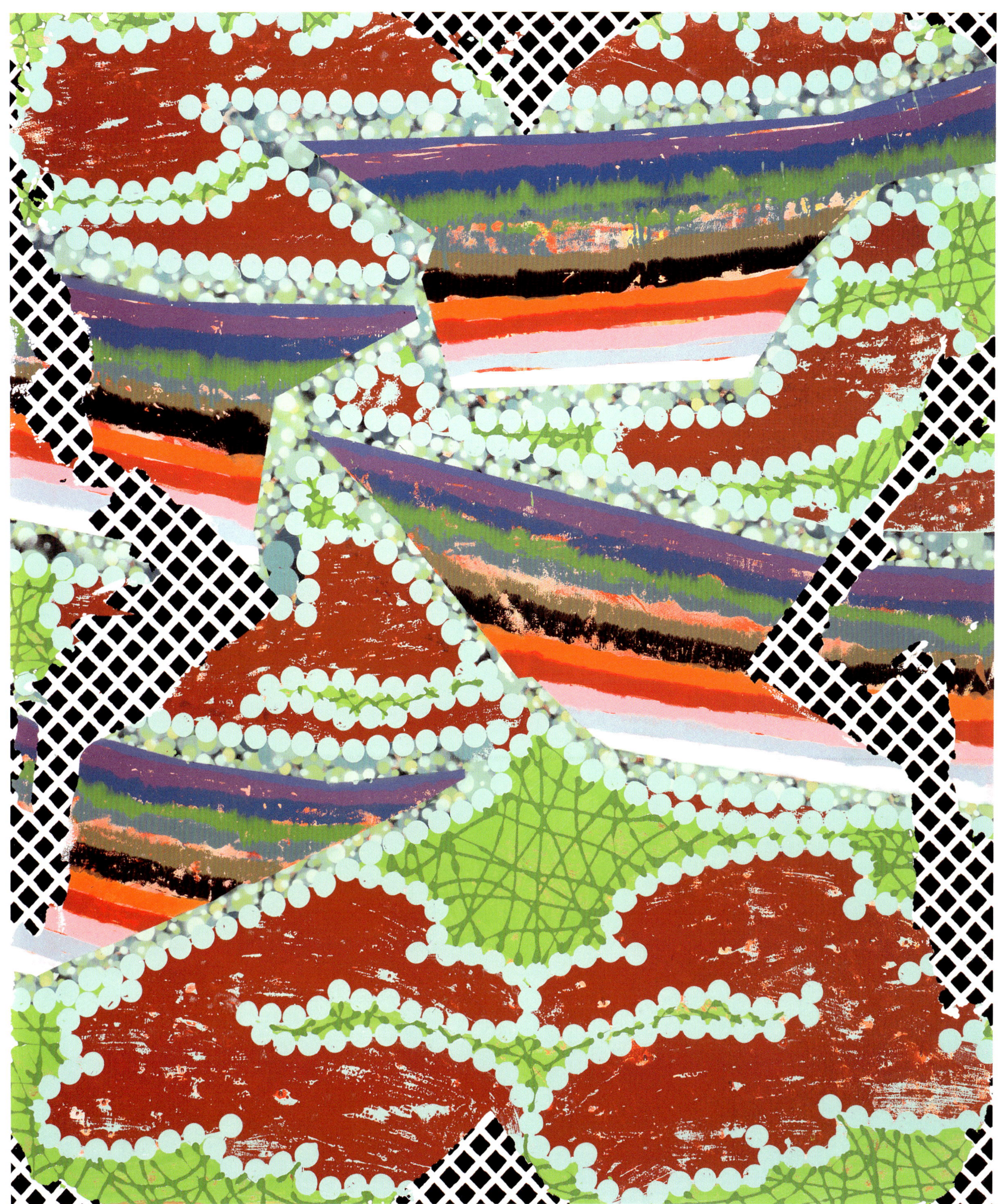

stichfest

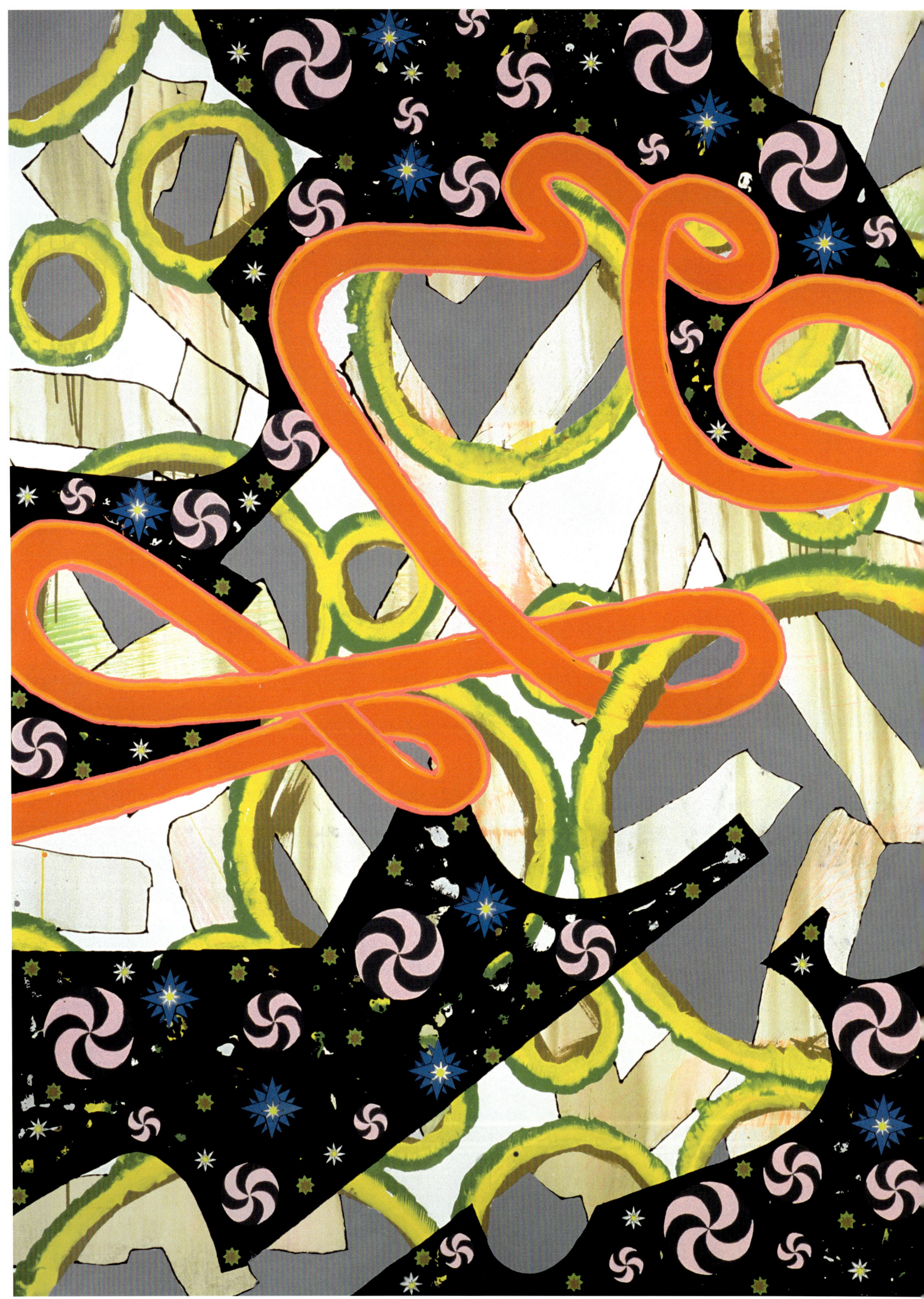

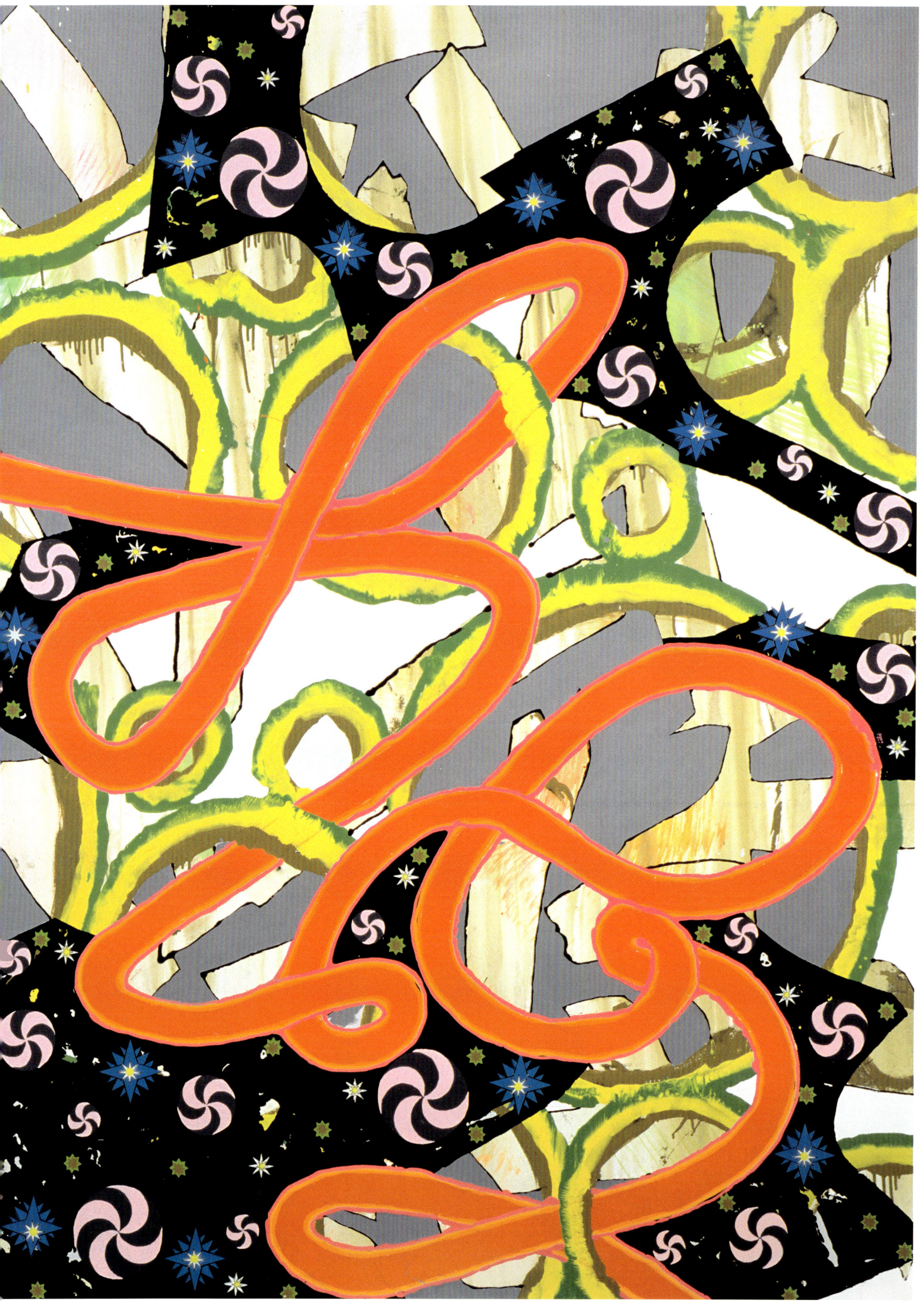

heartbeat

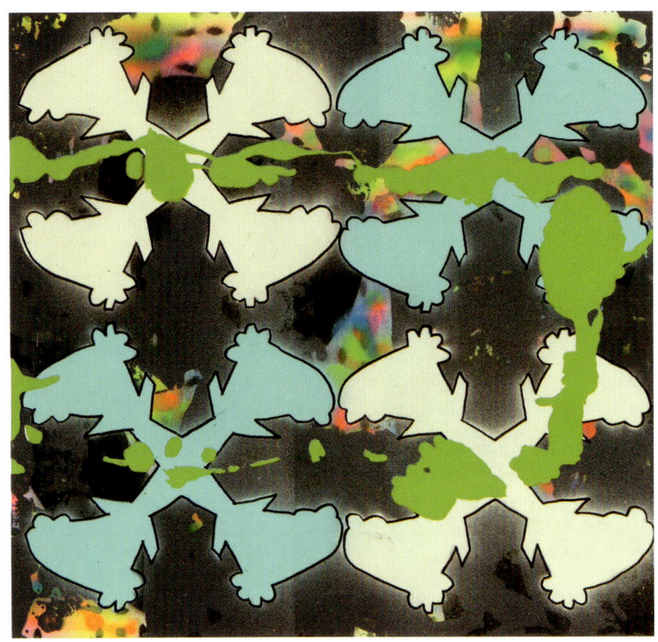

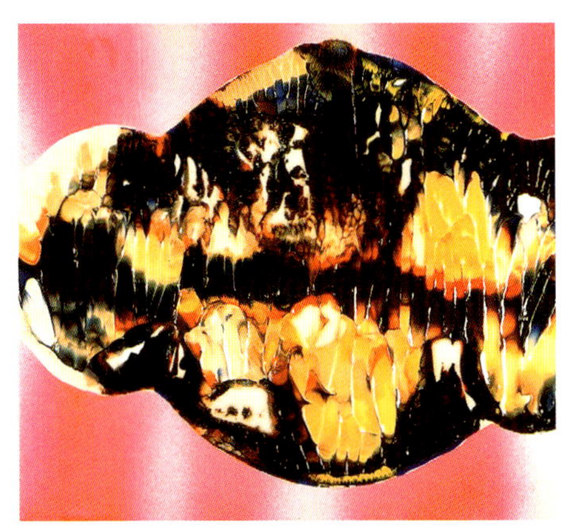

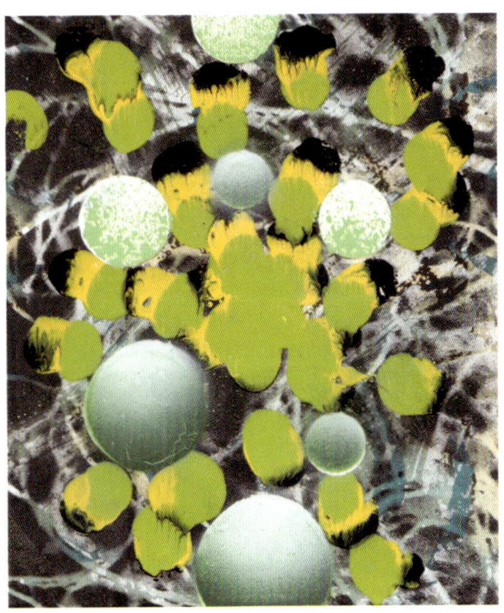

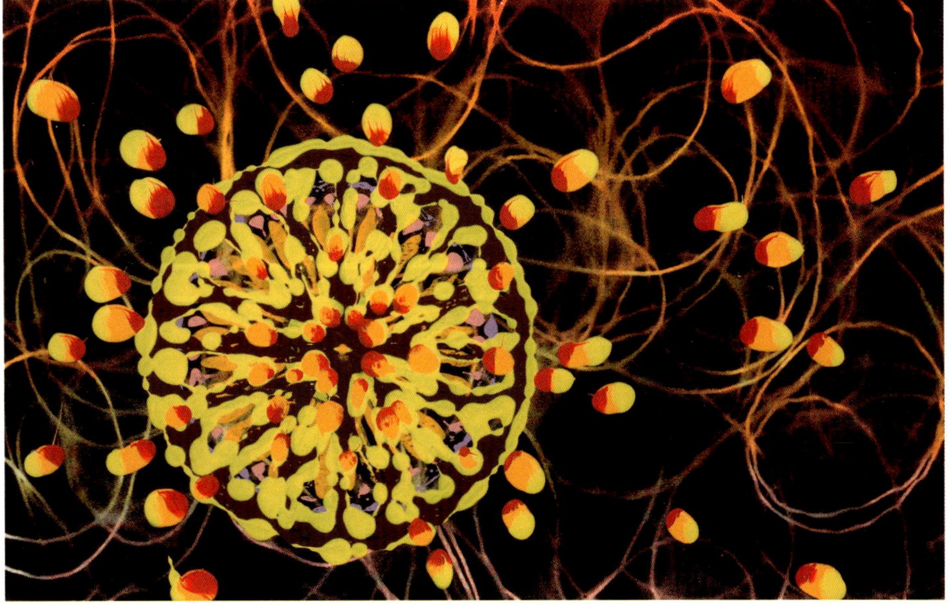

< Kopfankopfrennen
> von den blauen Bergen
< Moos
> Labor

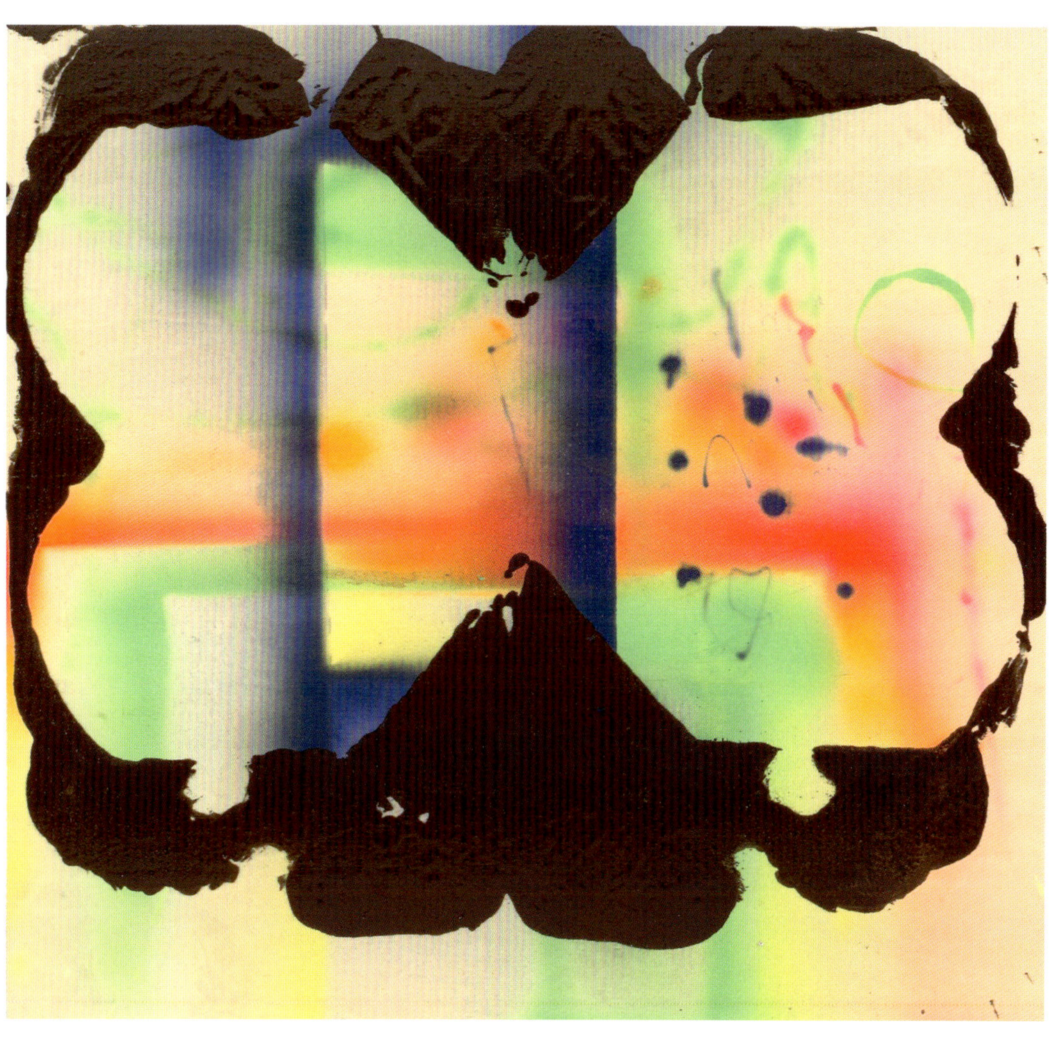

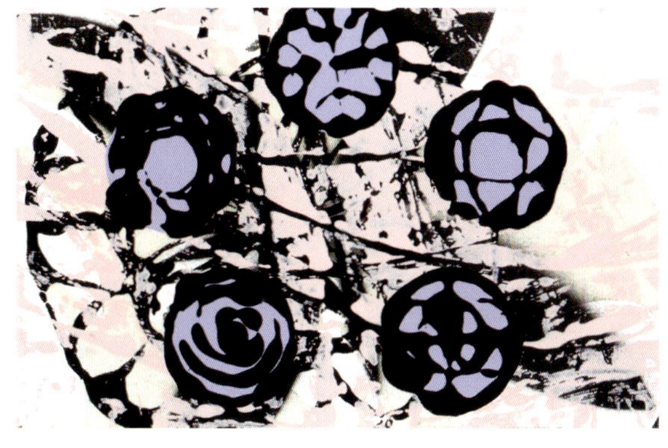

> Faltblatt
< Radar

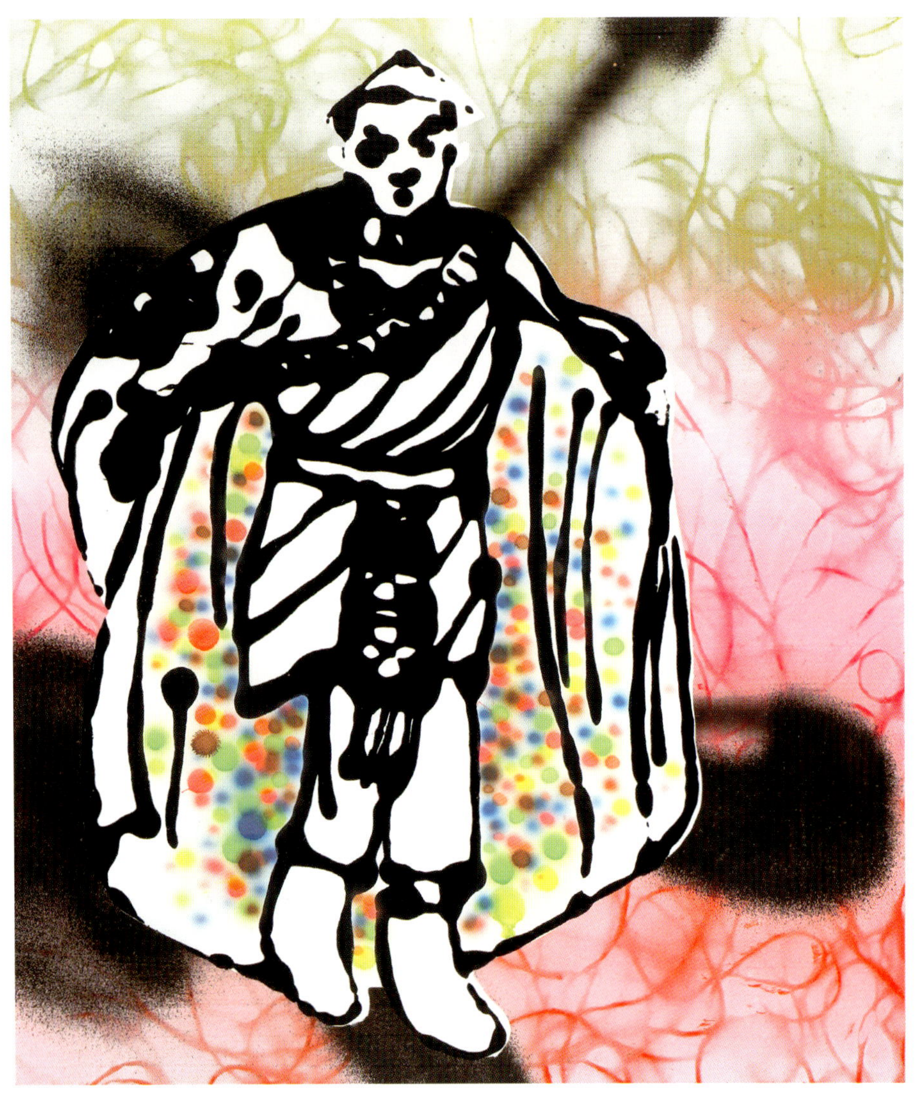

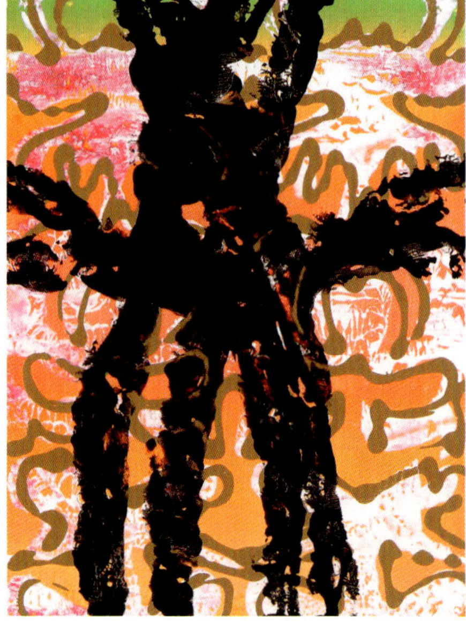

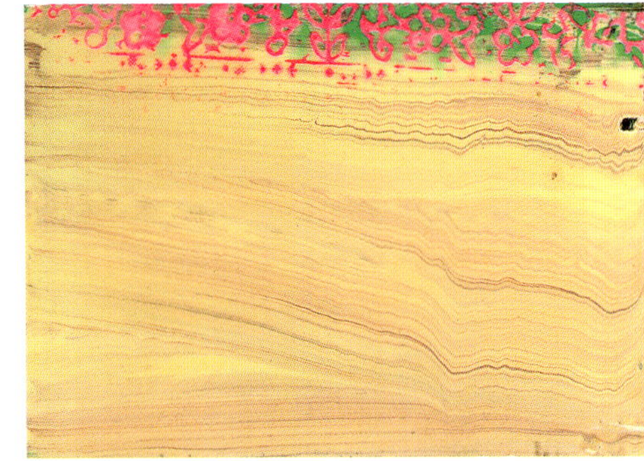

< magic
> Woodoo
< oasis

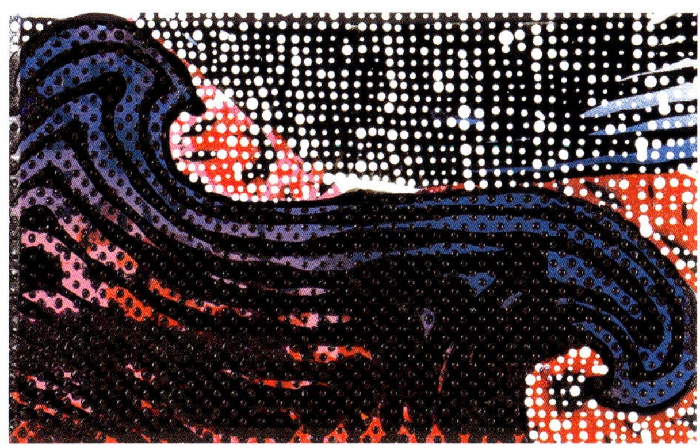

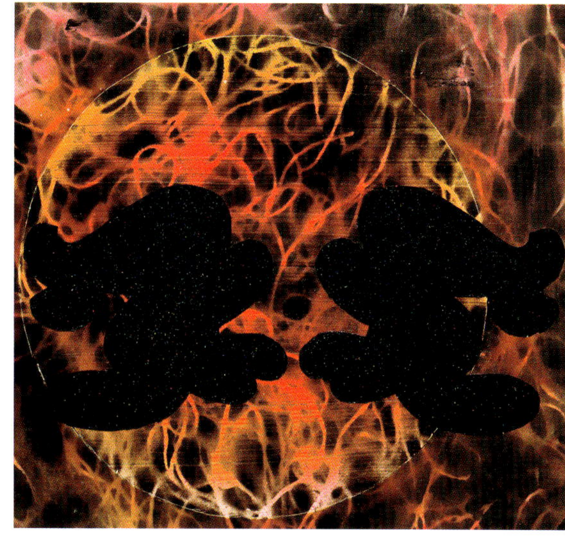

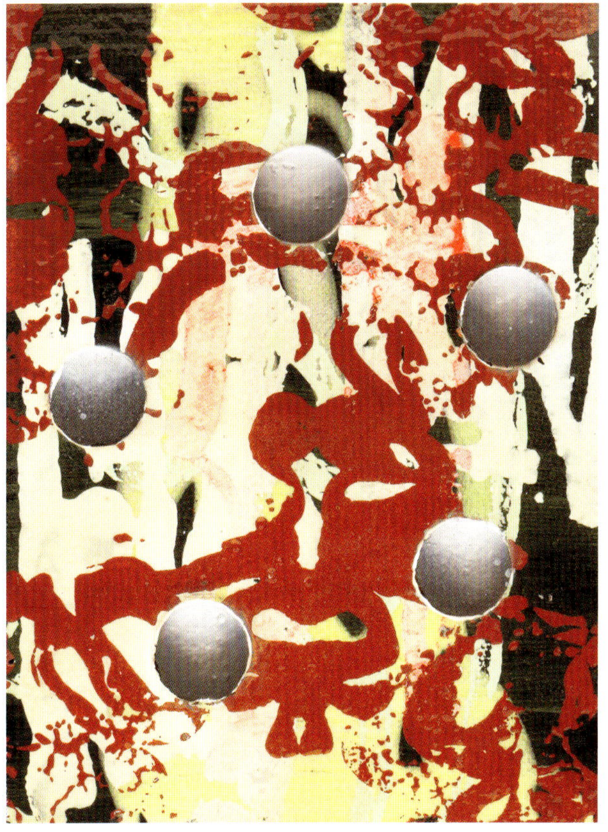

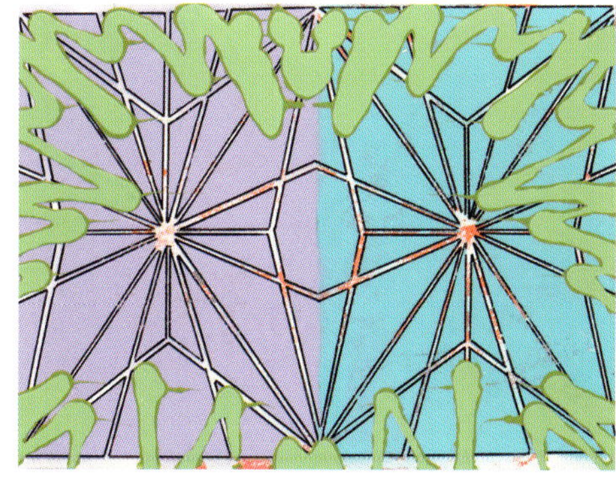

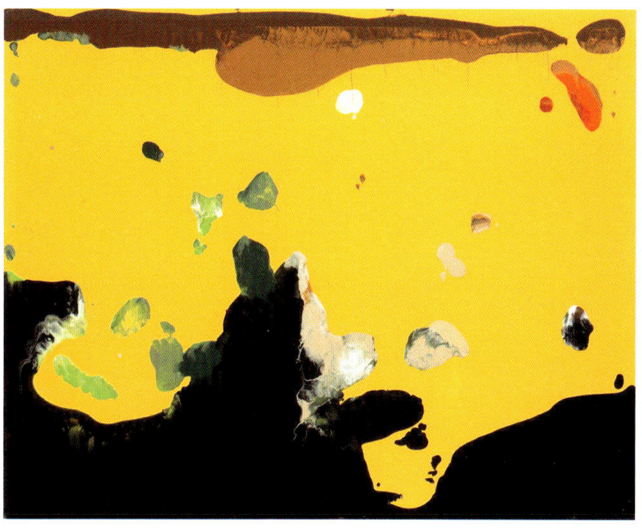

< big wave
> trüb
< kreisen
> 2 strukturierte Explosionen
> Berg, Bäume, Himmel

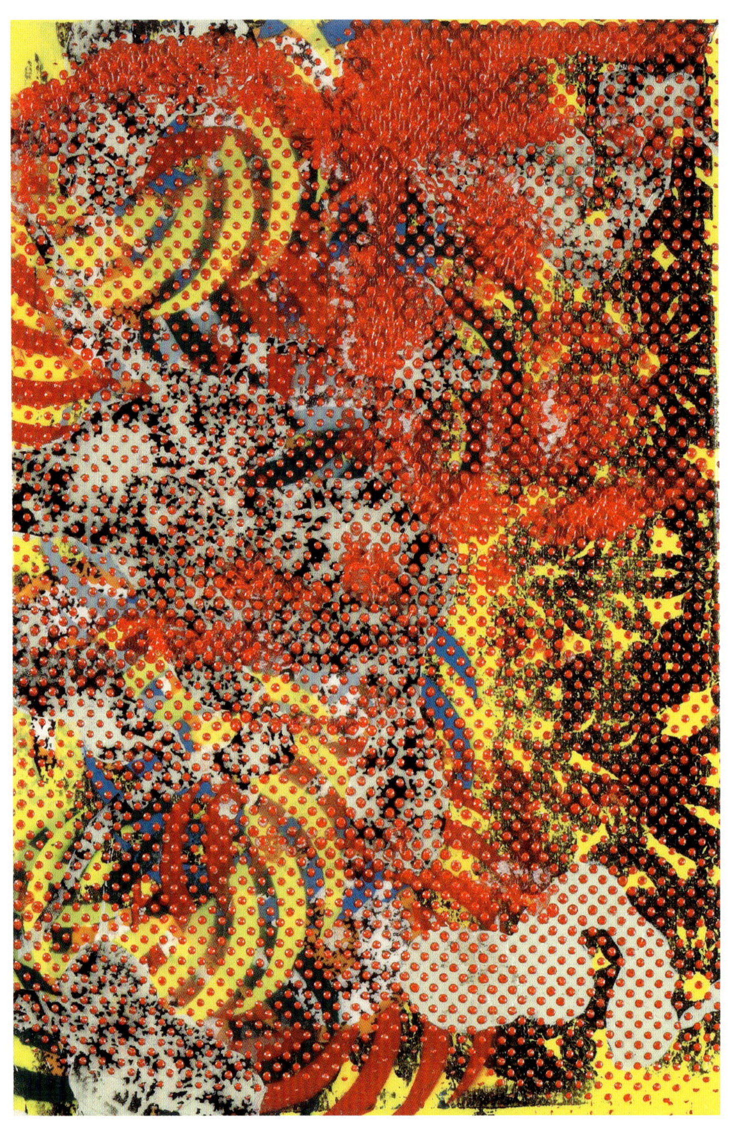

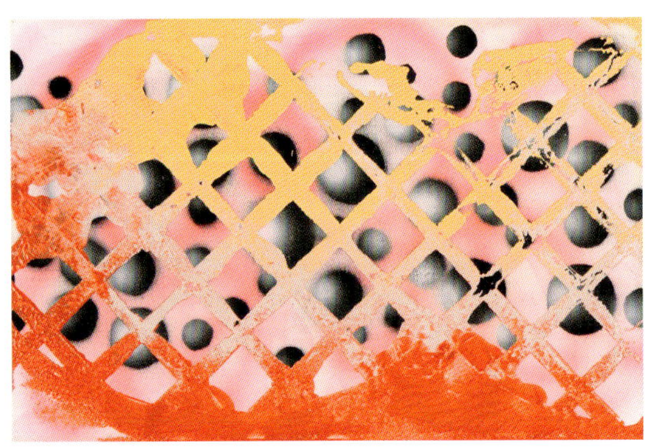

> Rotwelk
< bin vernetzt

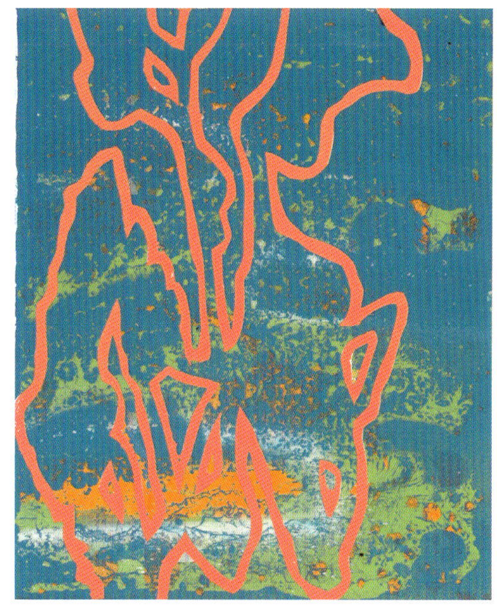

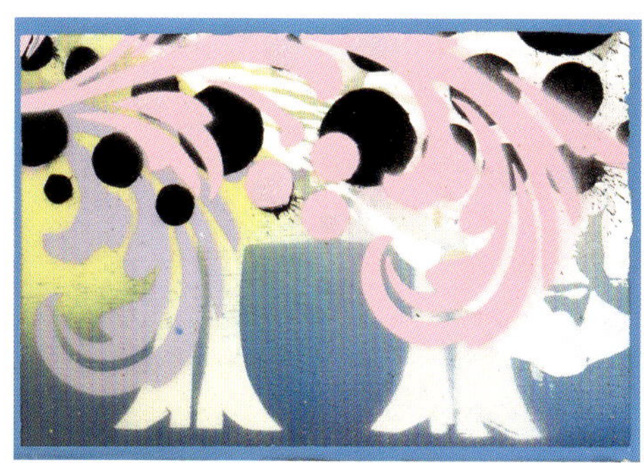

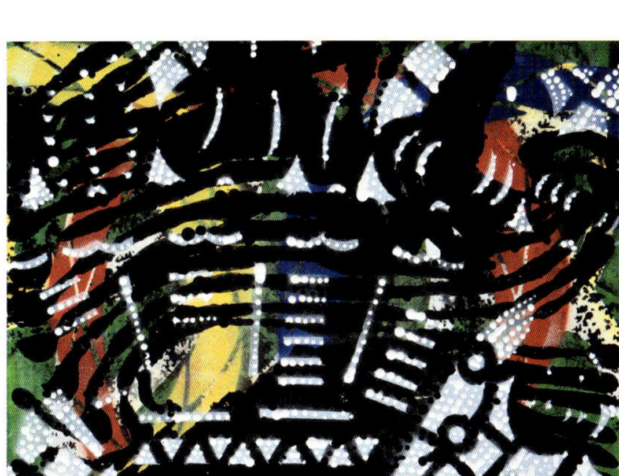

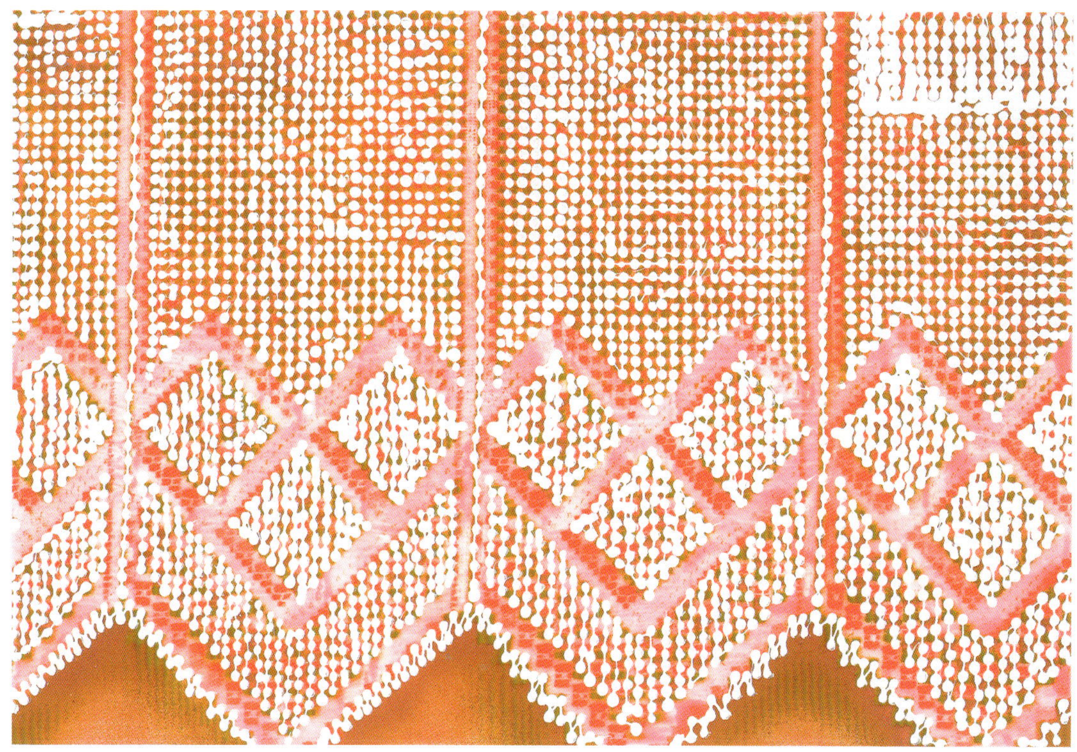

< banding
> high heels 1
< Fruchtkörbchen
> Hera

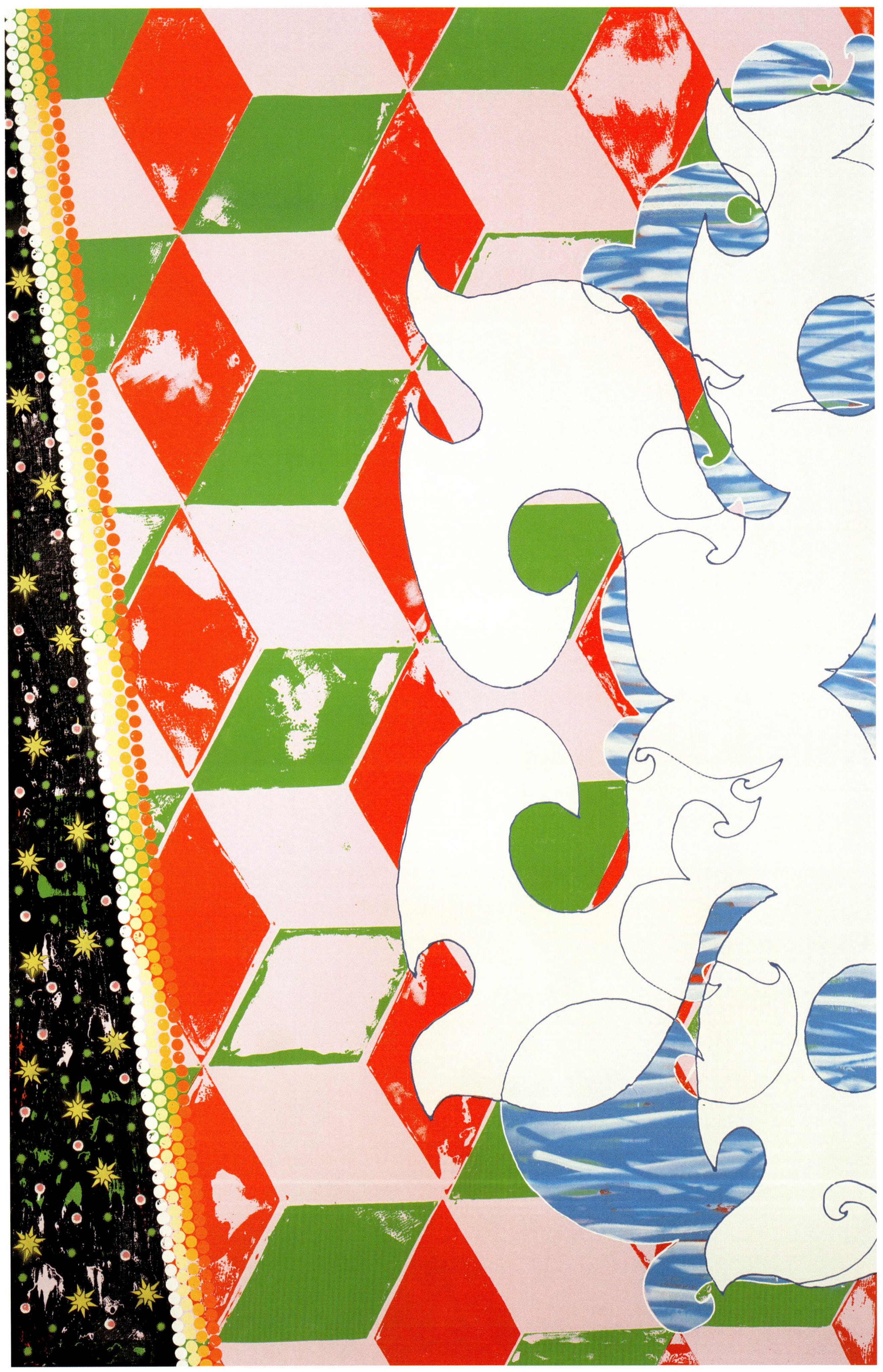

Wellenschlagen

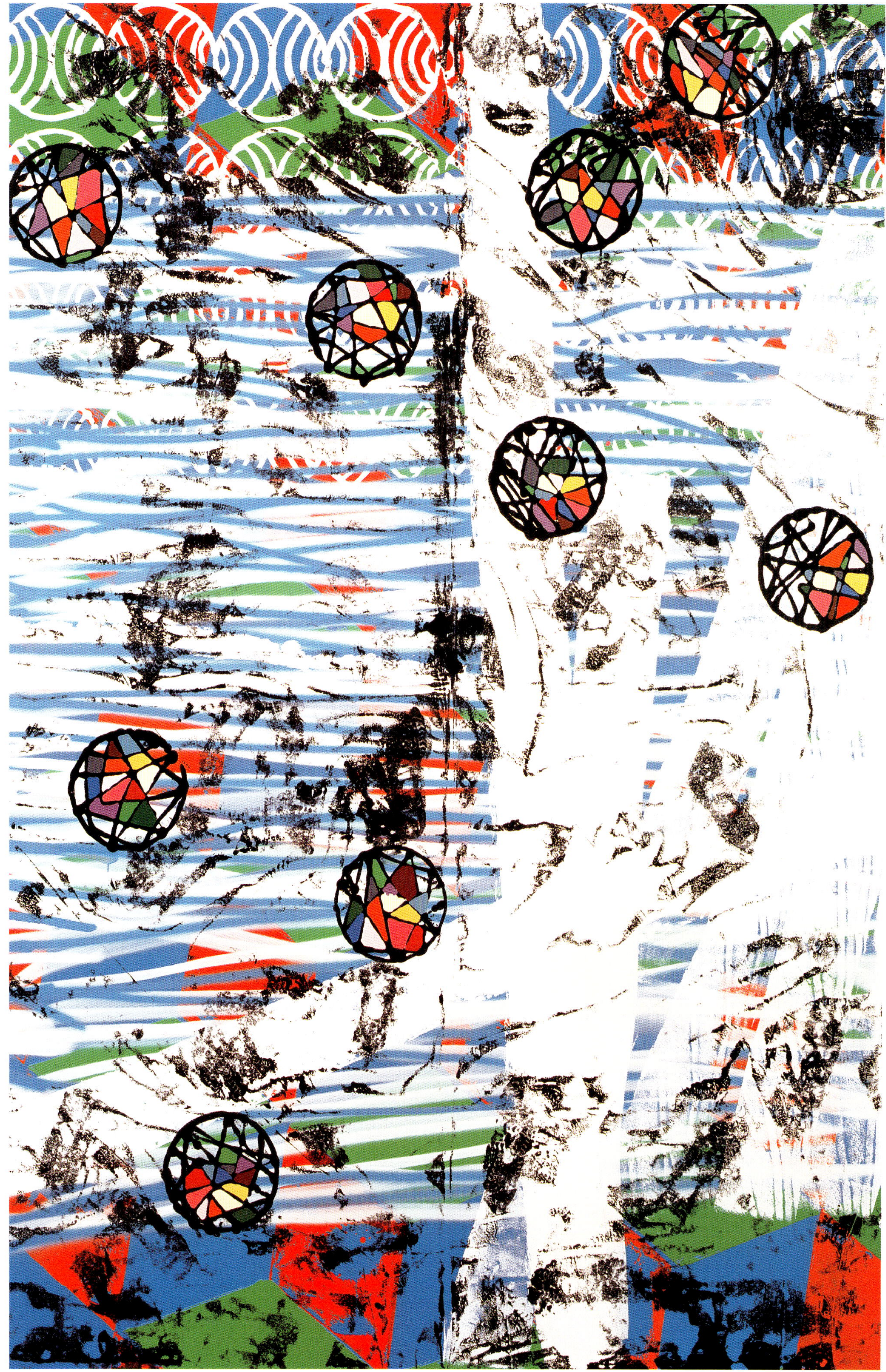

Flusser

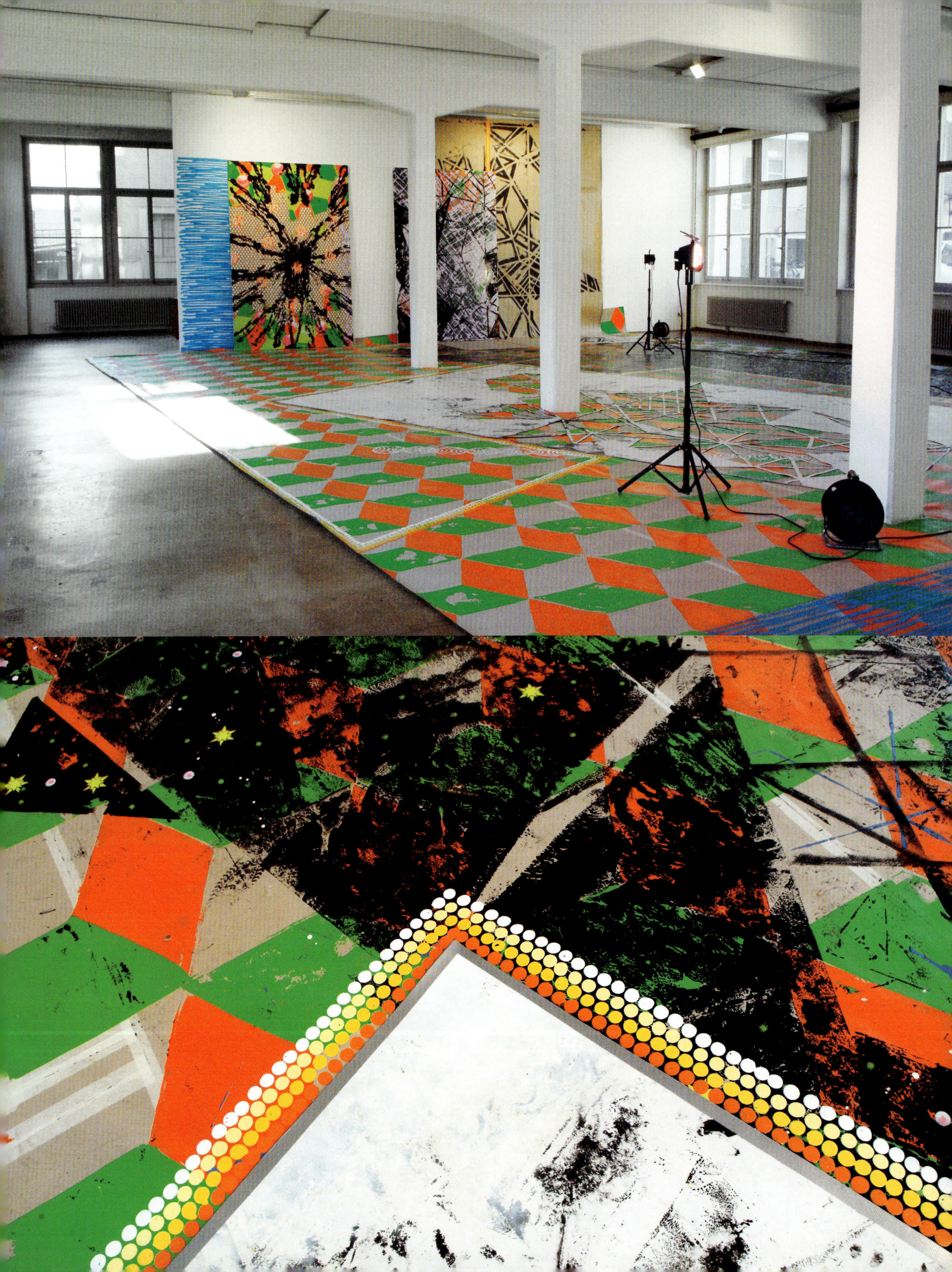

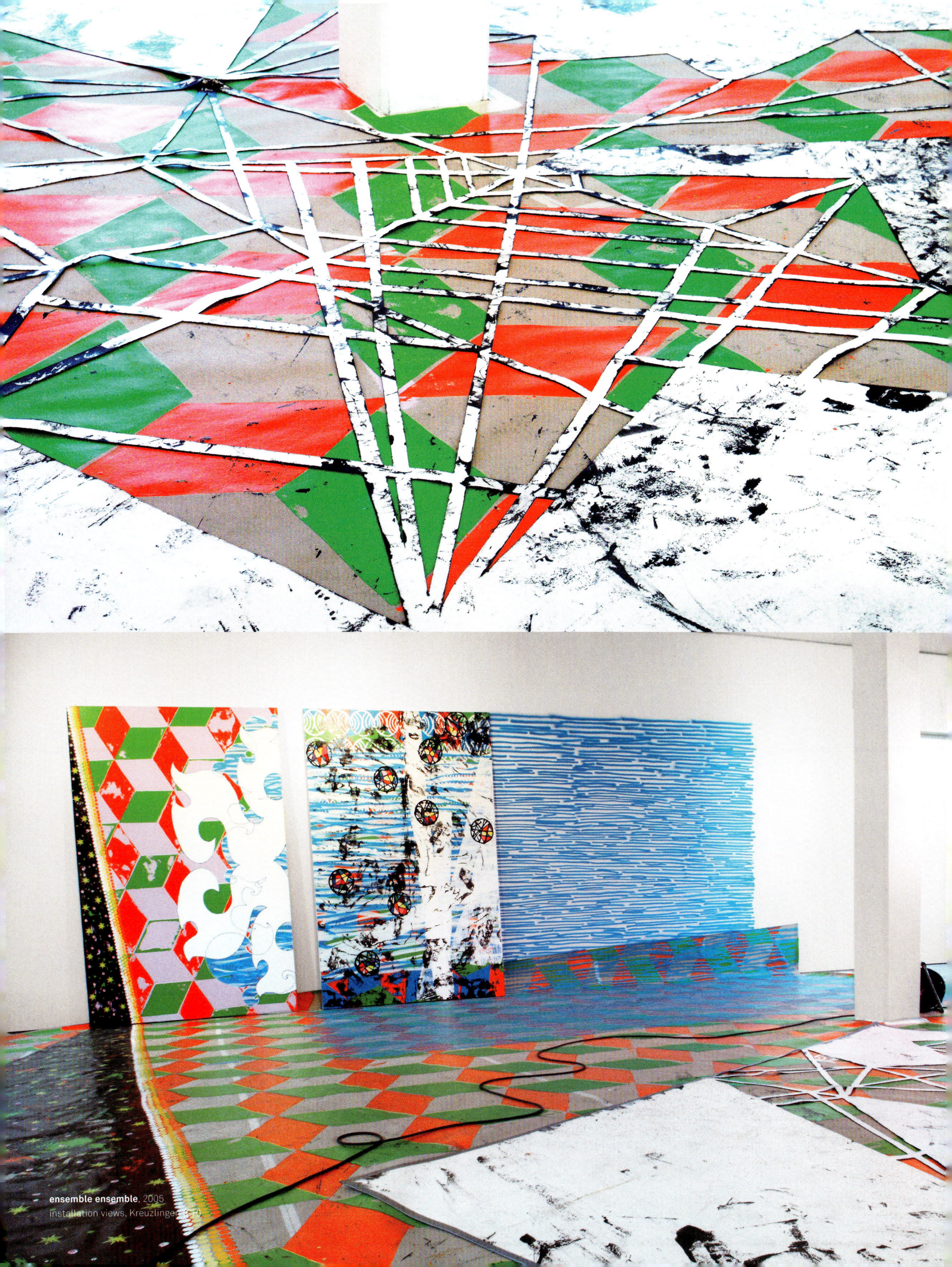

ensemble ensemble, 2005
installation views, Kreuzlingen (CH)

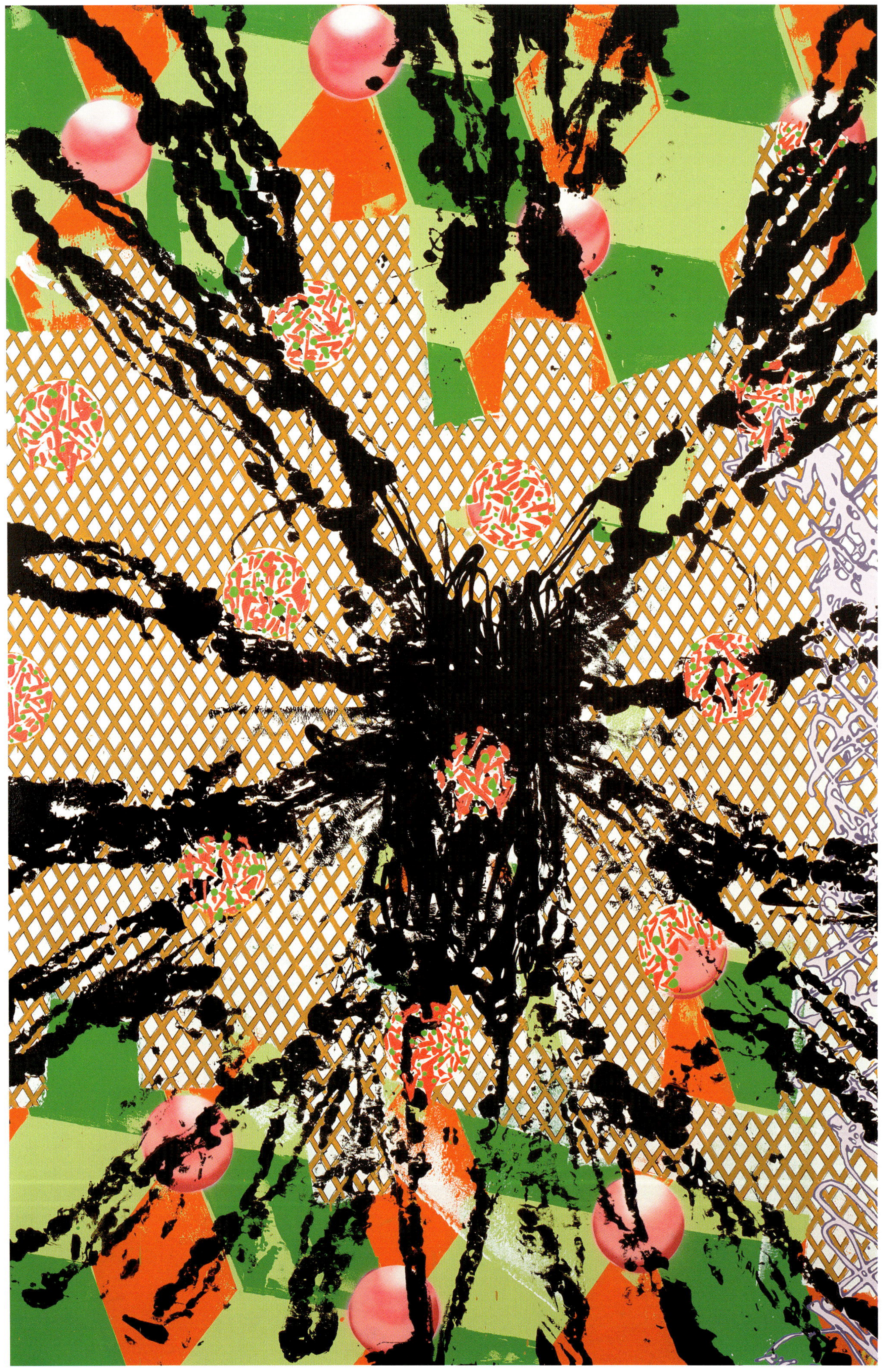

Humpty

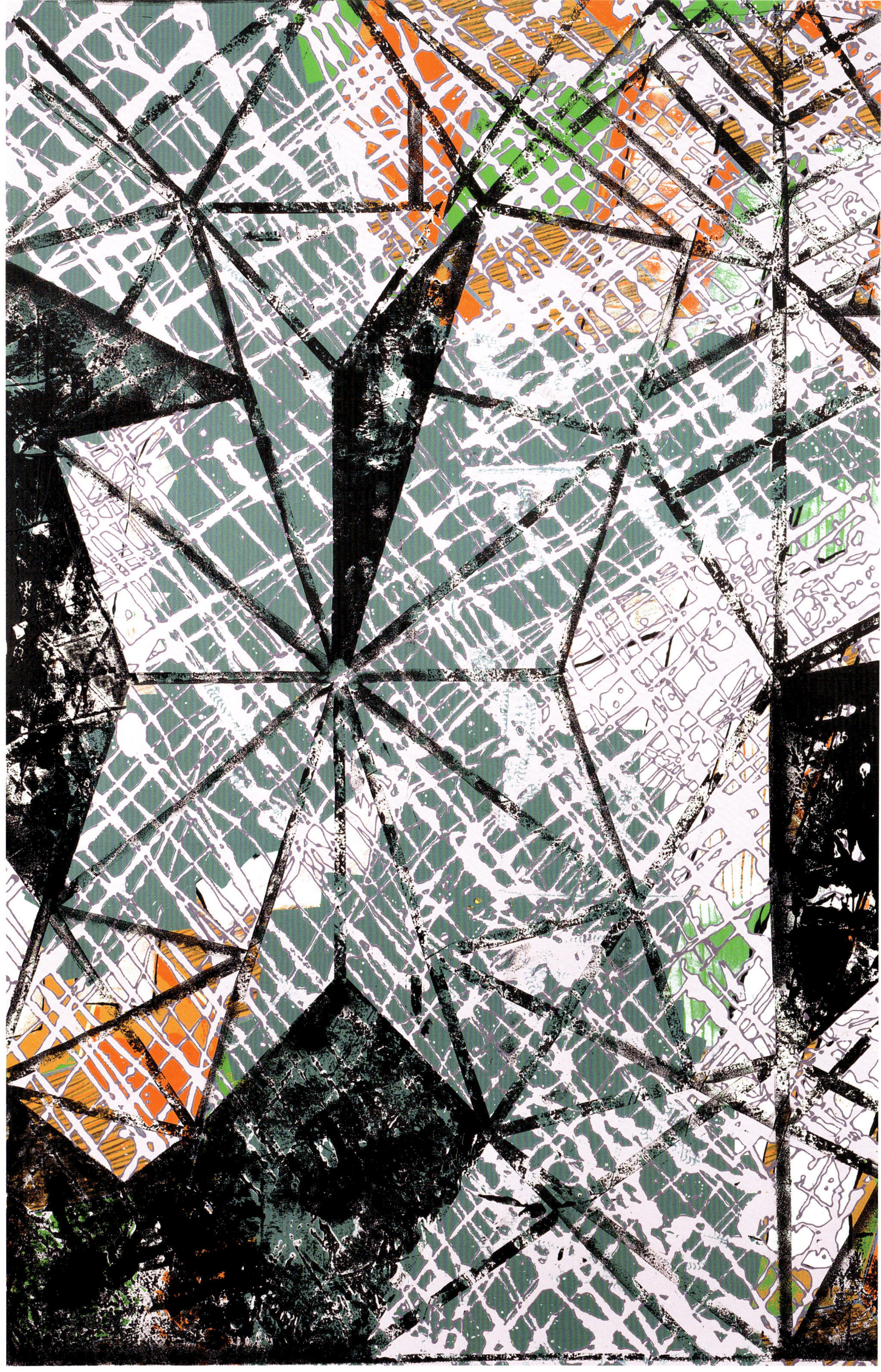

planen

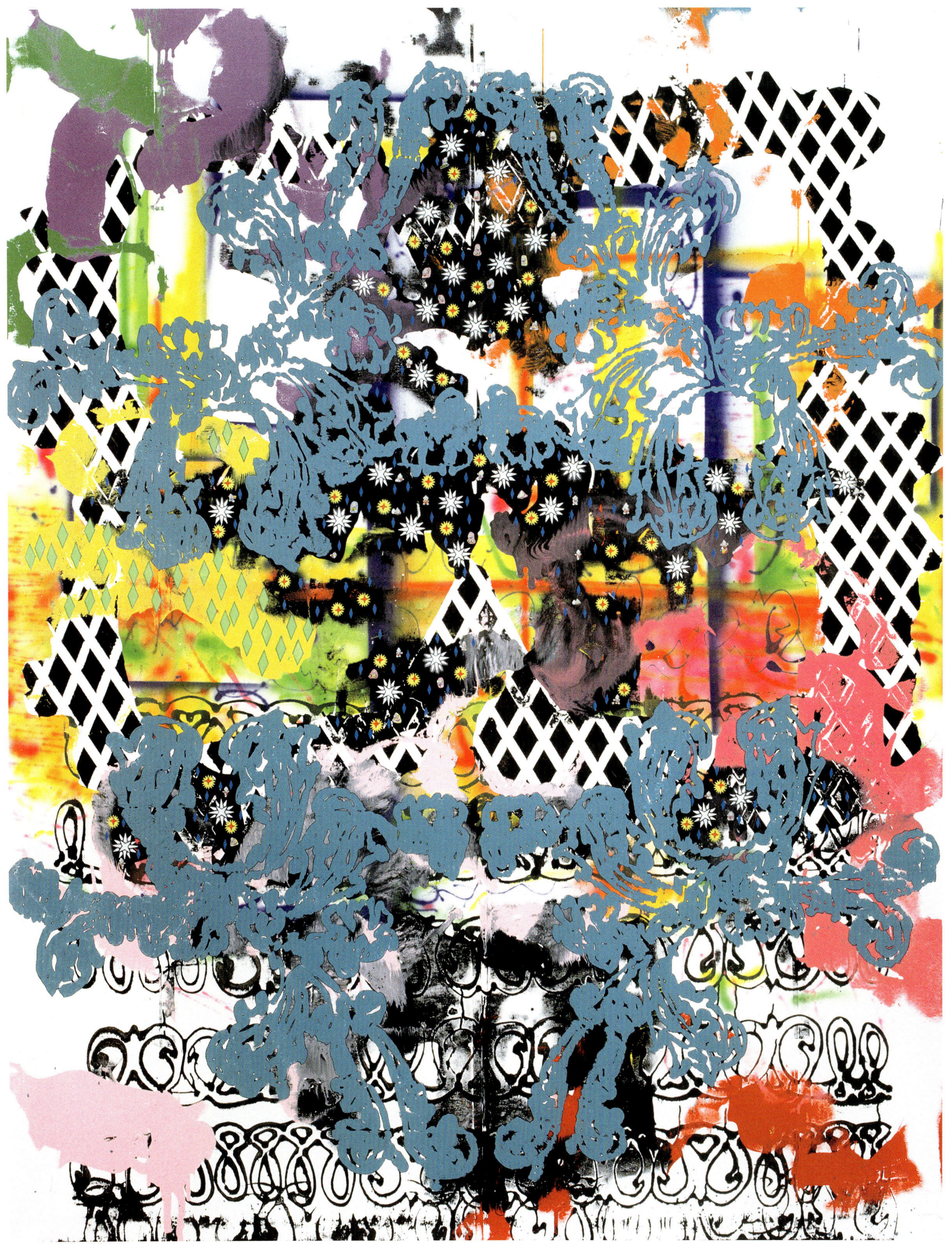

hinterlässt Spuren

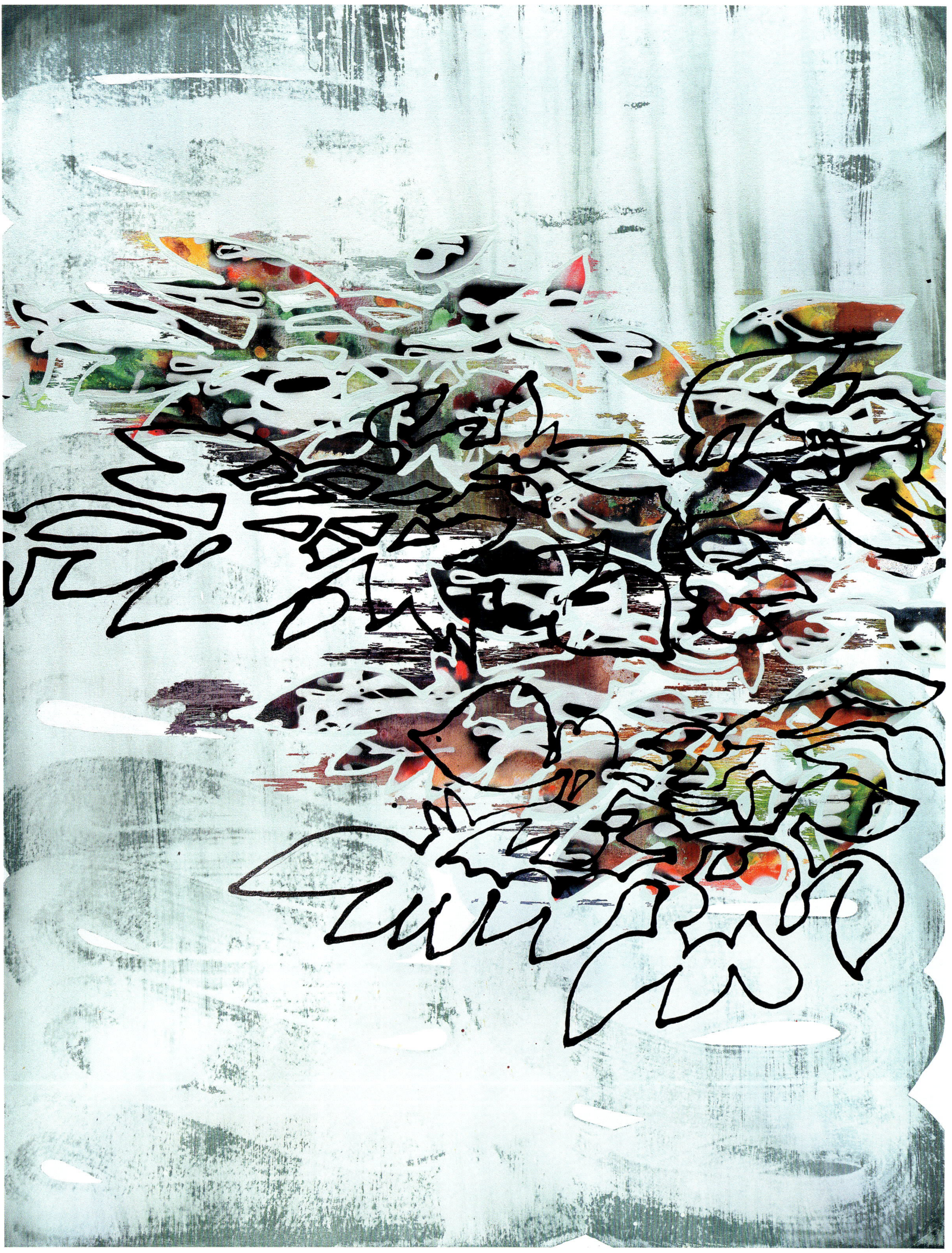

fast forward

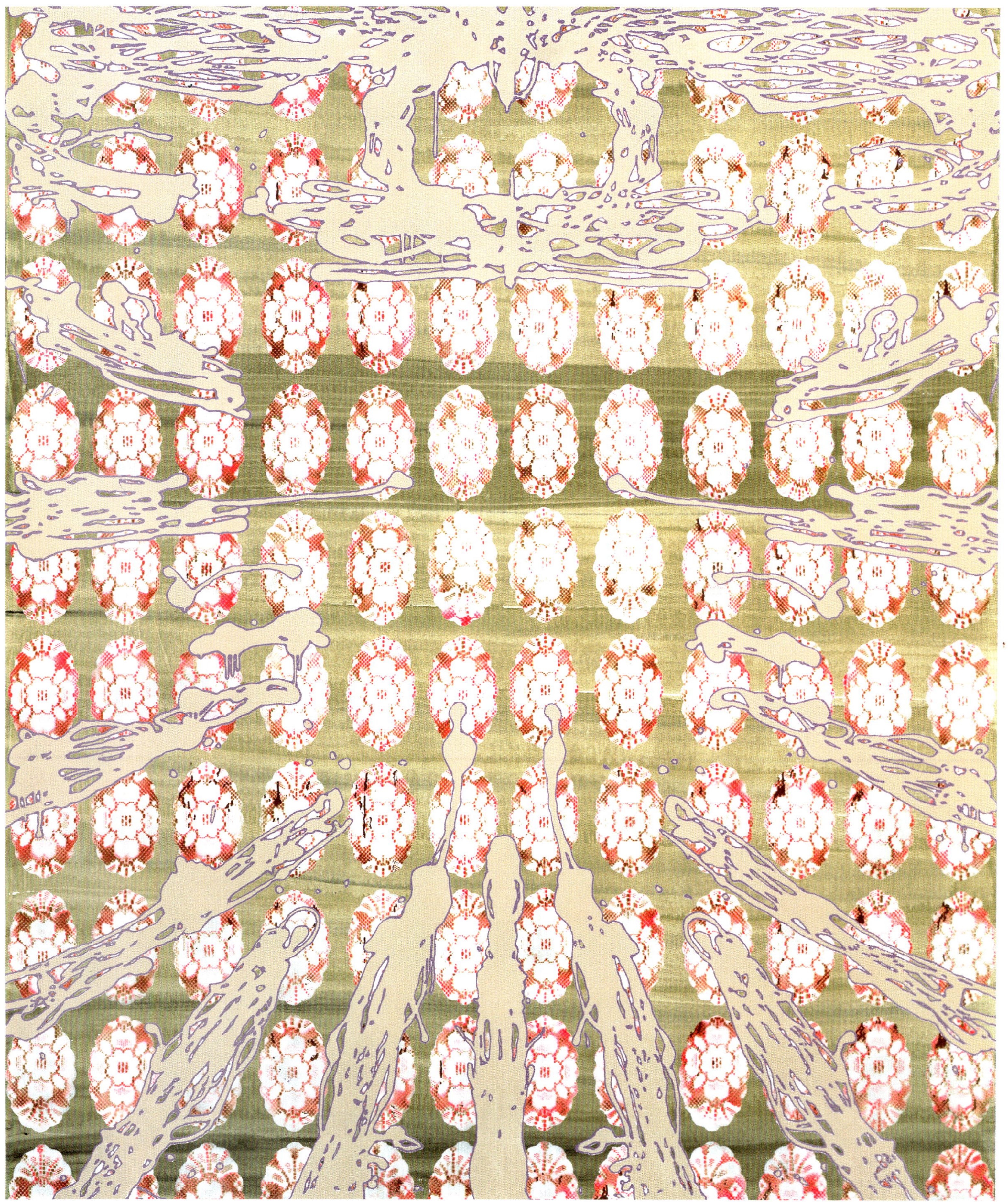

wing

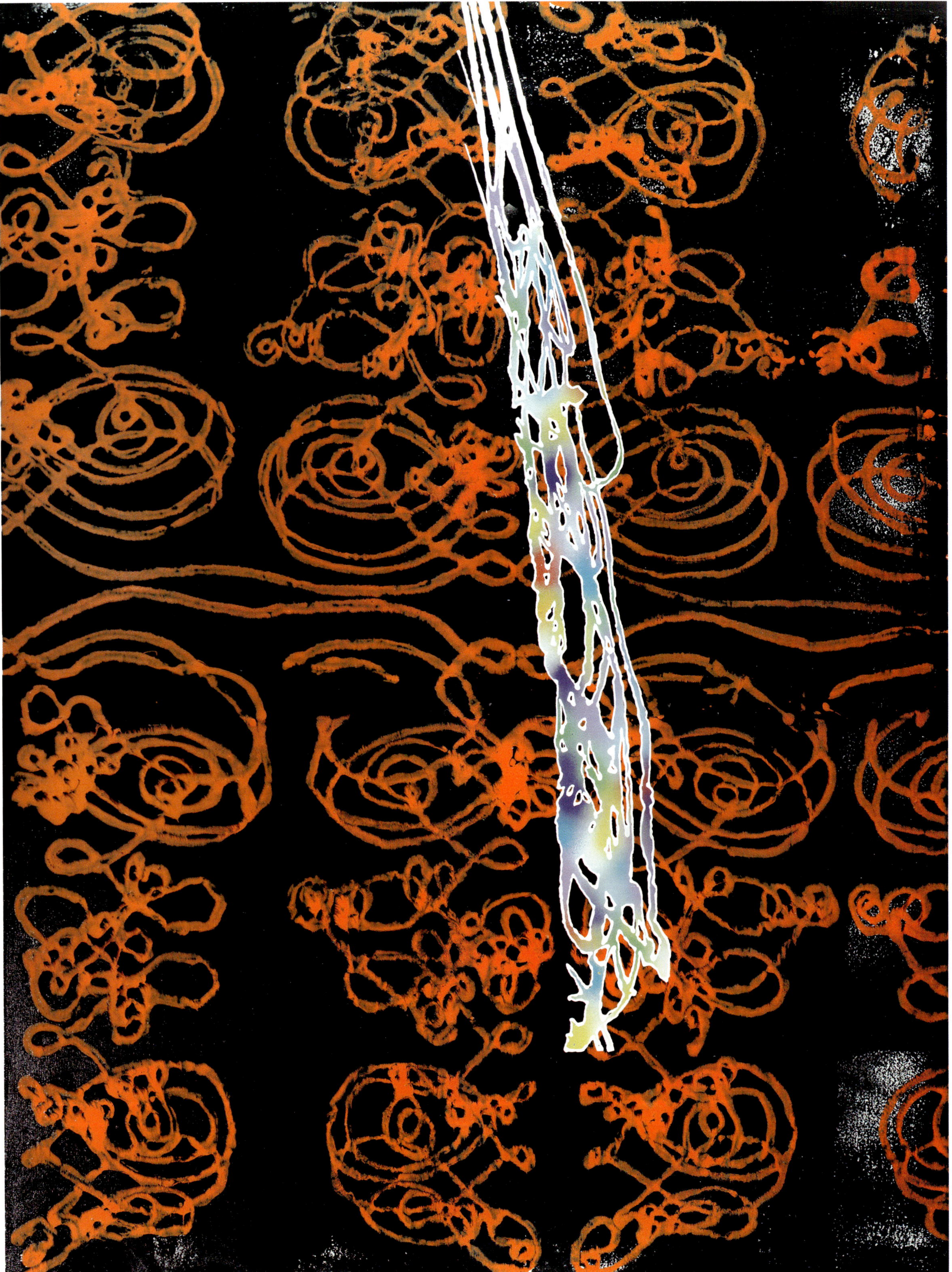

Riss

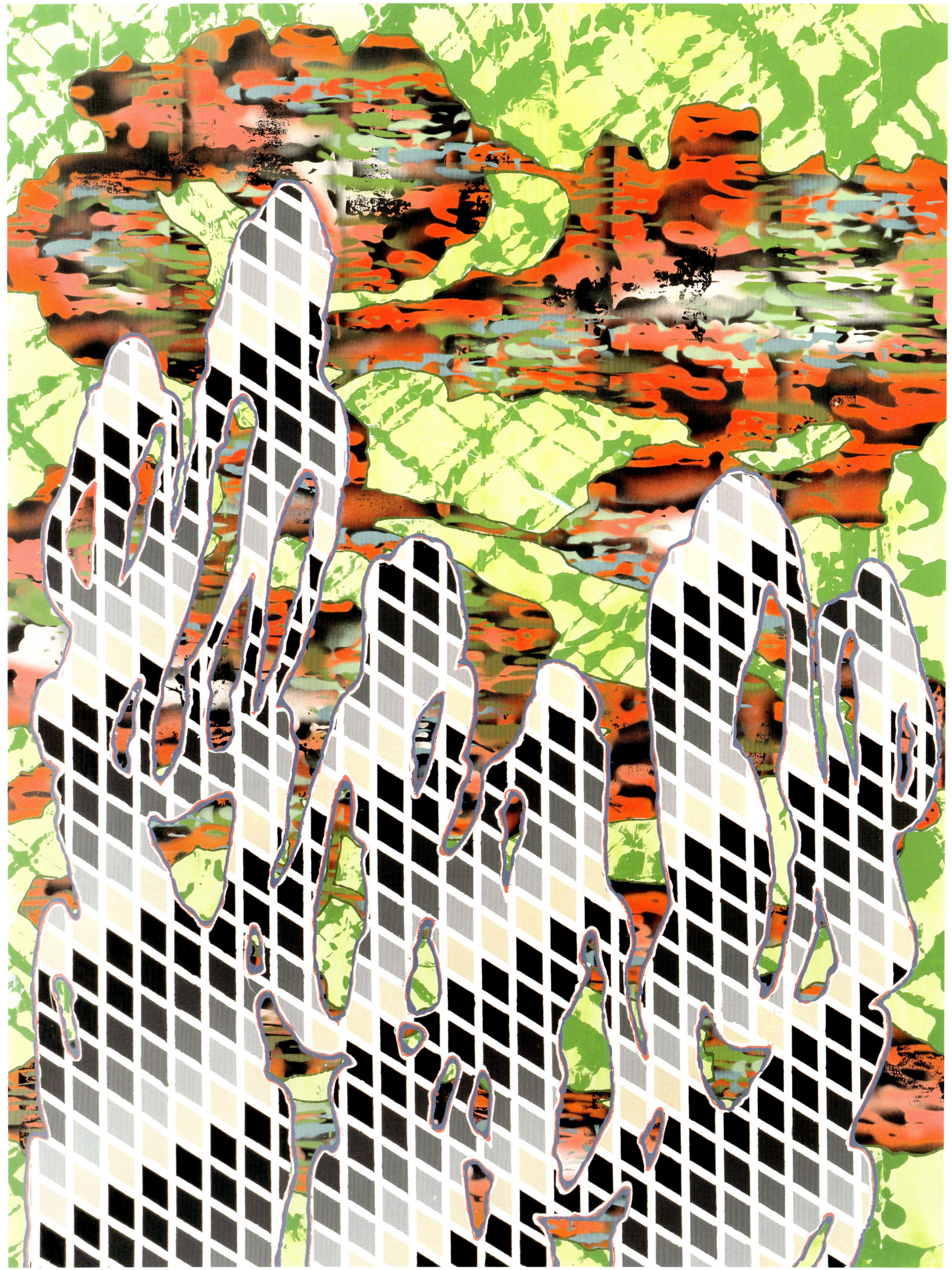

sandeln

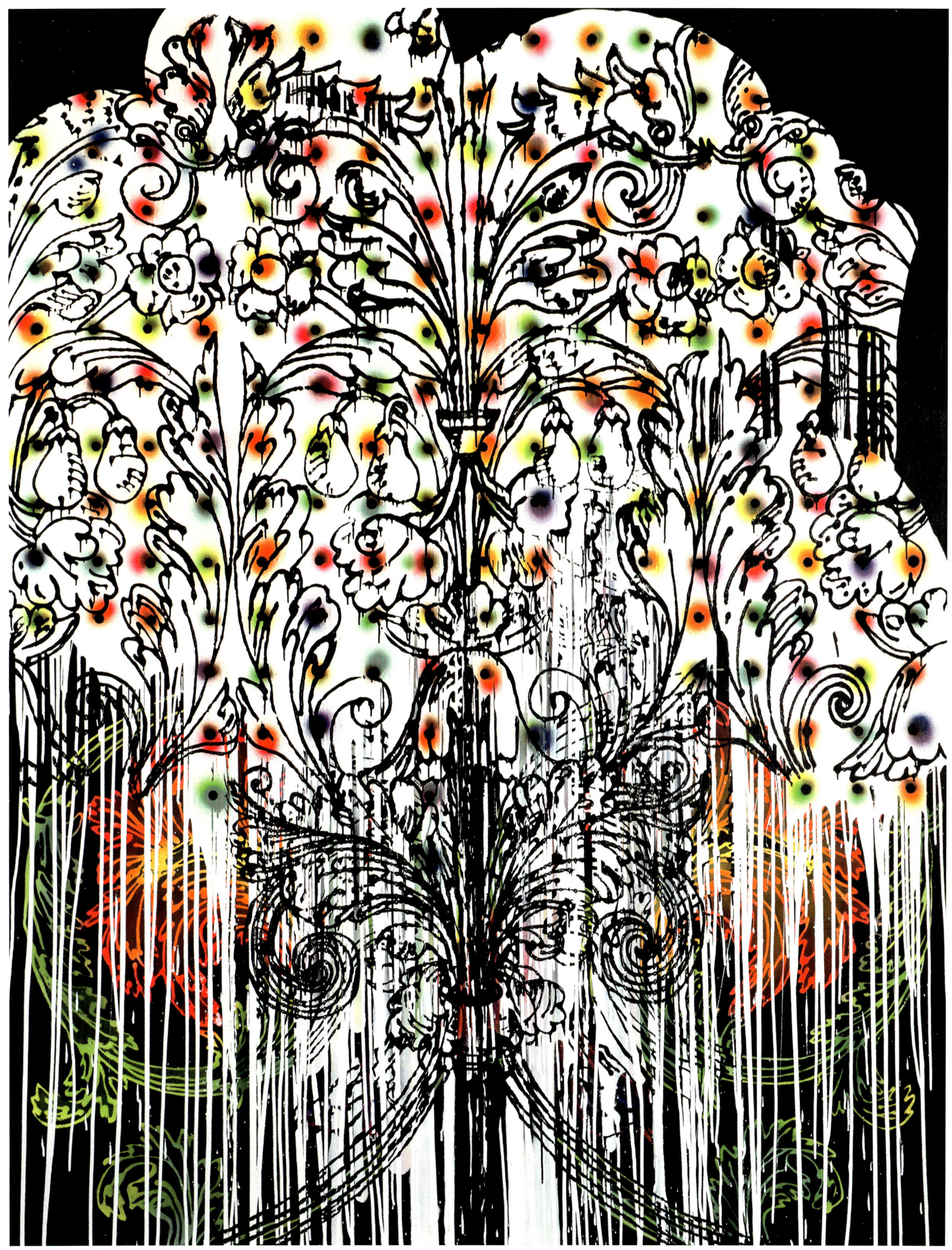

welken Birnbaum

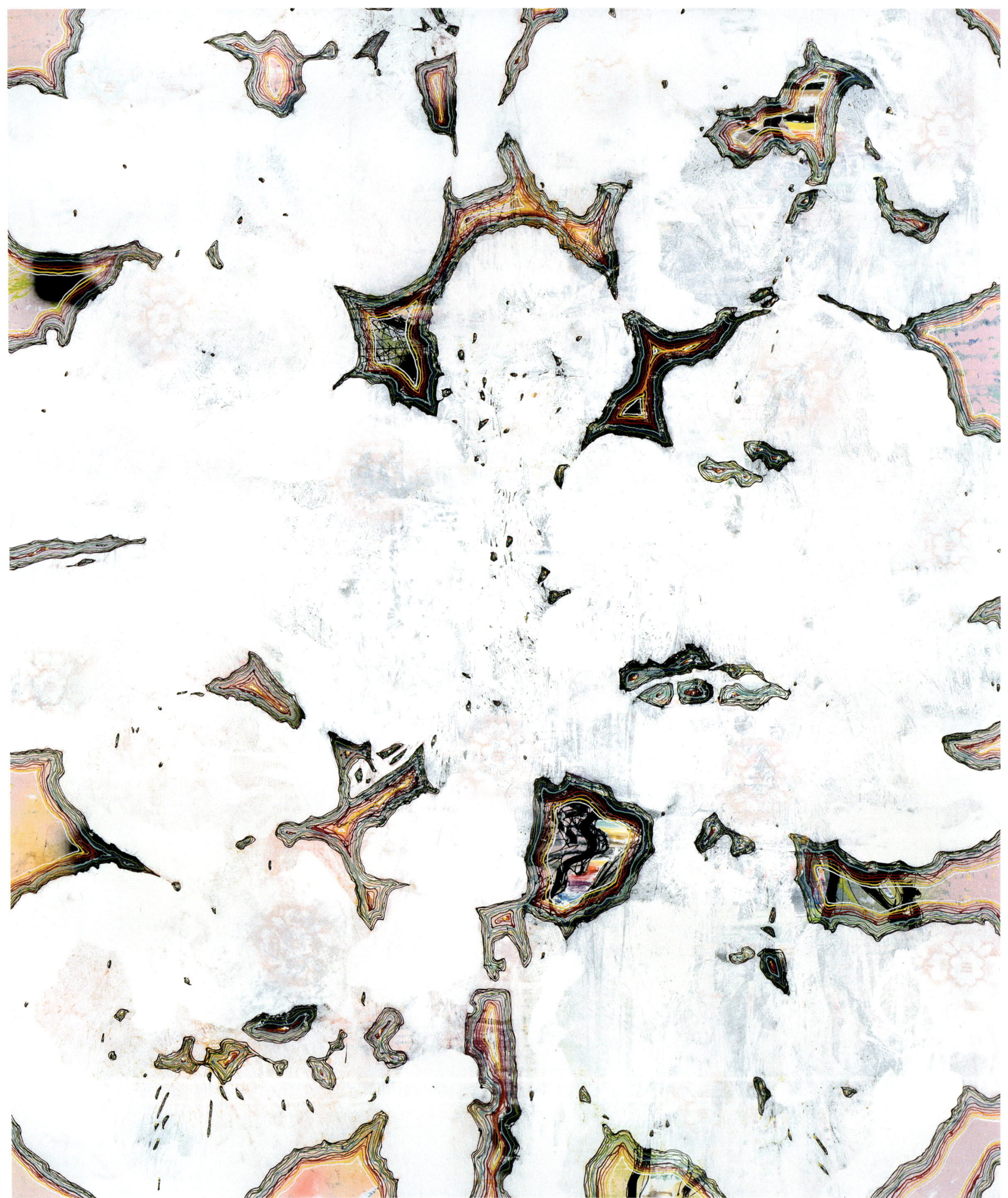

Winterschlaf

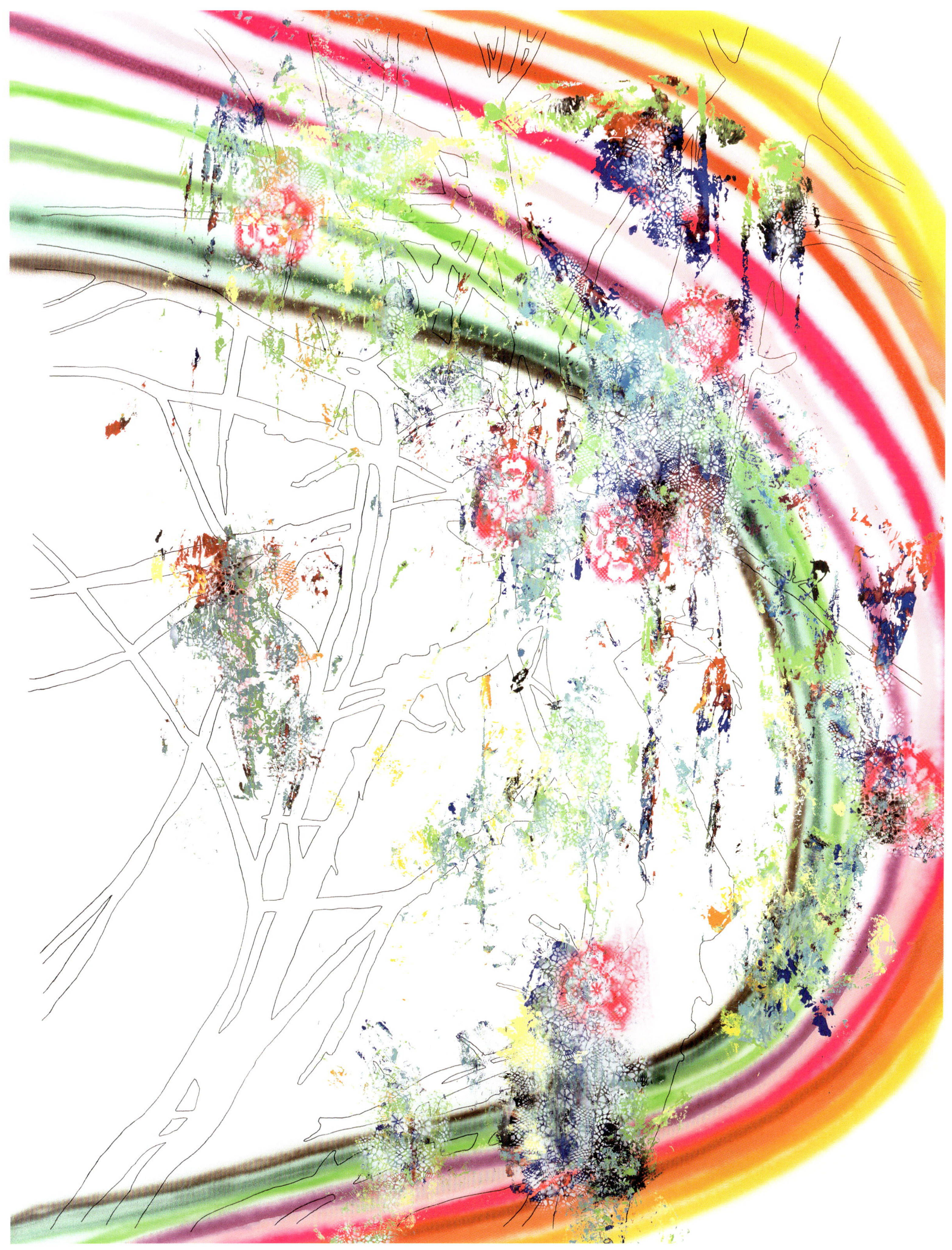

Trauerweide

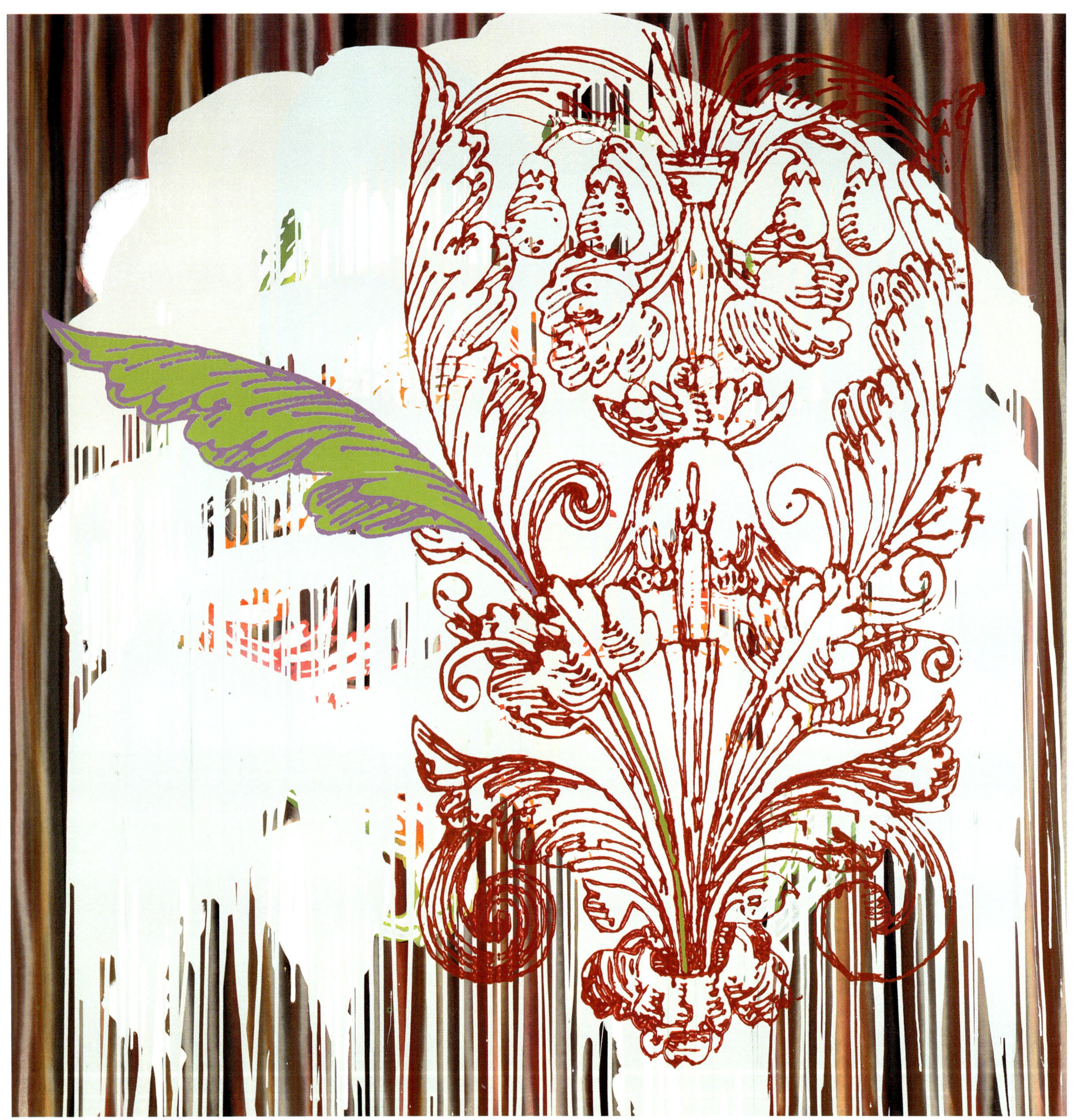

Unkraut

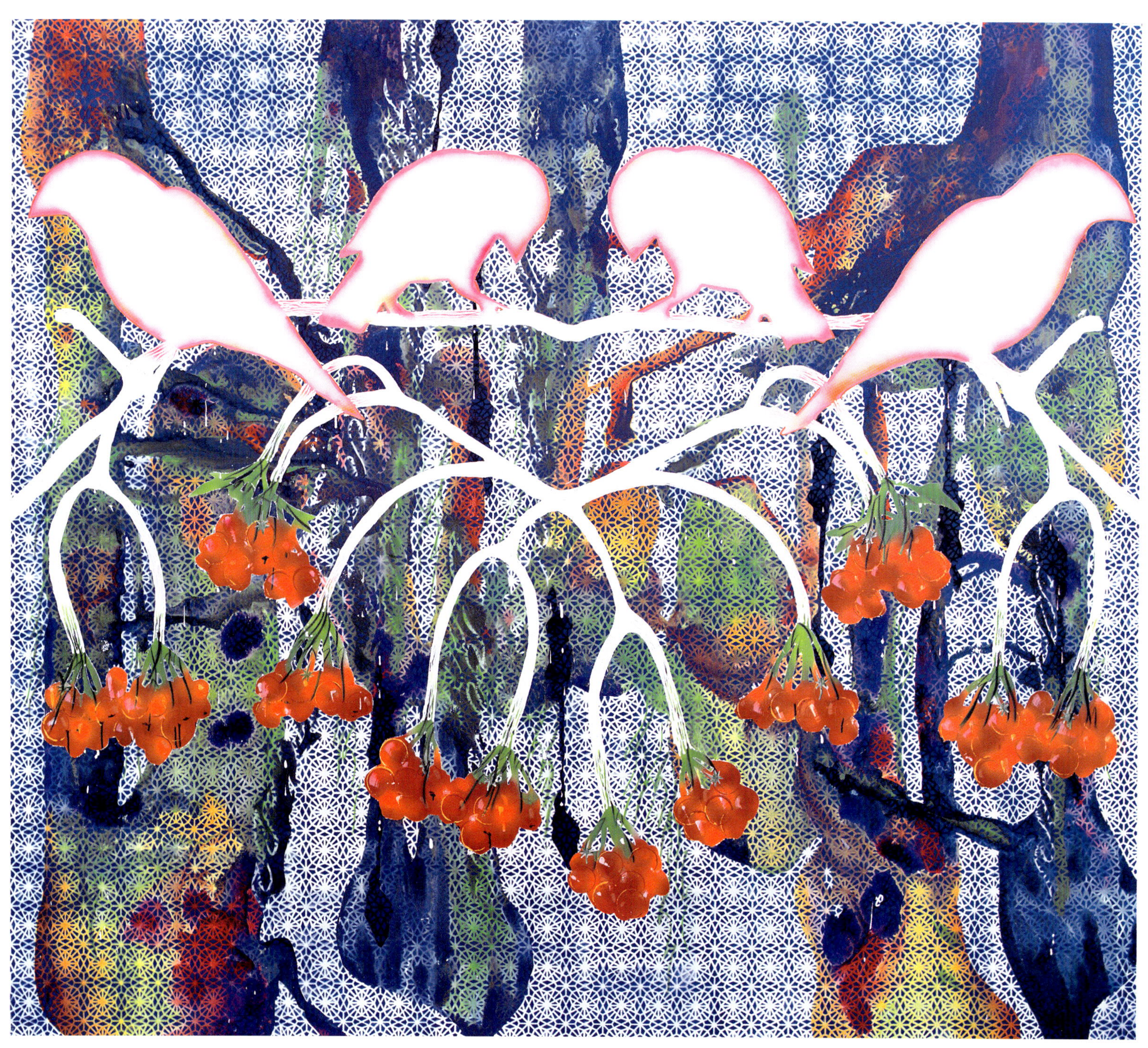

Tollkirschen

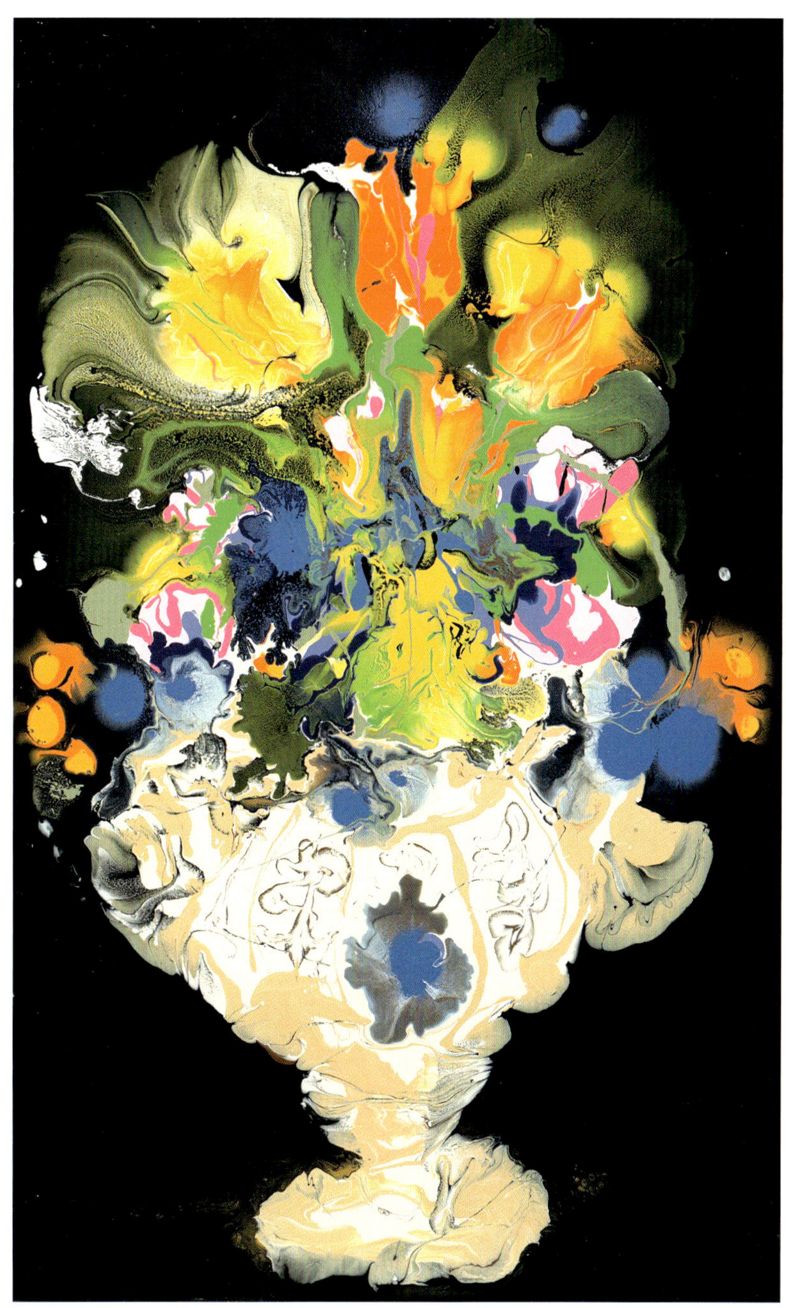

Groteskvase mit Blumen 1

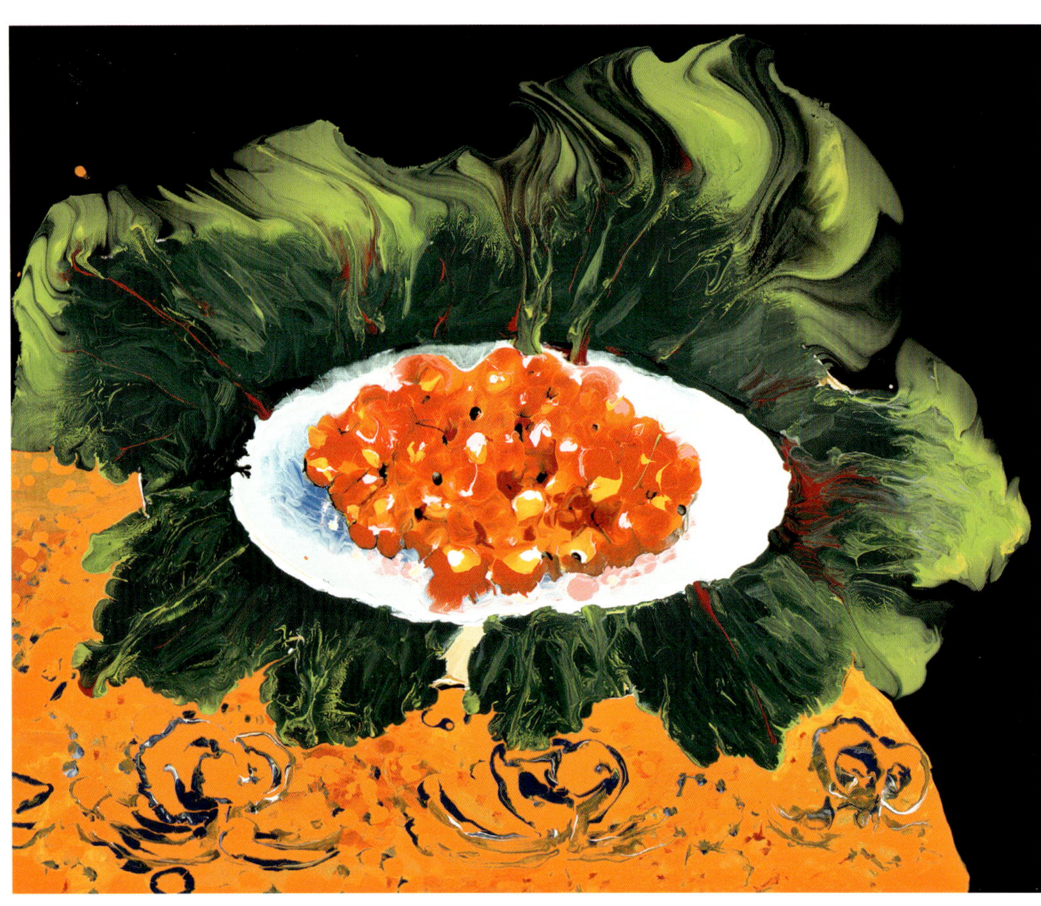

Walderdbeeren auf Zinnteller

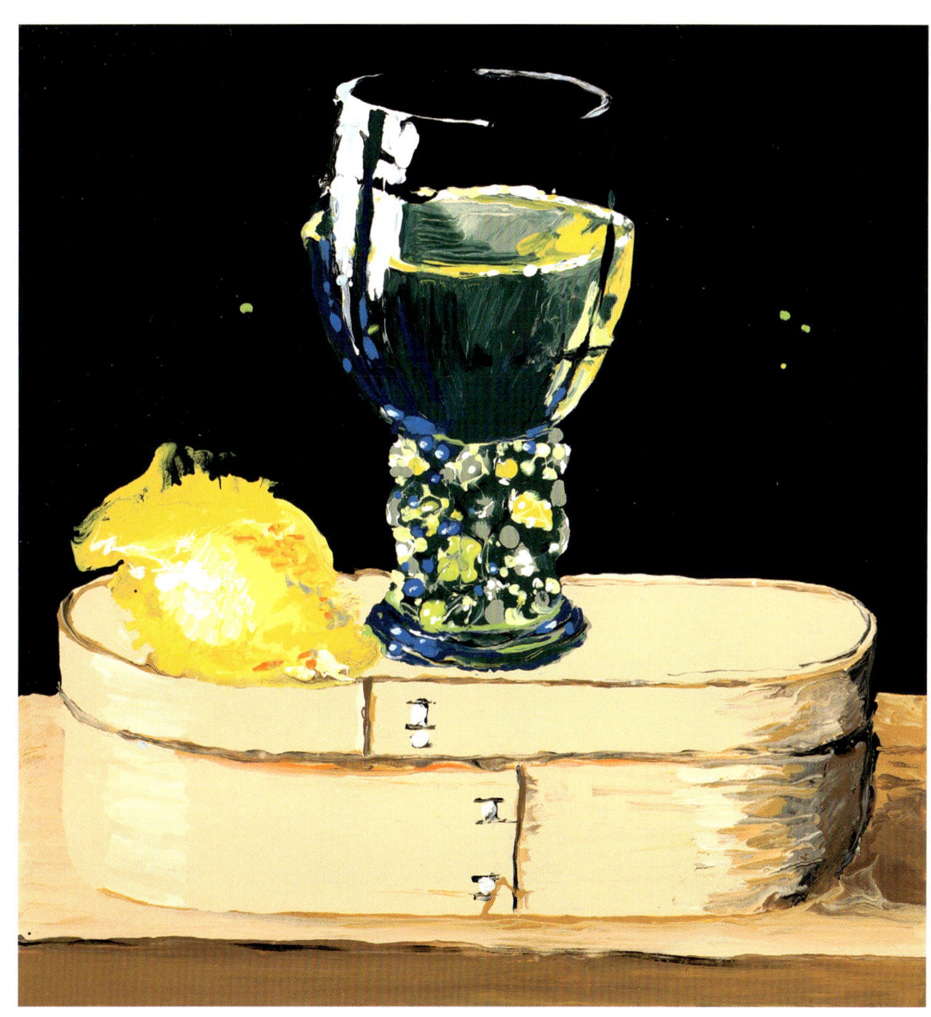

Spanschachtel mit Römer und Zitrone

Claudia Jolles

Stillleben?

In Zeiten des »Schöner Wohnens« haftet der Gattung Stillleben ein etwas merkwürdiger Beigeschmack an und lässt eher an einen bestimmten Lifestyle als an aktuelle Kunst denken. Entsprechend ungewöhnlich ist das Sujet für eine junge Malerin. Worum geht es Christine Streuli mit den neun kleinformatigen Gemälden von 2004? Die Früchteschalen, Blumenvasen, Spanschachteln oder Weingläser sind zwar sofort zu erkennen, doch ebenso unvermittelt löst sich bei näherer Betrachtung die Vertrautheit der häuslichen Realität auf – in einem rasanten Farbrausch, dem wir uns kaum entziehen können.

»Alla-prima-Malerei« wird hier geboten, eine Technik, die keine Korrektur, kein Zögern zulässt, die Schnelligkeit und Geistesgegenwart fordert und zugleich auf einer strengen Komposition basiert. Die industriellen Malmaterialien – Lack auf Alu – sind unprätentiös und weisen direkt in die Gegenwart. Doch das Motiv ist einer langen Bildtradition verhaftet.

So spontan die Malweise wirkt, so unverblümt greift Christine Streuli auf ein bestimmtes Vorbild zurück, und zwar auf den barocken Stilllebenmaler, den Strassburger Künstler Sebastian Stoskopff (1597–1657). Von ihm sind, nebst einer abenteuerlichen Lebensgeschichte, auch 69 Gemälde überliefert, darunter »sehr viele schöne curiose Werke von stillestehenden Sachen ... worinnen er fleissig gewesen.«[1] Die Gemälde stammen aus der eigentlichen Blütezeit des Stilllebens, das in den Niederlanden, in Flandern und später auch in Frankreich eine beliebte Gattung war. Denn über die scheinbar unbedeutenden Szenerien liessen sich verschlüsselte Botschaften kirchlich moralischer Natur in einer realistisch weltlichen Sprache übermitteln.

Sucht man nach Vorgängern aus etwas jüngerer Zeit, so fallen einem Künstler wie Cézanne, Braque, Gris, Morandi, Le Corbusier und vielleicht die Tasse von Meret Oppenheim ein. Den meisten der Erwähnten diente das Motiv der Überprüfung des Verhältnisses von Bild und Wirklichkeit. Es ging um räumliche Darstellung, um die bildliche Übersetzung eines dynamischen Wahrnehmungsprozesses, um malerische Fragen, um meditative Weltanschauung und – bei Meret Oppenheim – um Identität.

Bei Christine Streuli schwingen diese Fragestellungen nur bedingt mit. Wie eine verblasste Erinnerung aus entfernter Vergangenheit bieten ihr die barocken Vorbilder die beinahe neutralen Hintergründe für ihre Recherchen – ein freudscher Rückgriff auf lange Zurückliegendes als Projektionsfläche für aktuell virulente Fragestellungen.

Was geschieht bei diesen Anverwandlungen? Betrachten wir die *Groteskvase mit Blumen*, das früheste überlieferte Gemälde von Sebastian Stoskopff, so wirkt das Sujet gestelzt und symmetrisch gezähmt. Der Blumenstrauss ist säuberlich längs der Mittelachse – einer Tulpe – angeordnet. Ebenso ordentlich wie das Motiv wirkt die verschlüsselte Botschaft: Es handelt sich um ein klassisches Memento mori, eine Mahnung, sein Herz nicht an weltliche Güter – konkret den Tulpenwahn – zu verlieren. Seltene Tulpenzwiebeln wurden damals wie Aktien gehandelt. So schreibt Maria Sibylla Merian in ihrem Blumenbuch von 1680: »Ihrer viel haben schöne, köstliche Häuser, Landgüter, und alles, was sie gehabt, verkaufft, auch grosse, auf Zins ausgeliehene Geldsummen wieder eingezogen, und an solche Blumen gewagt, die weder Geruch noch Geschmack hatten; nur dass sie mit einer flüchtigen Augenweide lüsterne Hertzen eine kurze Zeit ergötzten.«[2] Auch die anderen Motive von Stoskopff mahnen an die Vergänglichkeit des irdischen Lebens, beispielsweise das zerbrechliche Weinglas, in welchem sich das Fenster als christliches Leidenskreuz spiegelt, die brennende Kerze, die sargähnlichen hölzernen Spanschachteln, die Zitrusfrüchte – Paradiesäpfel mit bitterer Schale und süssem Kern –, die ins Jenseits verweisenden schwarzen Hintergründe oder der Fisch als urchristliches Symbol.

Doch so moralisch eindeutig die Aussagen dieser Bilder auch sein mögen, so mehrschichtig ist die Realität, die sie verkörpern. Die weltliche Schönheit, die sie anprangern, liegt nicht nur ausserhalb ihrer selbst. Malerei ist immer auch Teil einer ästhetischen Kultur – und Ästhetik kann durch ästhetische Mittel nicht grundsätzlich in Frage gestellt werden. Vielleicht ist es gerade dieser innere Widerspruch zwischen wörtlicher Aussage und künstlerischer Realität, diese ganz grundsätzliche Schizophrenie, die den Wert und die Faszination dieser Bilder für Christine Streuli ausgemacht hat.

Jedenfalls hat sich Christine Streuli die latente Symbolik und Weltenschwere ihrer Vorbilder, diese bildungsbürgerliche Doppelmoral beherzt vom Leibe gemalt. Stattdessen baut sie auf dem inhärenten Widerspruch dieser Lehrstücke auf, auf deren ästhetischer Sinnenfreude und Lebenslust. So werden ihre Blumen- und Früchtestillleben zu explosiven Farbpetarden, welche die rechteckige Bildfläche zu sprengen und in einen dynamisch gekrümmten Raum zu überführen scheinen. Die leuchtroten Erdbeeren und das den Teller umwuchernde Grünzeug sind reine Energie, visualisieren einen dynamischen Verdrängungskampf, in welchem sich die statischen Umrisse der Motive beinahe aufgelöst haben.

»Stilleven«, »Stillleben«, »Nature Morte« oder »Riposo« suggerieren Stille, angehaltene Zeit und Reflexion. Christine Streulis Stillleben wirken wie eine Auszeit in ihrer Arbeit, eine motivische und technische Experimentierphase. Das Abtauchen bedeutet zugleich ein Sich-Verorten in einer bestimmten Malereigeschichte, der sie ein höchst zeitgenössisches Lebensgefühl entgegensetzt. Figurative Zwischenphasen hat die Künstlerin immer wieder eingefordert. Als kompakte, variantenreiche Gruppe, die motivisch eng an ein historisches Vorbild anknüpft, sind die Stillleben jedoch einzigartig.

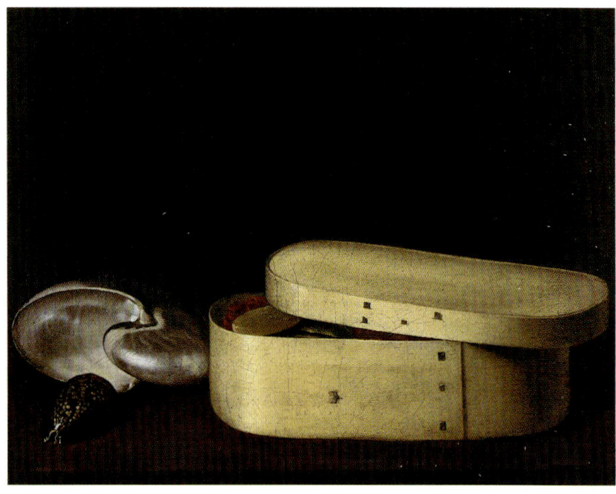

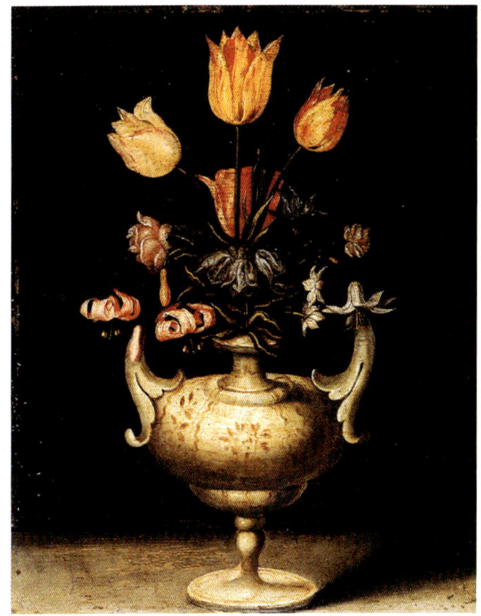

Wenn Christine Streuli ihre abstrakte Malerei beschreibt, hört sich dies an wie ein Kochrezept. Da werden Partien mit Schablonen und Bändern abgeklebt, übermalt, wieder abgelöst und weiterbearbeitet. Schicht um Schicht entstehen Räume, Muster und Rhythmen. Dieser bewusste Umgang mit Zufall und System prägt auch die Stillleben. Sie sprechen von Bewegung und Stillstand, von einem Aggregatzustand, der zugleich flüssig und starr sein könnte.

Aktion ist immer auch Interpretation, Historie fordert nicht nur Abgrenzung, sondern auch ein Neudenken des Gewesenen. Christine Streulis Gemälde zeigen, dass ein souveräner Umgang mit historischen und gelebten Widersprüchen zukunftstauglich ist. Denn Vertrautheit mit dem Terrain hilft beim Absprung ins Neuland. Gerade in ihrer Bipolarität liegt die energetische Aufladung der Werke – eine Aufladung, die hilft, das eigene Tun neu zu takten und Widersprüche nicht aufzuheben, sondern als kreative Zündfaktoren gezielt zu nutzen.

1 Birgit Hahn-Woernle, *Sebastian Stoskopff*, Verlag Gerd Hatje, Stuttgart 1996, S. 35.
2 Maria Sibylla Merian, *Neues Blumenbuch – Allen Kunstverständiger Liebhabern zu Lust, Nutz und Dienst, mit Fleiss verfertiget*, Nürnberg 1680. Aus: Anita Albus, *Die Kunst der Künste, Erinnerungen an die Malerei*, Eichhornverlag, Frankfurt am Main, 1997/2005, S. 247.

< Sebastian Stoskopff
Spanschachtel und Nautilus, 1630ies Jahre, Oil on canvas, 46 × 61 cm
Privatbesitz, Deutschland

> Sebastian Stoskopff
Groteskvase mit Blumen, before 1625
Oil on oak wood, 29,5 × 23,5 cm,
Musée des Beaux-Arts, Strassburg

Claudia Jolles

Still life?

In times shaped by carefully beautified interiors, the genre of still life has a strange aftertaste and brings to mind a specific lifestyle rather than current art. The subject is thus quite unusual for a young painter. What was Christine Streuli's intention with her nine small-sized paintings of 2004? Although we can immediately discern the fruit bowls, flower vases, chip-board boxes or wine glasses, on closer consideration the familiarity of domestic reality dissolves – in a swift intoxication with color the tug of which we find it hard to resist.

On offer here is "alla prima painting", a technique that does not allow any corrections or hesitation and instead calls for swiftness and a presence of mind, not to mention a strict composition. The industrial materials used – lacquer on aluminum – are unpretentious and kindle clear associations with the present day. Yet the motifs are entrenched in a long pictorial tradition.

However spontaneous the method of painting seems to be, Christine Streuli relies on a specific predecessor, namely Baroque painter of still lifes, the Strasbourg-based artist Sebastian Stoskopff (1597–1657). He has bequeathed us not only a very colorful biography but also 69 paintings including "a very many beautiful and curious works of things standing still … a field where he was very assiduous."[1] The paintings stem from the real heyday of the still life – a popular genre in the Netherlands, Flanders and later France, too. Because the ostensibly unimportant scenarios were a means of conveying messages of a religious/clerical nature in a realistic secular idiom.

If one looks for somewhat more recent precursors, then the obvious choices would be artists such as Cézanne, Braque, Gris, Morandi, Le Corbusier and perhaps the cup painted by Meret Oppenheim. Most of those mentioned used the motif to explore the relationship between image and reality. The emphasis was on spatial representation, the pictorial translation of a dynamic perceptual process, painterly issues, meditative world views and (in the case of Meret Oppenheim), on identity.

In Christine Streuli's work we can sense the presence of these issues only to a minor degree. Like a faded memory from some distant past, she uses the Baroque images as an essentially neutral backdrop to her own research – it is a Freudian reliance on something long past as the screen onto which currently virulent issues can be projected.

What happens during these appropriations? If we consider *Groteskvase mit Blumen*, the earliest painting by Sebastian Stoskopff to survive, the subject matter seems stilted and trammeled by symmetry. The bouquet of flowers is arranged carefully along the central axis – a tulip. The cryptic message seems as orderly as the motif: It is a classical memento mori, admonishing the viewer not to give his heart over to worldly goods – explicitly the craving for tulips. At that time, rare tulip bulbs were traded like shares. Thus Maria Sibylla Merian wrote in her flower compendium of 1680 that "Many of them have beautiful, precious houses, country estates, and everything they own they have sold, redeeming large sums of money lent against interest, and have dared commit it to such flowers as have neither a scent nor a taste, but merely bring delight to the pleasure-seeking heart for a brief period when glanced upon."[2] The other motifs chosen by Stoskopff also warn us that life on earth is transient; for example, there is the fragile wineglass, in which we see a window reflected as if it were the cross of Christ's passion, or the burning candle, the coffin-like chip-wood boxes, the citrus fruit – the apples of Paradise with their bitter peel and sweet flesh – the black backgrounds alluding to death, or fish as the original Christian symbol.

However unequivocal the statements made by these images may be, the reality they embody is ambivalent. The worldly beauty they denounce not only lies outside them, as painting itself is always part of an aesthetic culture – and aesthetics can not in principle be cast into question by aesthetic means. Perhaps it is precisely this inner contradiction between literal statement and artistic reality, this quite fundamental schizophrenia, that constitutes the value and fascination these pictures have for Christine Streuli.

At any rate, Streuli has energetically set about committing the latent symbolism and secular gravitas of these precursors, this educated middle-class hypocrisy, to paint. She relies on the inherent self-contradiction of these didactic pieces, taking up their aesthetic sensual joy and joie de vivre. Thus her still lifes of flowers or fruit become explosive petards of color, which burst the rectangular pictorial surface asunder and seem to lead to some dynamically curved space. The bright red strawberries and the rampant greenery around the plate are pure energy, visualizing a dynamic war of attrition in which the static outlines of the motifs have almost dissolved into nothingness.

"Stilleven", "Stillleben", "Nature Morte" or "Riposo" all suggest silence, time stood still, reflection. Christine Streuli's still lifes seem to constitute a time-out in her own work, a phase or experimentation in terms of motifs and techniques. Her immersion in the subject also entails her finding a place in a specific history of painting, to which she juxtaposes a highly contemporary joie de vivre. She has repeatedly called for figurative interim phases. However, as a compact, highly diverse group, with motifs that run close to their predecessors in history, her still lifes are unique.

When Christine Streuli describes her abstract painting, it sounds as if she were recounting a recipe. Sections are masked with stencils or tape, painted over, the coverings removed, and then worked up. Layer after layer gives rise to spaces, patterns and rhythms. This conscious approach to chance and method also applies to her still lifes. They attest to movement and standstill, to an aggregate state that can be both fluid and rigid at once.

Action is always also interpretation, history calls not only for delineation but also for a new interpretation of what was. Christine Streuli's paintings show that a masterful approach to historical and lived contradictions is a viable path forwards. Because a familiarity with the terrain helps to leap into virgin territory. The work's energy derives precisely from their bipolarity – it is energy that helps give her own work a new rhythm and does not negate the contradictions, but instead consciously uses them as creative triggers.

1 Birgit Hahn-Woernle: *Sebastian Stoskopff*, Verlag Gerd Hatje, Stuttgart 1996, p. 35.
2 Maria Sibylla Merian: *Neues Blumenbuch – Allen Kunstverständiger Liebhabern zu Lust, Nutz und Dienst, mit Fleiss verfertiget*, Nuremberg 1680. Ex: Anita Albus: *Die Kunst der Künste, Erinnerungen an die Malerei*, Eichhornverlag, Frankfurt/Main 1997/2005, p. 247.

Translation: Jeremy Gaines

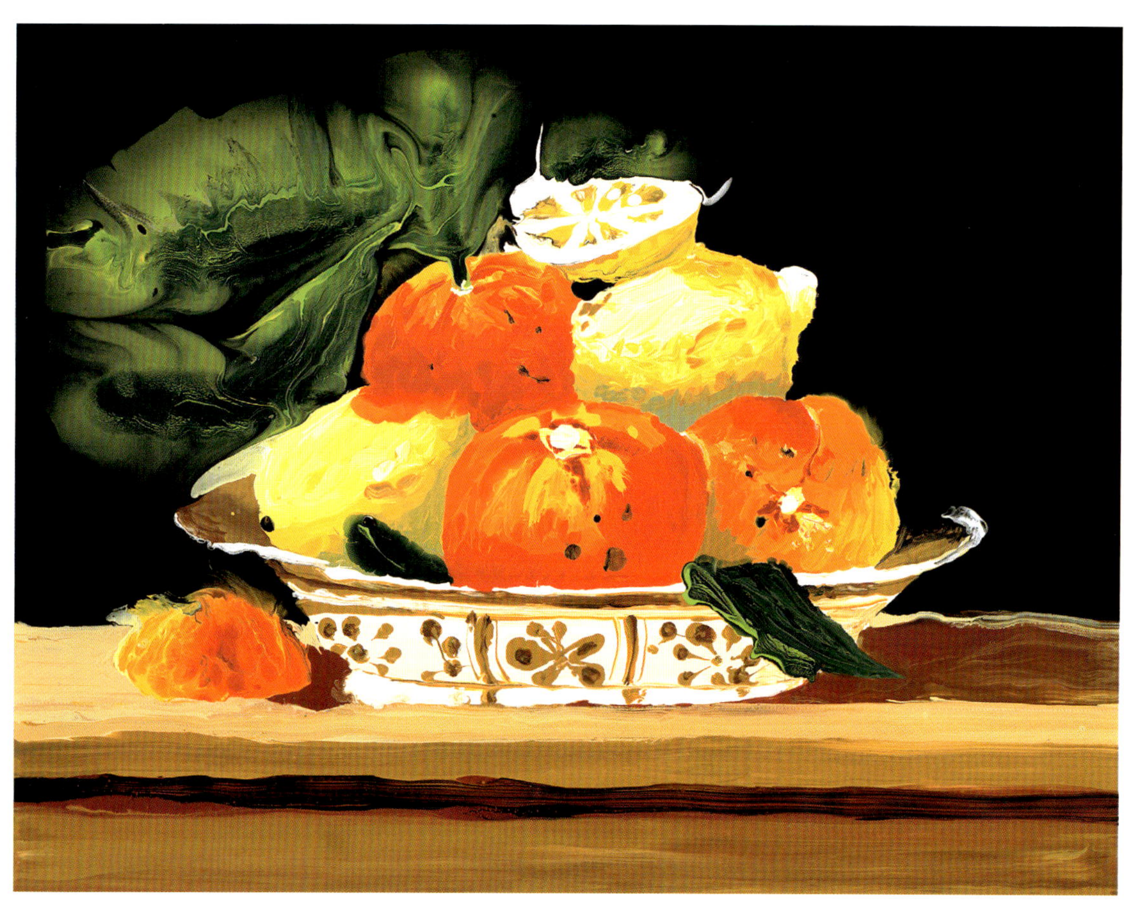

Zitrusfrüchte in Porzellanschale

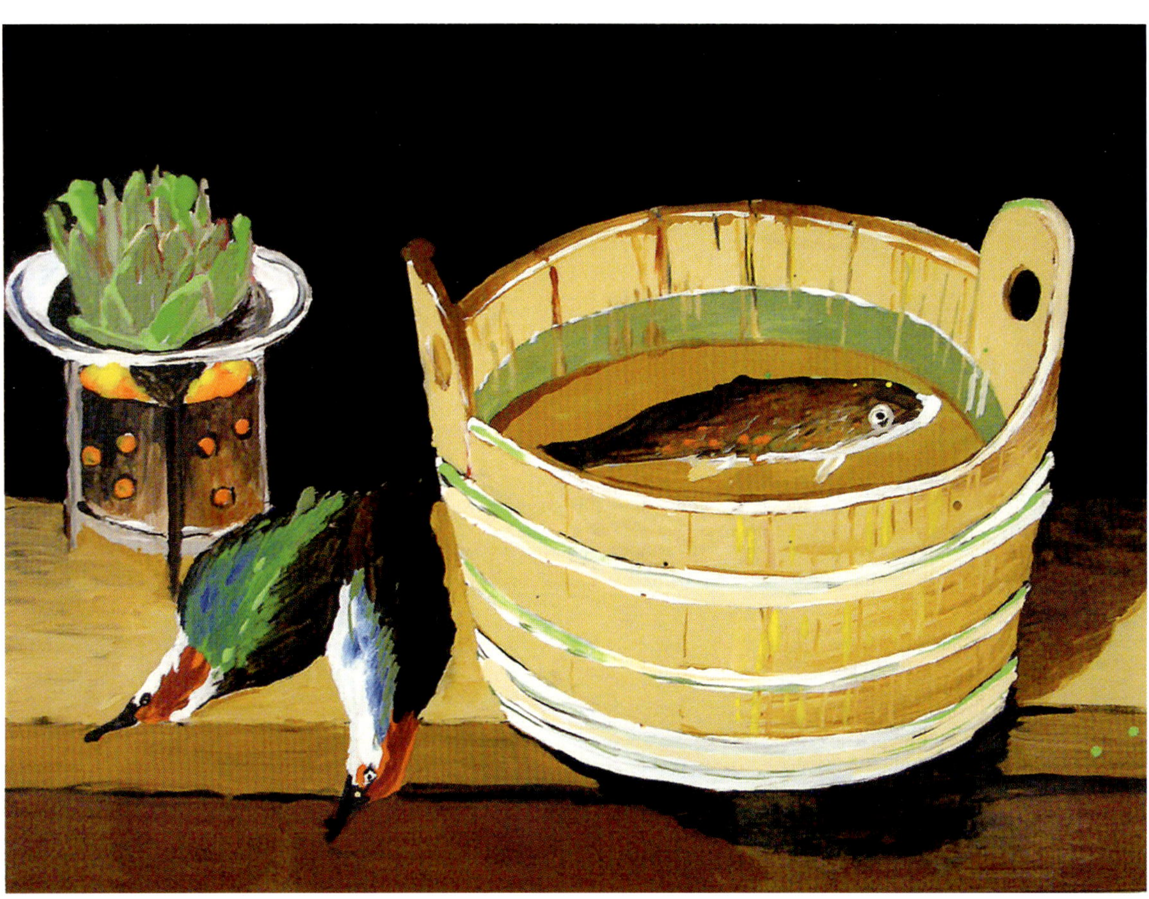

Glutherd, Spechte und Wasserzuber mit Karpfen

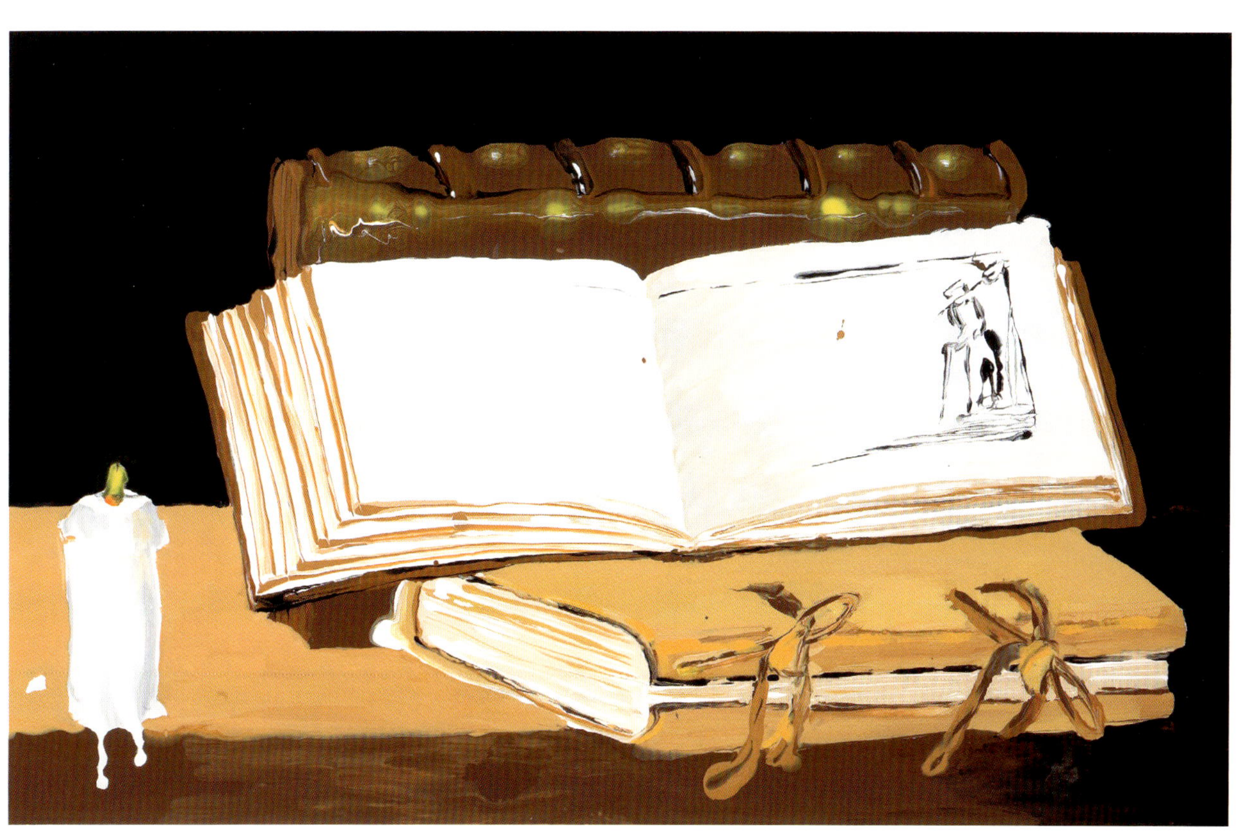

Stillleben mit Büchern und Kerze

... Ich hatte mich damals so für Stoskopff interessiert, weil er ein so »querer«, seltsamer Künstler war und eigentlich vielleicht auch wahnsinnig untypische Stillleben für seine Zeit gemalt hatte. Ich habe seine Malerei mit der »Spanschachtel« im Met in NY lieben gelernt ... ein kleines, unscheinbares, schwarzes, düsteres Ding ... gefüllt mit kandierten Früchten.

Das Unheimliche und die Schärfe in seiner Arbeit liegen meines Erachtens darin, dass seine Bildassemblagen im Gegensatz zu denjenigen seiner Zeitgenossen (z.B. Claez, Heda oder Flegel) nie von einer aktiven, eben erst unterbrochenen Szenerie reden ... Ich hatte bei der Betrachtung seiner Gemälde nie den Eindruck von: »Die Zitronenrinde fällt jetzt gerade runter« oder: »Das Buttermesser wurde vor 2 Sekunden noch benutzt.« Keine Wasser- oder Schweissperlen, keine Krümel, nichts erinnert bei Stoskopff an diese »videostillartig« festgehaltene Gegenwart.

Seine Bilder sind cool, tief eingefroren – die ganze Symbolik wird auf locker konzeptuelle Art und Weise präsentiert, fast plump hingestellt ... keine übertriebene Inszenierung. Die Gegenstände werden in der Bildmitte oder links und rechts angeordnet, keine Friemelei, kein Krimskrams. Die Situationen lassen suggerieren, dass es dort auf diesem dargestellten Tisch schon ewig so ausgesehen hat und dass es durchaus auch noch Tage oder Wochen so ausgesehen haben könnte ... falls nicht irgendjemand doch irgendeinmal dies oder das weggeräumt hat. Und von »aufgeräumt« kann sowieso nie die Rede sein, da die Situationen nie chaotisch, schmuddelig oder gar schmutzig wären. Das finde ich grossartig an seiner Malerei! Diese Schwere und Gelassenheit zugleich, diese Trägheit des Liegenlassens und diese leichtfüssige, unprätentiöse Gleichgültigkeit.

Und da kommt natürlich auch meine Gedankenwelt zur Malerei ins Spiel: Es geht um Widersprüche ... um Zufall und Konzept, um warm und kalt, um cool und beherzt, um Bewegtes und Eingefrorenes, um das Hier und Jetzt, noch bevor eine Idee/ein Bild um- oder verbaut werden kann.

Das spielte ich damals auch bei meiner Stilllebenserie durch: cooles, hartes Material, industrielle Farben, nass in nass: Das klare Konzept kann dabei nur bis zu einem bestimmten Punkt durchgezogen werden ... Und plötzlich setzt das Warme ein, das Verführerische und das »Gehen- und Geschehenlassen«, das Hier und Jetzt, ohne dass ich mit dem Pinsel noch etwas ein- oder ausrenken konnte.

Christine Streuli aus einer E-mail an Claudia Jolles

... Back then I was so interested in Stoskopff because he was such an "off-beat", strange artist and actually perhaps painted still lifes that were incredibly untypical of his day. I came to love his paintings when viewing his "chip-wood box" in the Met in NY ... a small, unobtrusive, black and somber thing ... filled with candied fruit.

The mysterious and acuity of his work stems in my opinion from the fact that his pictorial assemblages contract so strongly with those of his contemporaries (such as Claez, Heda or Flegel) as they never speak of an active scene just interrupted ... When viewing his paintings I have never felt that "The lemon peel is just about to fall off," or "the butter knife was used just two seconds ago". There are no drops of water or beads of sweat, no crumbs; nothing in Stoskopff's work brings to mind the present as captured "as if in a video still".

His pictures are cool, deep frozen – all the symbolism is depicted in a loosely conceptual manner, almost abruptly ... there is no exaggerated staging. Then objects are arranged in the center of the picture or to the left and right, no little frills or bits and pieces. The situations intimate that things on the table shown have been that way since eternity and may have stayed that way for days or weeks ... unless someone did clear away this or that, after all. And there can be no talk of things getting "cleared up", as the situations are never chaotic, messy or even dirty. This is what I find so marvelous in his painting! That gravity and leisure in one, that turgidity of leaving things be, coupled with that light touch in the unpretentious indifference.

And that is of course the point where my own thoughts on painting come to bear: I strongly focus on these contradictions ... on chance and concept, on warm and cold, on the cool and the brave, on the animated and the frozen, on the here-and-now, before an idea/image can be altered or obscured.

That is what I tried out back then with my series of still lifes: cool, hard material, industrial paints, wet on wet: You can only realize a clear concept up to a certain point ... And suddenly warmth sets in, with it the seductive and the "be and let be", the here and now without me being able to adjust things for the better or the worse using a brush.

Christine Streuli from an email to Claudia Jolles

Translation: Jeremy Gaines

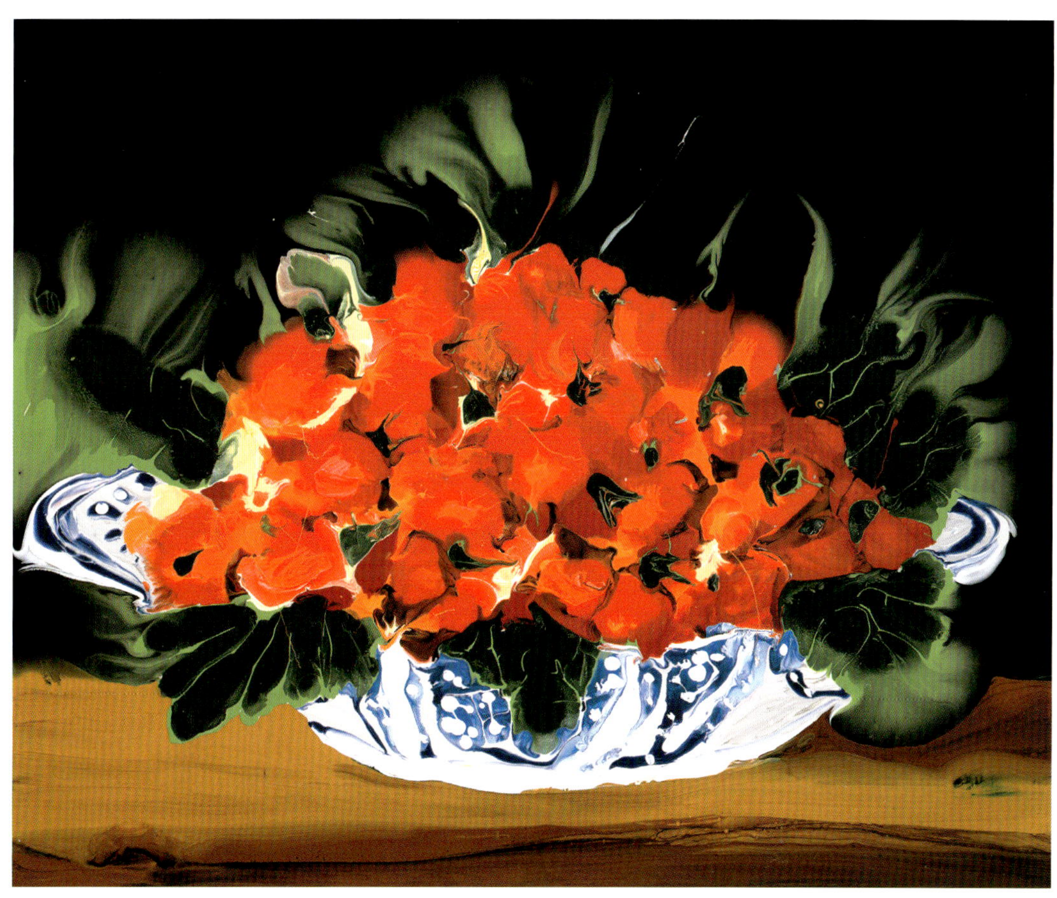

Erdbeerschale

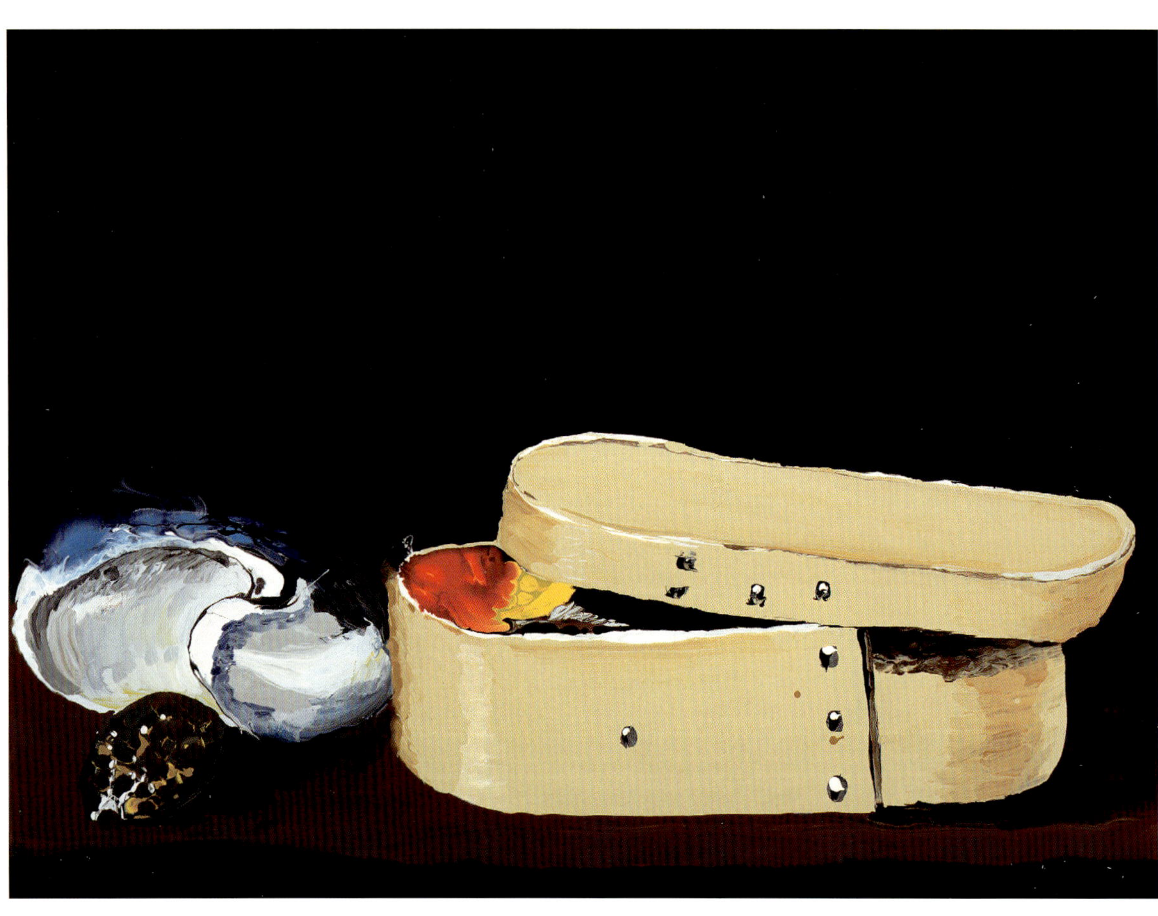

Spanschachtel und Nautilus

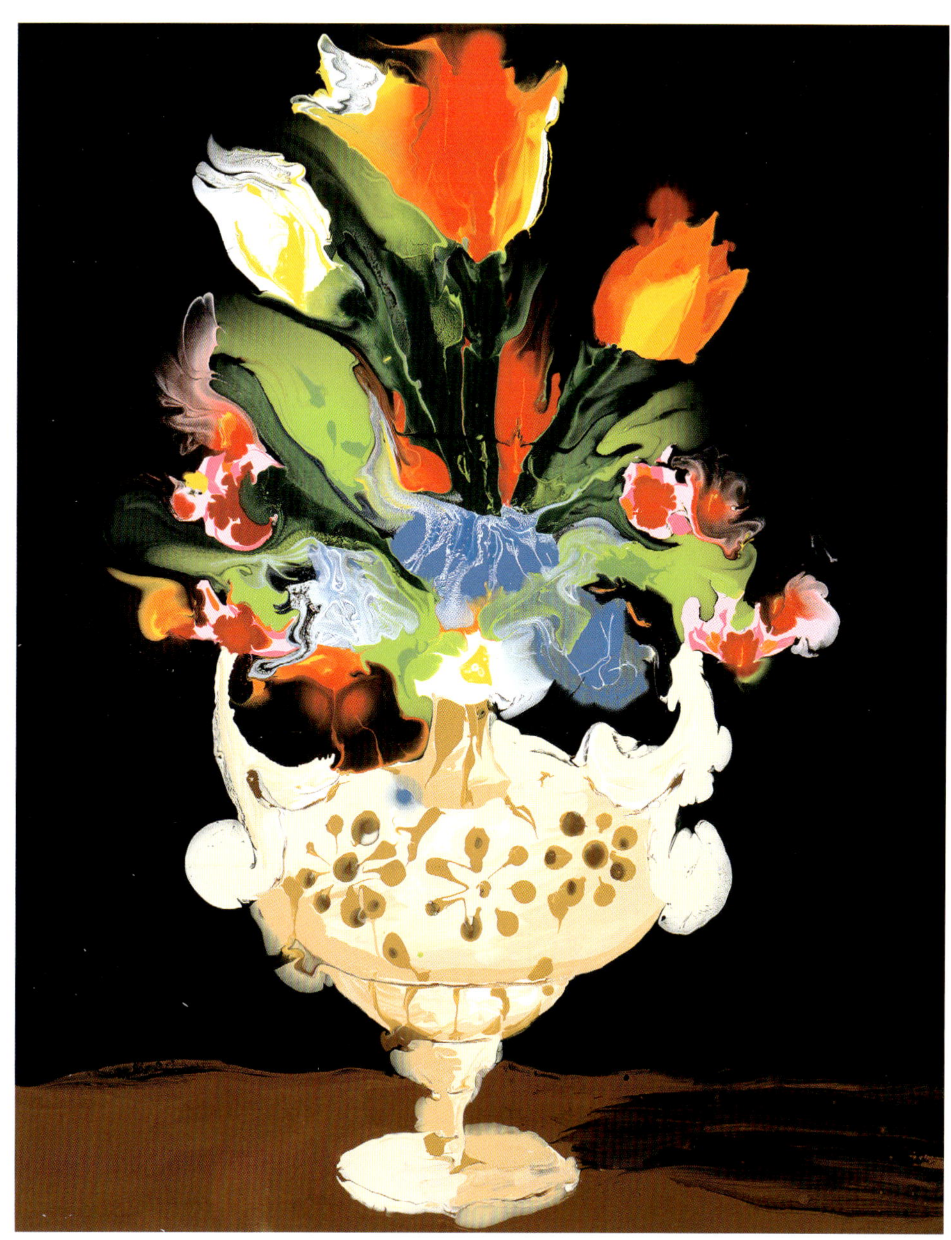

Groteskvase mit Blumen 2

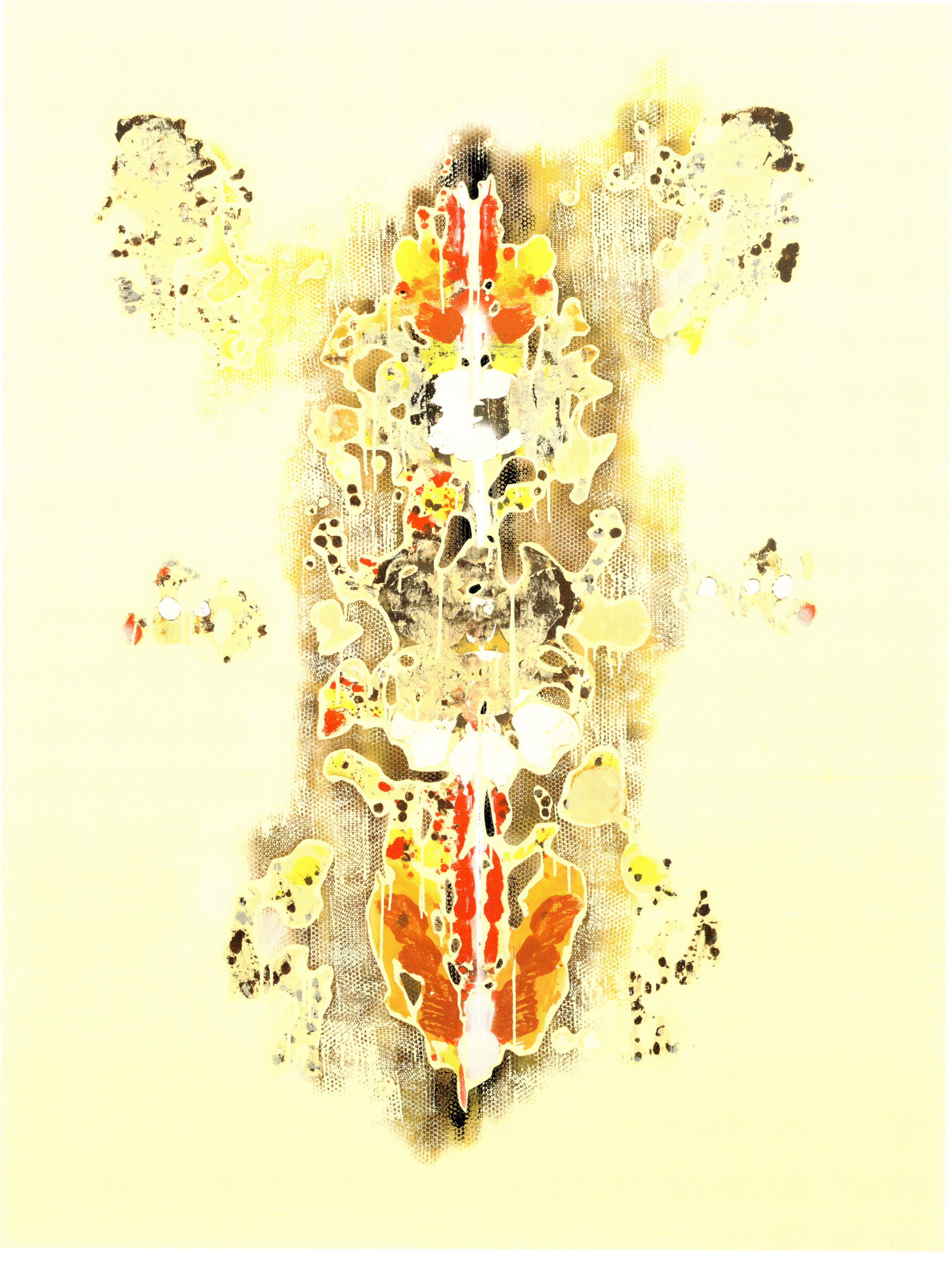

Rorschach

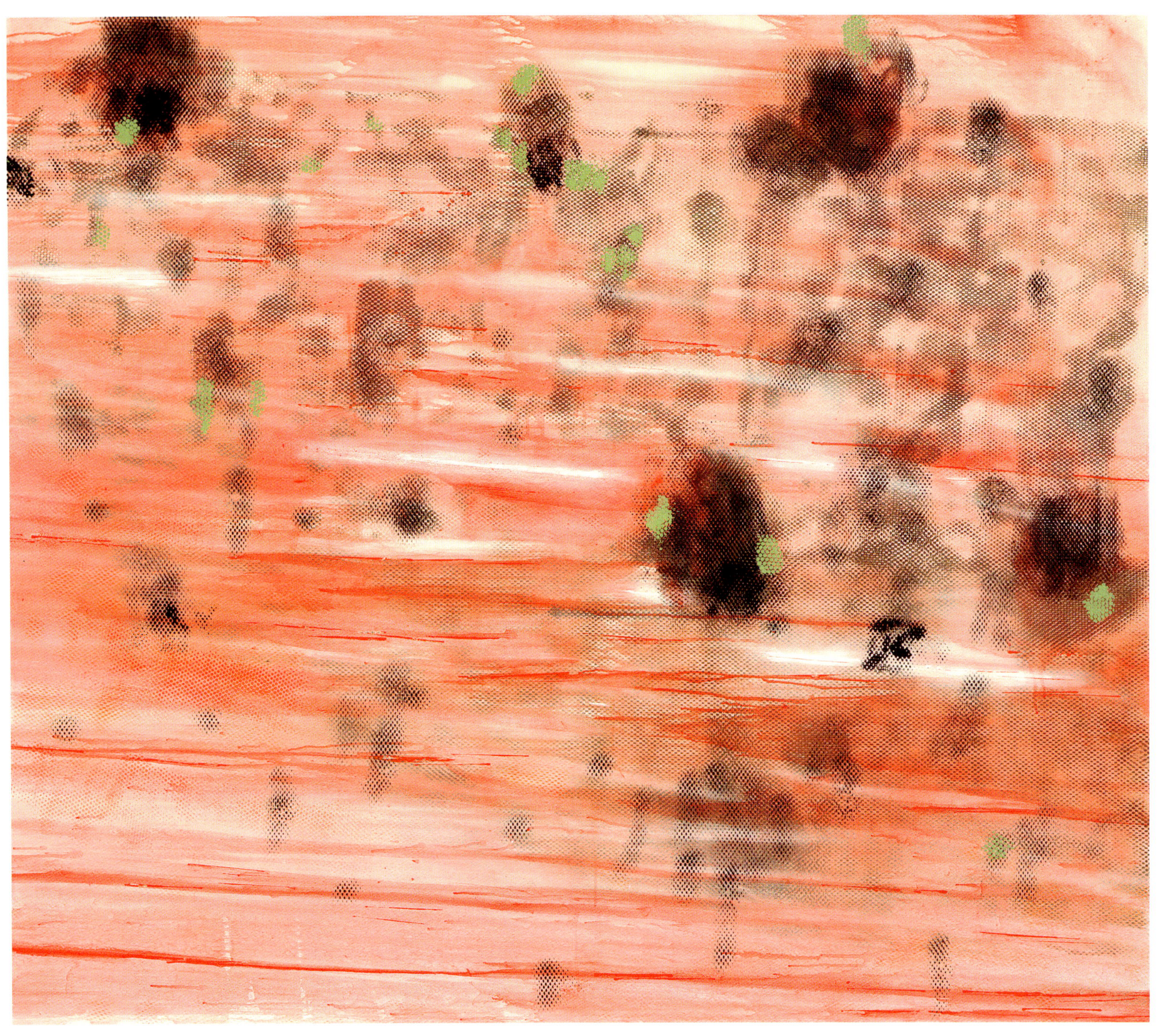

wasteland

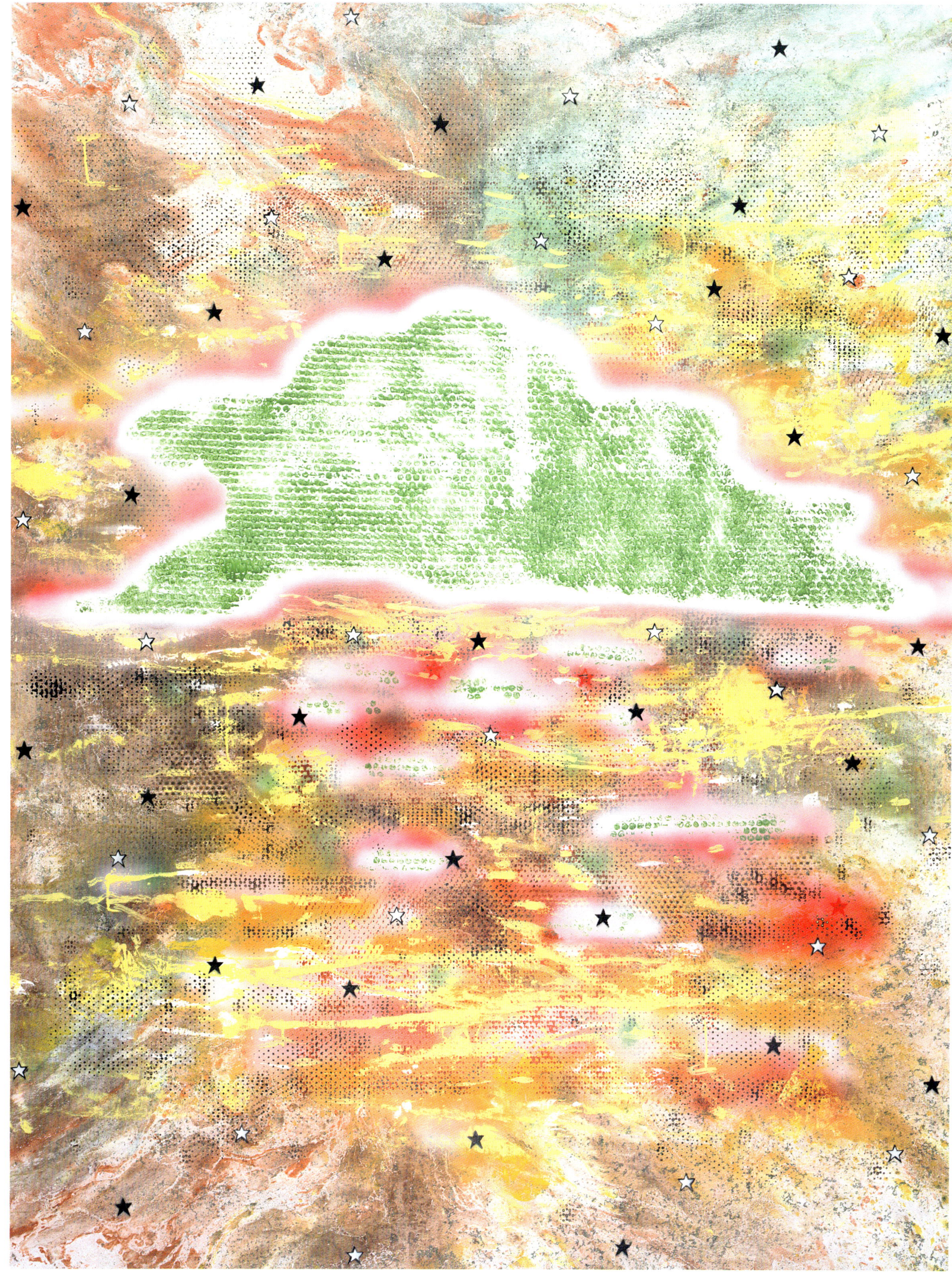

Liebespaar

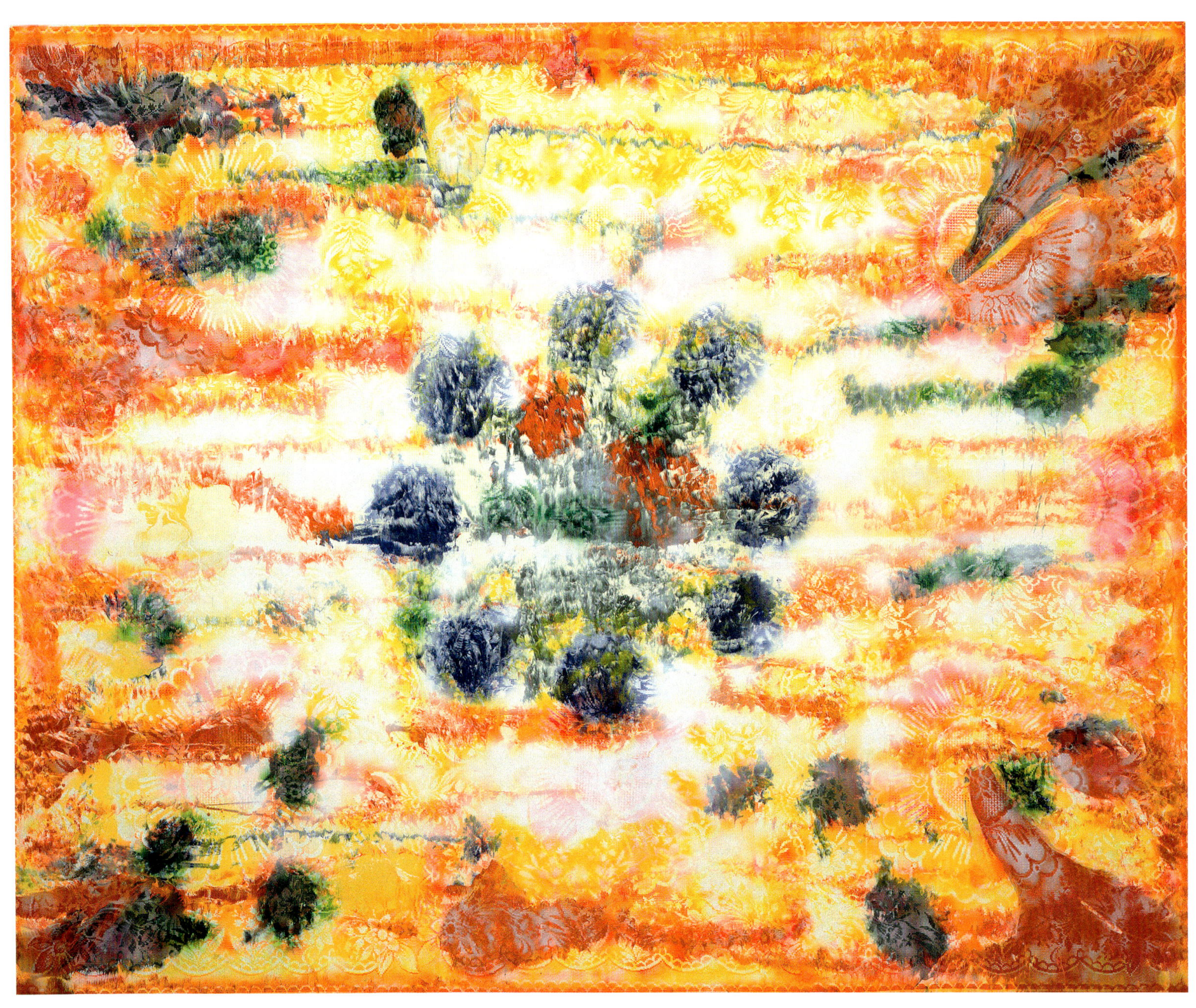

Spa

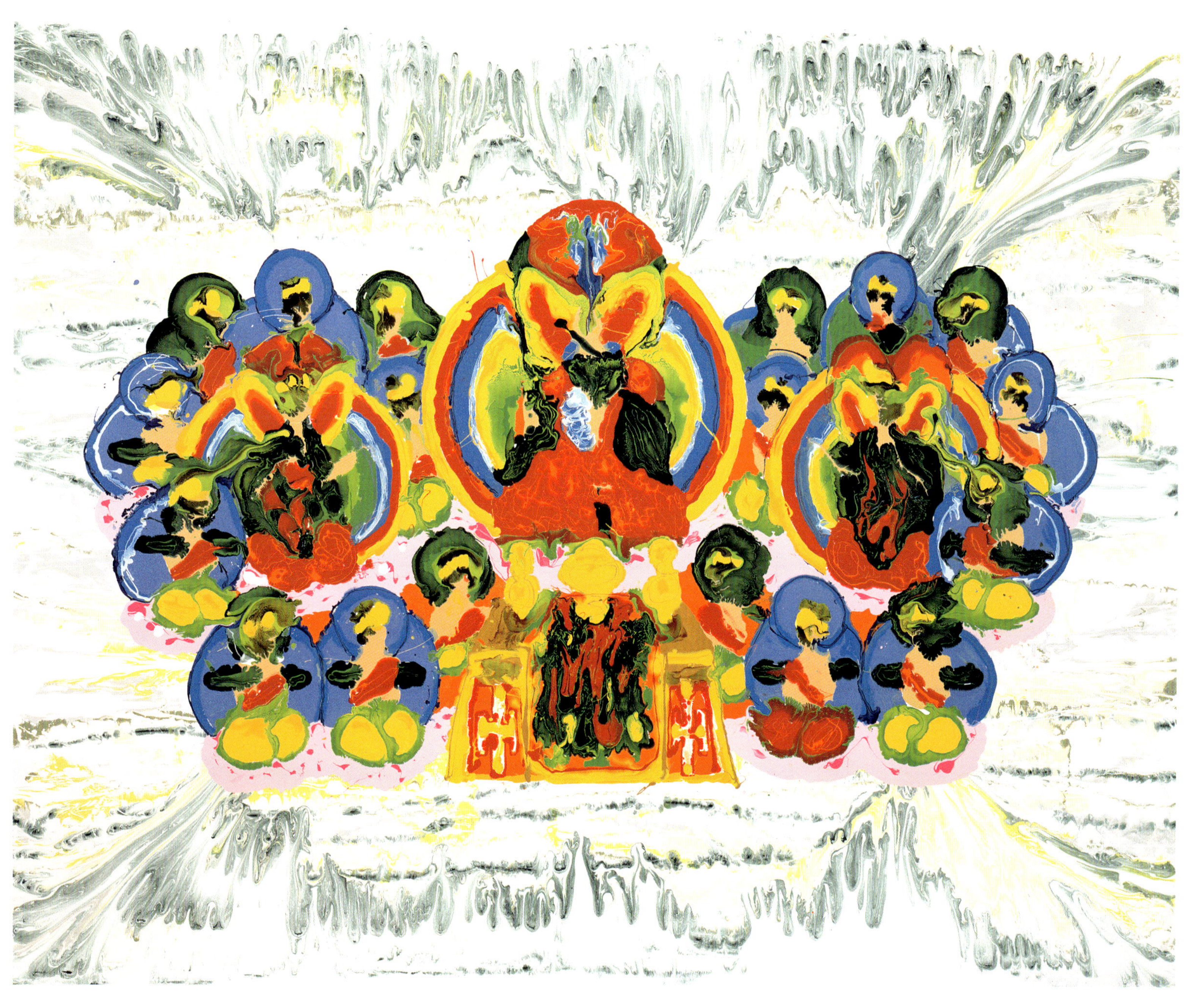

Delphi

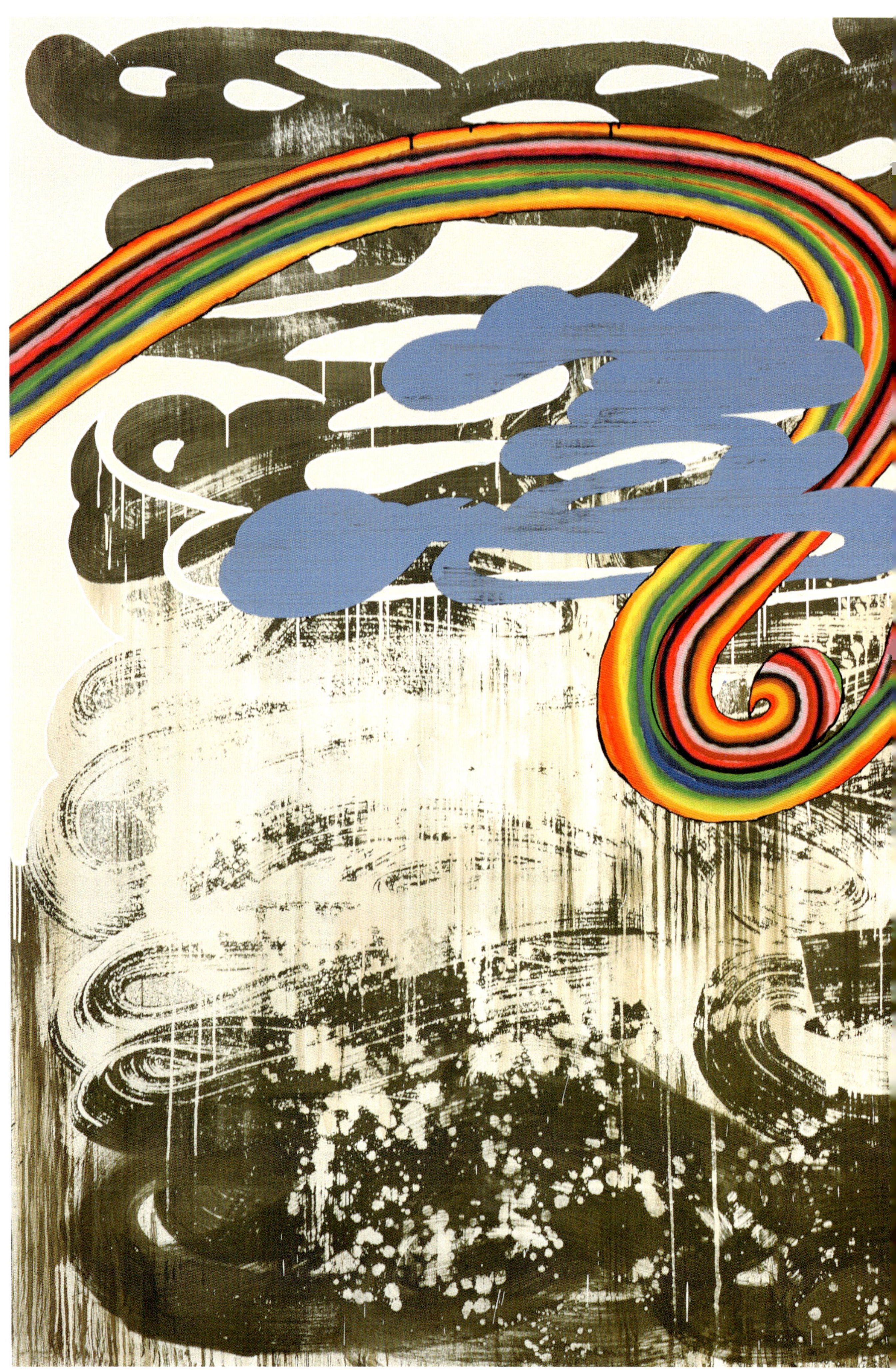

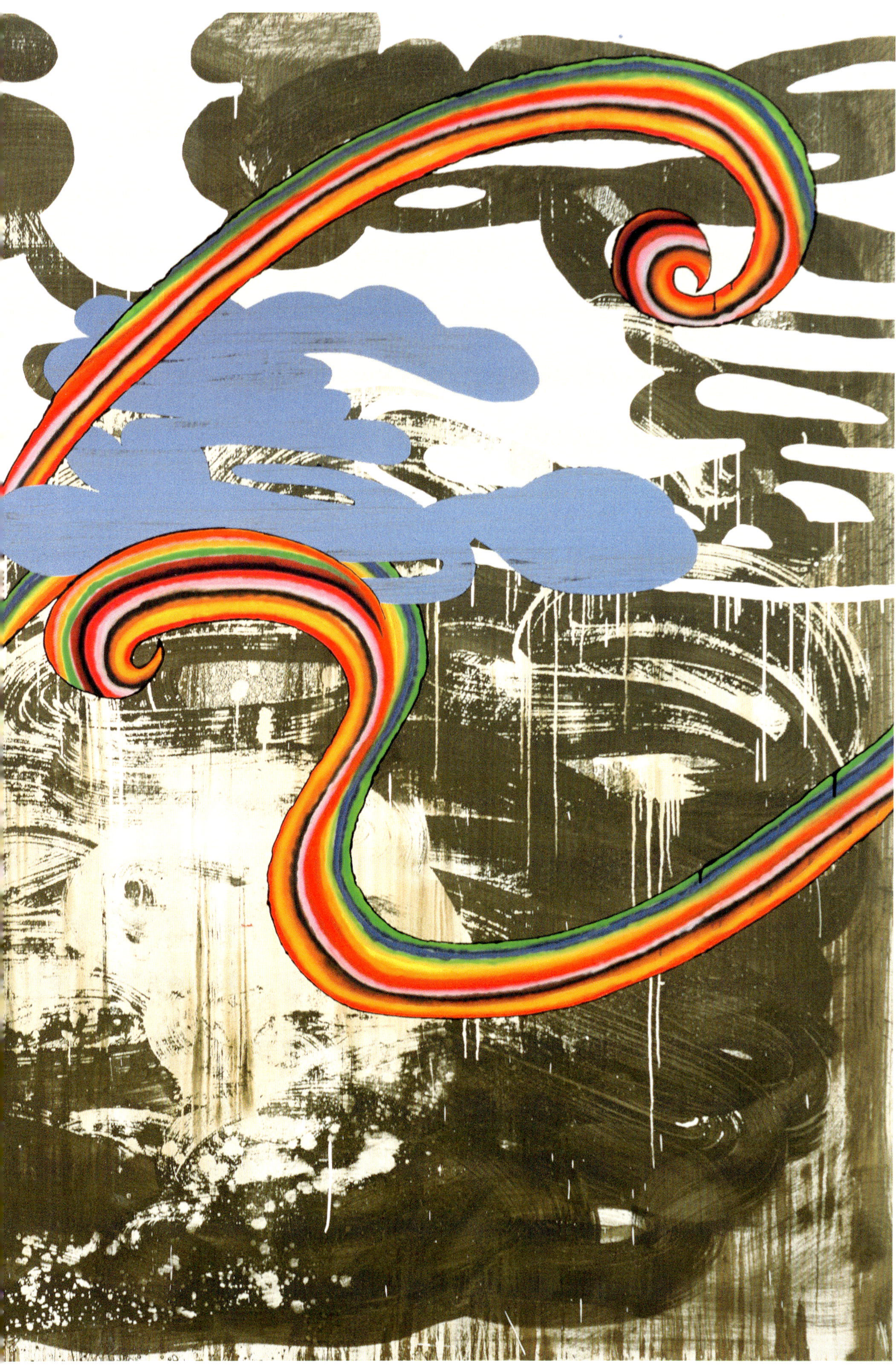

Ich lieb Dich, ich lieb Dich nicht…

Obwohl einem immer wieder Malerinnen und Maler in den Sinn kommen, mit deren Werken man die Bilder von Christine Streuli in einer imaginären Malereiausstellung in einen Dialog setzen möchte, sind ihre Malerei und ihre Bilder unverwechselbar. Es wären Maler (nicht nur zeitgenössische) der abstrakten – der man ihre Bilder prima vista eher zurechnen möchte – ebenso wie der figurativen Richtung, der sich die Künstlerin, wie man aus ihrem Sprechen über Malerei herauszuhören versucht ist, enger verbunden zu fühlen scheint. Und wenn wir ihrem Grossformat mit dem überraschenden Titel **Ich lieb Dich, ich lieb Dich nicht…** *erst mal wie einem abstrakten Gemälde begegnen, so reizt es doch auch zu einer inhaltlichen Lesart – was für die Malerin in Ordnung gehen dürfte, auch wenn ihre bildnerische Intention gewiss nicht in diese Richtung zielte. Am Anfang stand eine Bildidee, die in Malerei umgesetzt werden wollte, und gewiss nicht die Absicht, eine Idee mit einem Bild zu illustrieren. Der Titel verweigert einen einfachen Zugang, im Gegenteil, er führt zuerst mal von der alleine visuellen Beschäftigung mit dem Bild weg – auf dass wir der Malerei nochmals von einer anderen Richtung her begegnen mögen.*

Das Bild entstand 2004, als die Künstlerin an einer Werkgruppe für eine Ausstellung im Kunstmuseum Bonn arbeitete, es handelt sich um eines der ersten in einem solch grossen Format. Christine Streuli möge mir verzeihen, dass ich ihr Bild kurz zerlege. Obwohl viele Entscheide sicher erst auf der Leinwand gefällt werden, sind die Gemälde von der Malerin immer gut begründet, also die Richtung weisend bereits grundiert. Der Bildgrund wirft dabei quasi seine Schatten voraus, darauf reagiert oder antwortet das Geschehen an der Oberfläche. Die horizontale Teilung des Grundes legt eine landschaftliche Lektüre des Bildes nahe. Über einem erdfarbenen Grund unten in der selben tonigen Farbe wolkige Gebilde oben – nicht als freie Komposition, sondern offensichtlich aus Schablonen generiert, die sich ihrerseits wieder als strengere Formalisierung der freien Malbewegung des Bildgrundes unten zu erkennen geben: Sie reflektieren jene.

Die Formen antworten sich, wie so oft in dieser Bildwelt, entlang der Horizontalen ebenso wie der Vertikalen rorschachartig. »Wüst und öde« kommt mir die Landschaftsallusion unten vor: Und sie erinnert damit an das Ungeordnete des ersten Tages (so die lutherische Übersetzung des hebräischen Tohuwabohus am Beginn der Genesis). Über der horizontalen Trennlinie zwischen unscharfer unterer und schärferer oberer Hälfte schweben wieder sich à la Rorschach-Test entsprechende blaue Wolkenformationen. Darunter und darüber, oben und unten verbindend, die drei das Öde und Wüste konterkarierenden – also: durchkreuzenden – festlich bunten Banderolen. Auf dieses Widersprüchliche, gleichzeitig Ernste und Heitere, spielt auch der Titel an, auf den scheinbar spielerischen Umgang von jungen Verliebten mit der schweren, über Glück und Unglück entscheidenden Frage. Aber Streuli biegt die ängstliches Herzklopfen bereitende Frage, ob er sie denn liebe, listig um in eine Provokation. Wir nehmen ernst, dass Bilder der Betrachtung als Subjekte begegnen können, so die Betrachtung denn bereit ist, gemalte Bilder als zur Aussage fähige Subjekte zu respektieren – und gehen also davon aus, dass mit diesem Titel das Bild zu uns, den Betrachtern, spricht: So wie sich in ihm das wüst Öde mit barock üppiger Festlichkeit verbindet, so zieht es uns mit seiner sinnlichen Attraktivität an, um uns im nächsten Moment wieder auf Distanz zu halten. Immer wieder arbeitet Christine Streuli in ihrer Malerei mit solchen tatsächlichen oder angeblichen Gegensätzen.

Beat Wismer

Irrespective of the fact that one can always think of artists whose works one might like to engage in a dialogue with those of Christine Streuli in some imaginary exhibition, her painting method and her paintings are unmistakable. The dialogue partners in question would be (not just contemporary) artists of both an abstract leaning – to which, prima vista, her paintings might be ascribed – and a figurative leaning – to which the artist seems to feel a certain affinity, to judge by what she says about painting. And even if we initially see her large format work with the surprising title **Ich lieb Dich; ich lieb Dich nicht…** *as an abstract painting, it also tempts us to read something into it, which the artist would probably accept us doing, even though her artistic intention surely does not aim in this direction. In the beginning was an idea which she wanted to render in a painting, and certainly not any intention to illustrate an idea through an image. The very title prevents any simple approach; on the contrary, at first it impedes a purely visual preoccupation with the work – in order that we might encounter painting again from a different direction.*

Streuli produced the painting in 2004, when she was working on a group of paintings for an exhibition at the Kunstmuseum Bonn; it is one of her first in such a large format. Hopefully the artist will forgive me for taking that work apart briefly. Although many decisions are only made on the canvas, this artist's paintings are always well grounded, meaning that the thrust is already given by the ground. The pictorial ground thus casts its shadow in advance, so to speak, and what happens on the surface is in response to this. The horizontal division of the ground suggests viewing the painting as a landscape: below, an earth-coloured ground, above, cloud-like forms in the same earthy shade – not freely composed but clearly generated using stencils, which in turn are recognisable as a more strict formalisation of the free painterly movement of the pictorial ground below: this they reflect.

As so often in this particular pictorial world, the forms respond to one another along both the horizontals and the verticals, Rorschach-like. For me, the allusion to landscape below seems "desolate and bleak", and thus recalls the "chaos of the first day" (as in Luther's translation of the Hebrew tohuwabohu at the beginning of Genesis). Above the horizontal dividing line, between blurred lower and sharp upper half, hover blue cloud formations, again Rorschach-like. Below and above them, linking top and bottom, are three festively colourful scrolls, thwarting, i.e., cutting across the dreary wilderness. The work's title also refers to this contradictory element, which is both serious and cheerful, to the apparently playful behaviour of young lovers in the face of that grave question so decisive for their happiness or unhappiness. Streuli makes a clever provocation out of this heart-stopping question as to whether he loves her. We seriously assume that we, the observers, can encounter paintings as subjects, if we the observers are willing to acknowledge painted images as subjects capable of expression – and so assume that through its title the painting speaks to us, the viewers: just as it links the barren wasteland with abundantly baroque festivity, so too it draws us to it through its sensual attractiveness, only to then set us at a distance. Christine Streuli's paintings always harbour such actual or apparent contradictions.

Beat Wismer

Translation: Pauline Cumbers

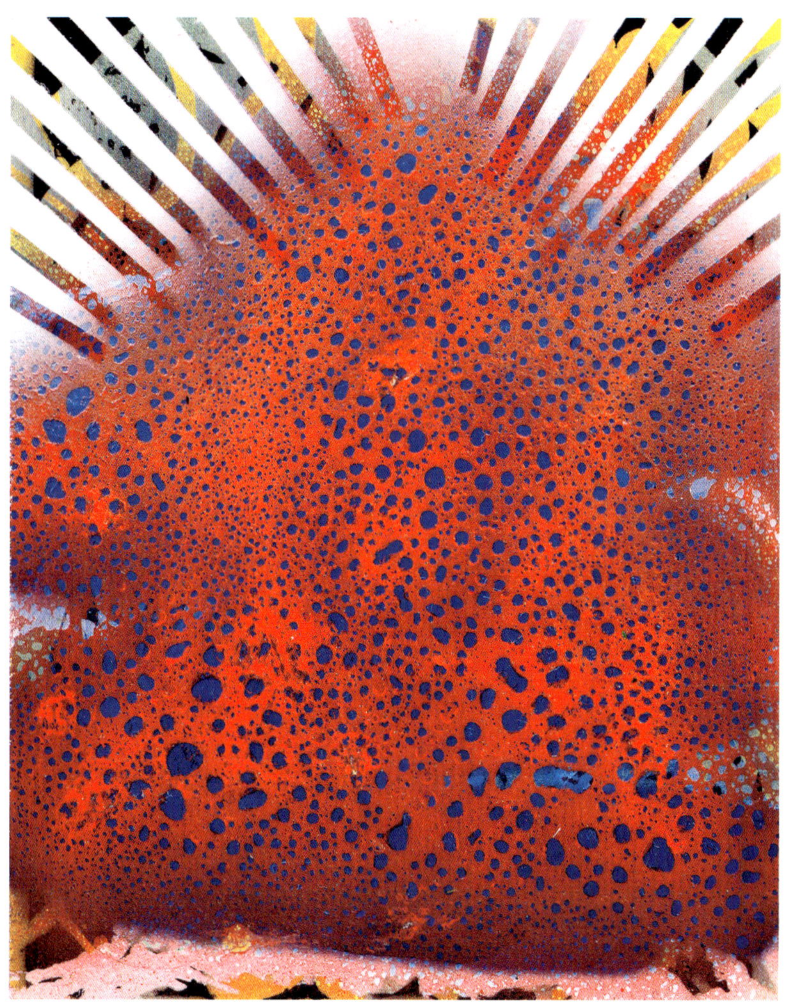

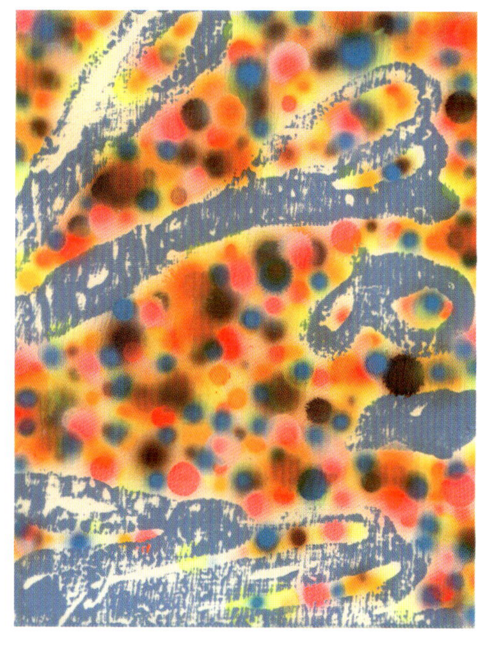

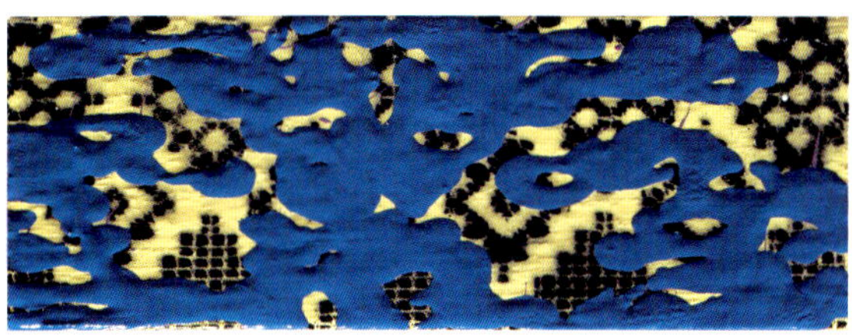

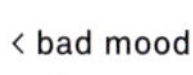

< bad mood
> champ
< stille Wasser
> Teddy

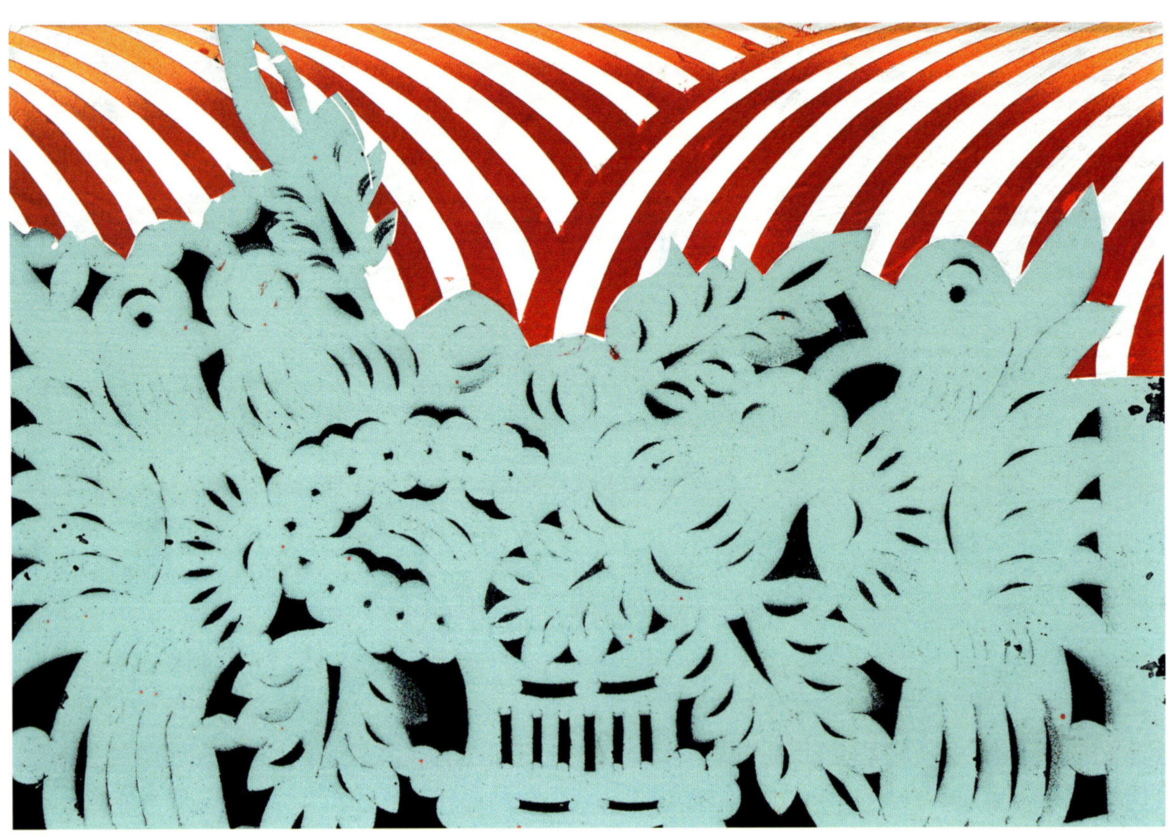

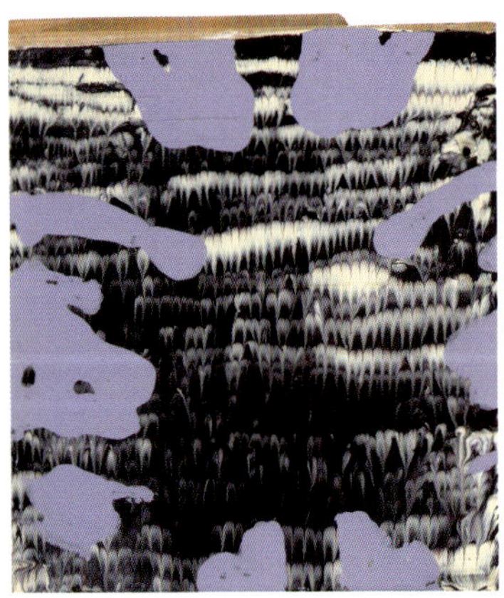

> la Rondella
< Egypt Eagle

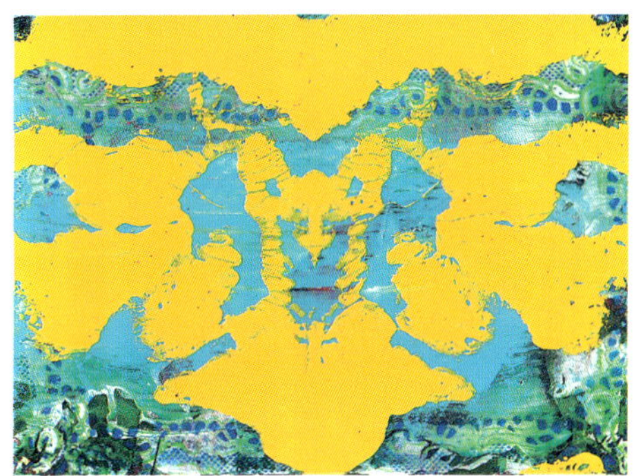

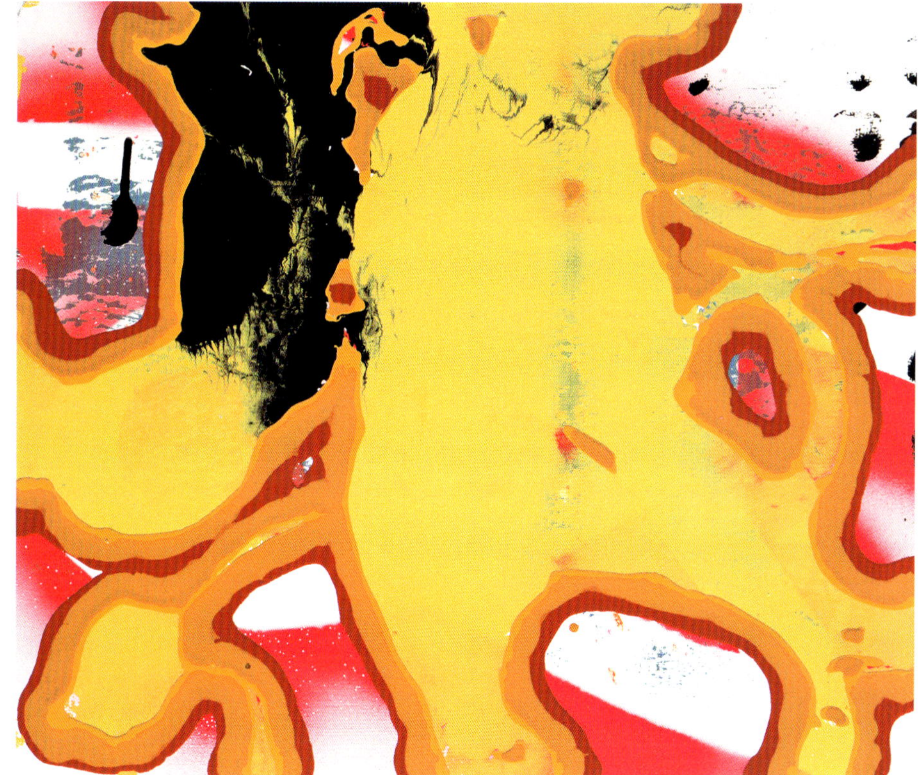

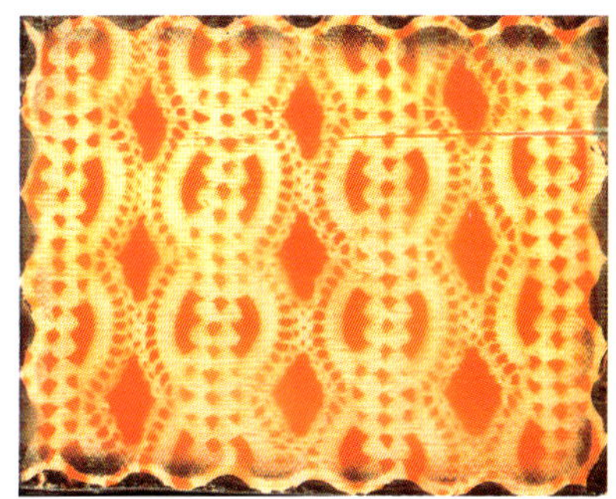

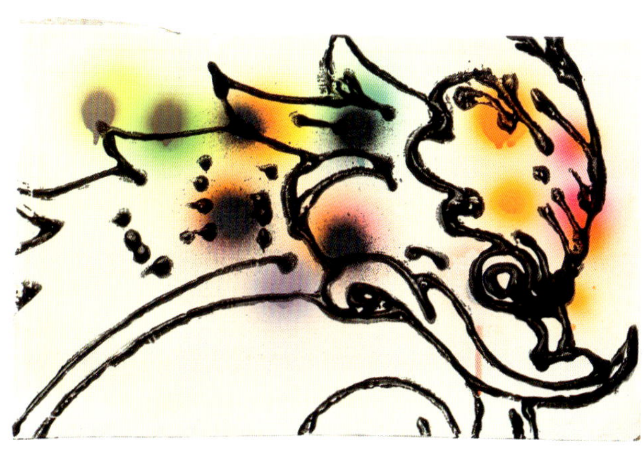

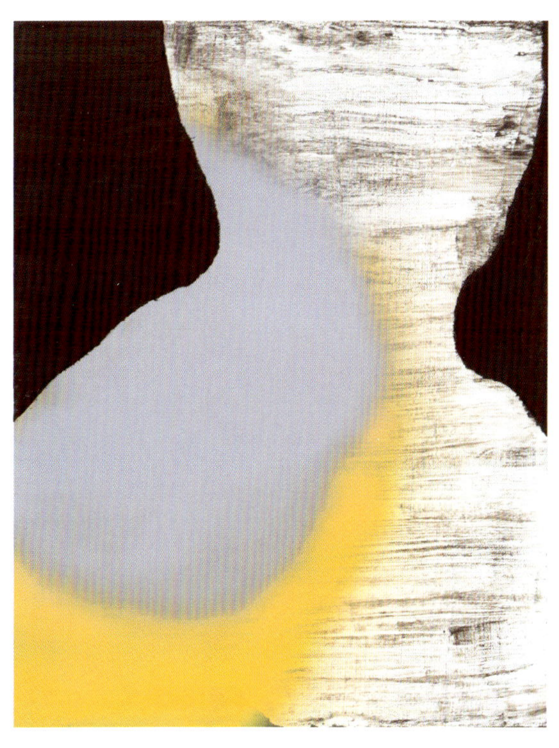

> blacking in my mind
< smart bomb
< handmade in Egypt
> Schlangenfrass
< Beitrag an das Familienalbum

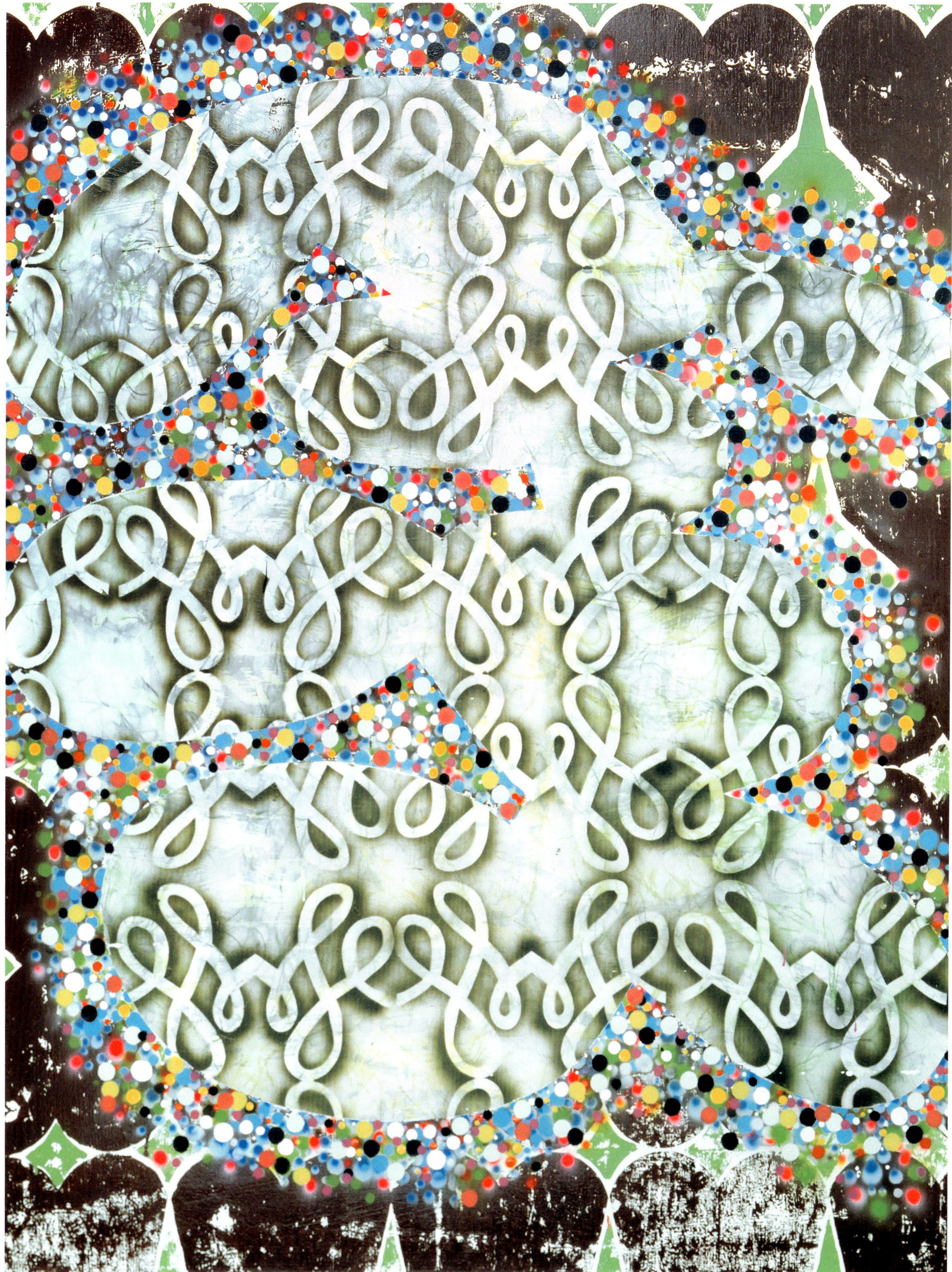

Kies

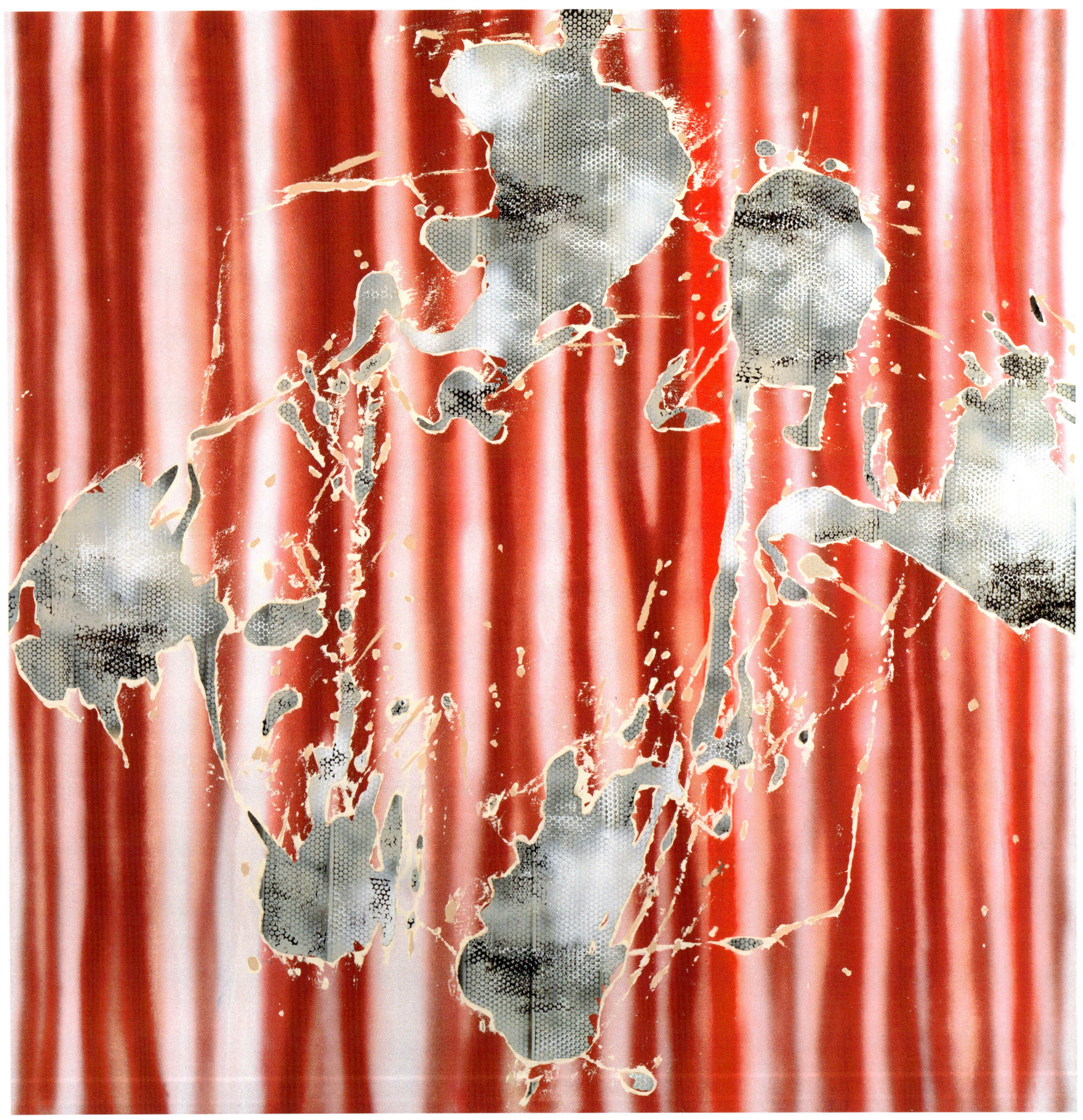

Schlangenleder

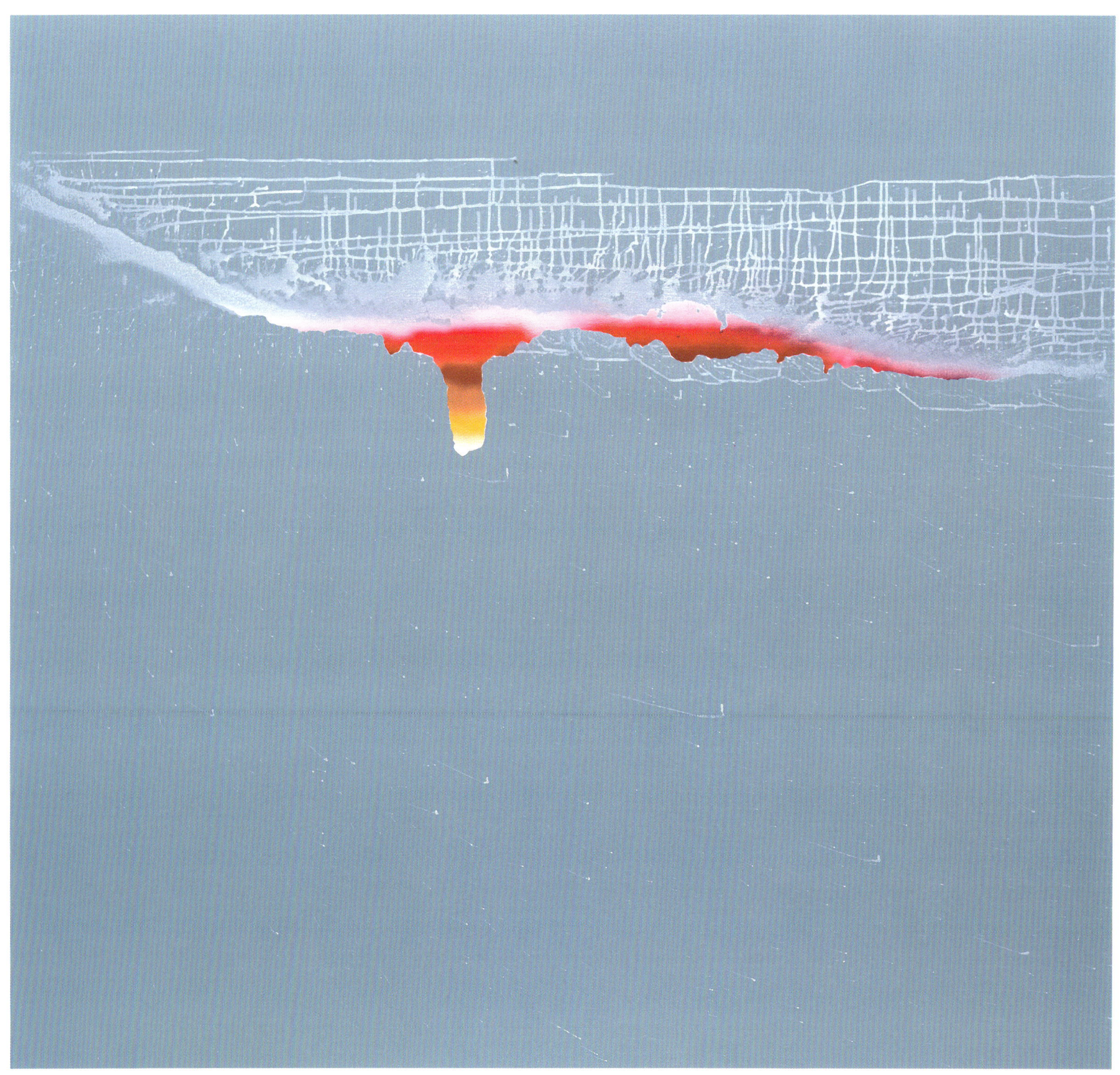

Delta

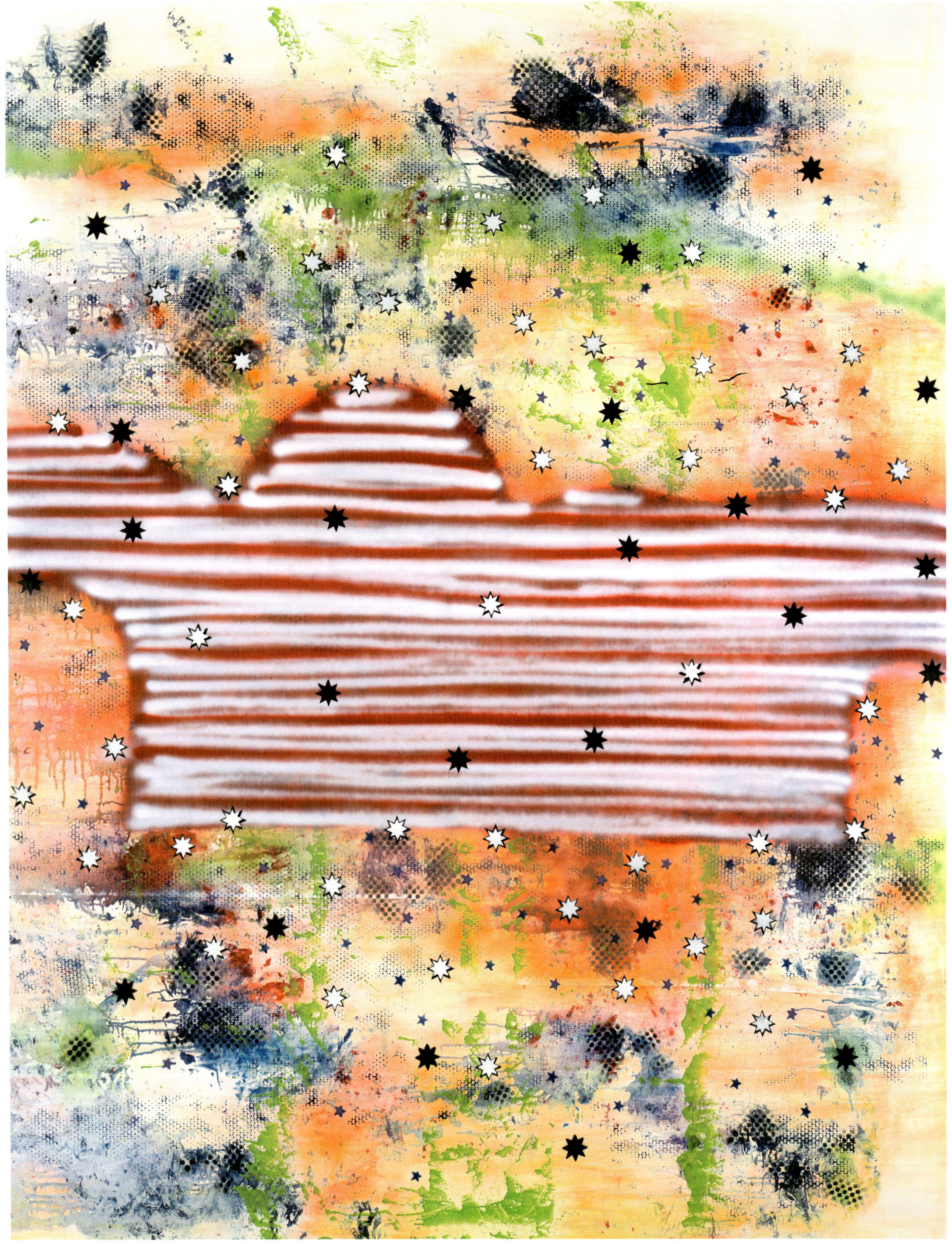

Aussteiger

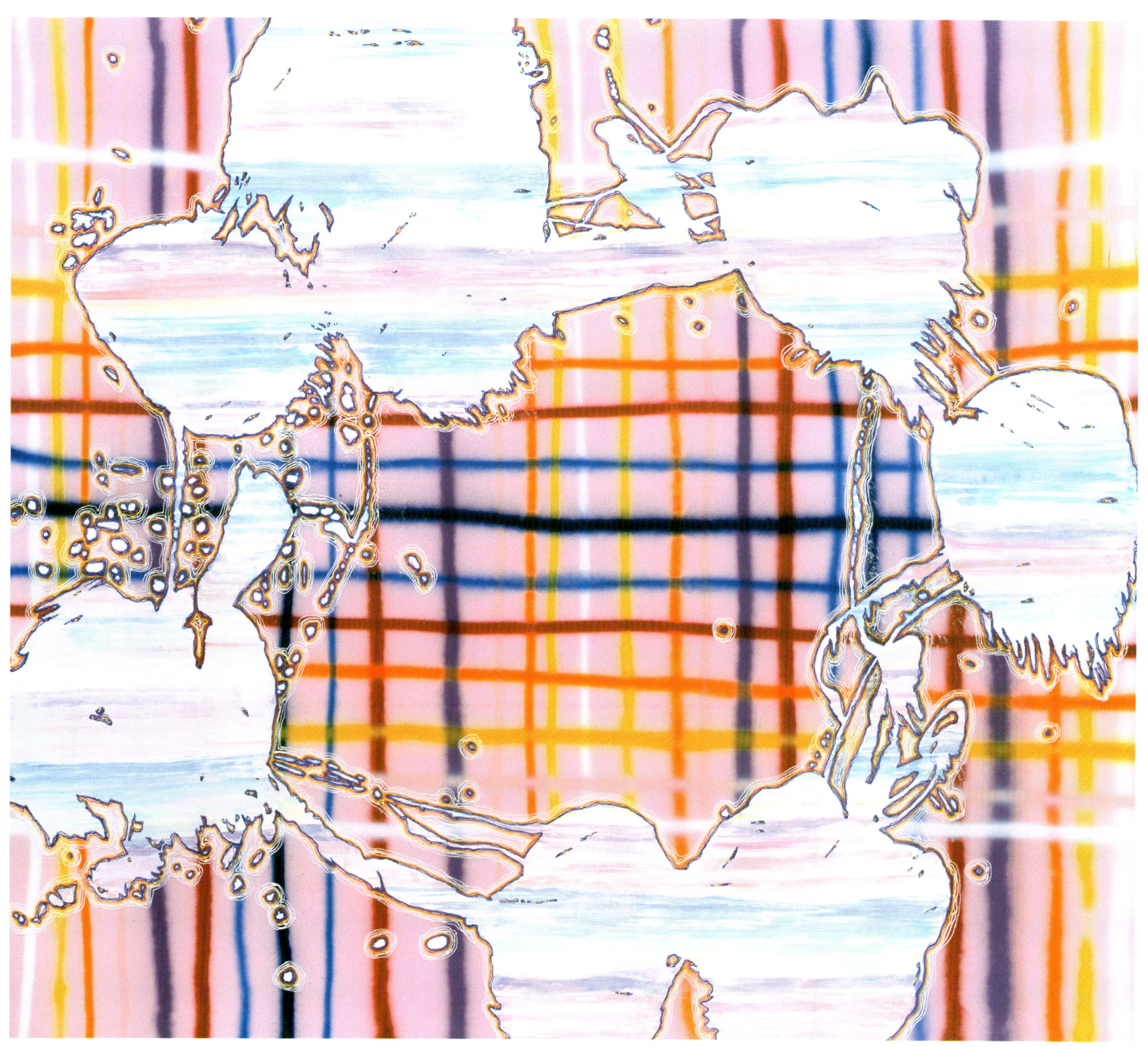

Windhund

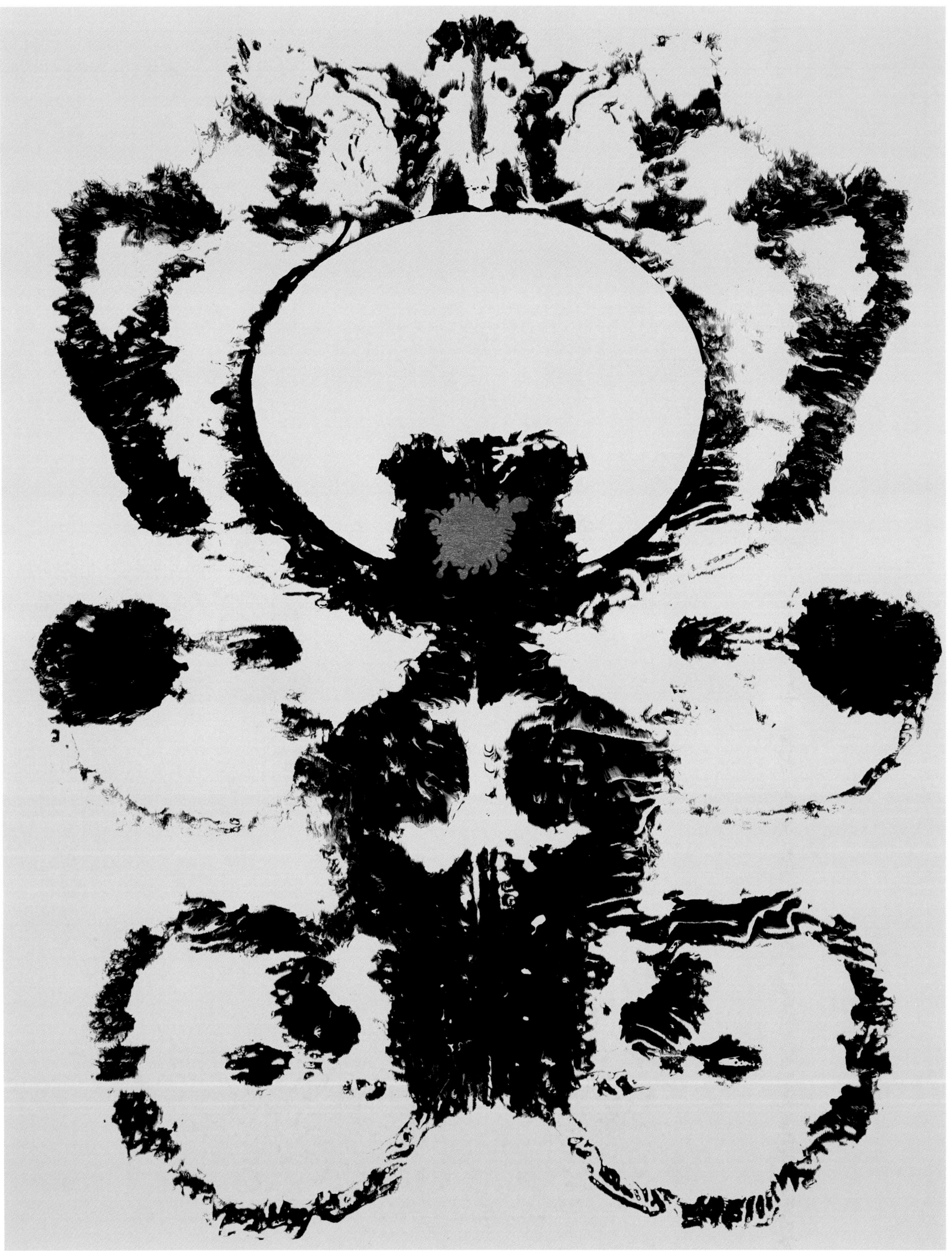

Puppe

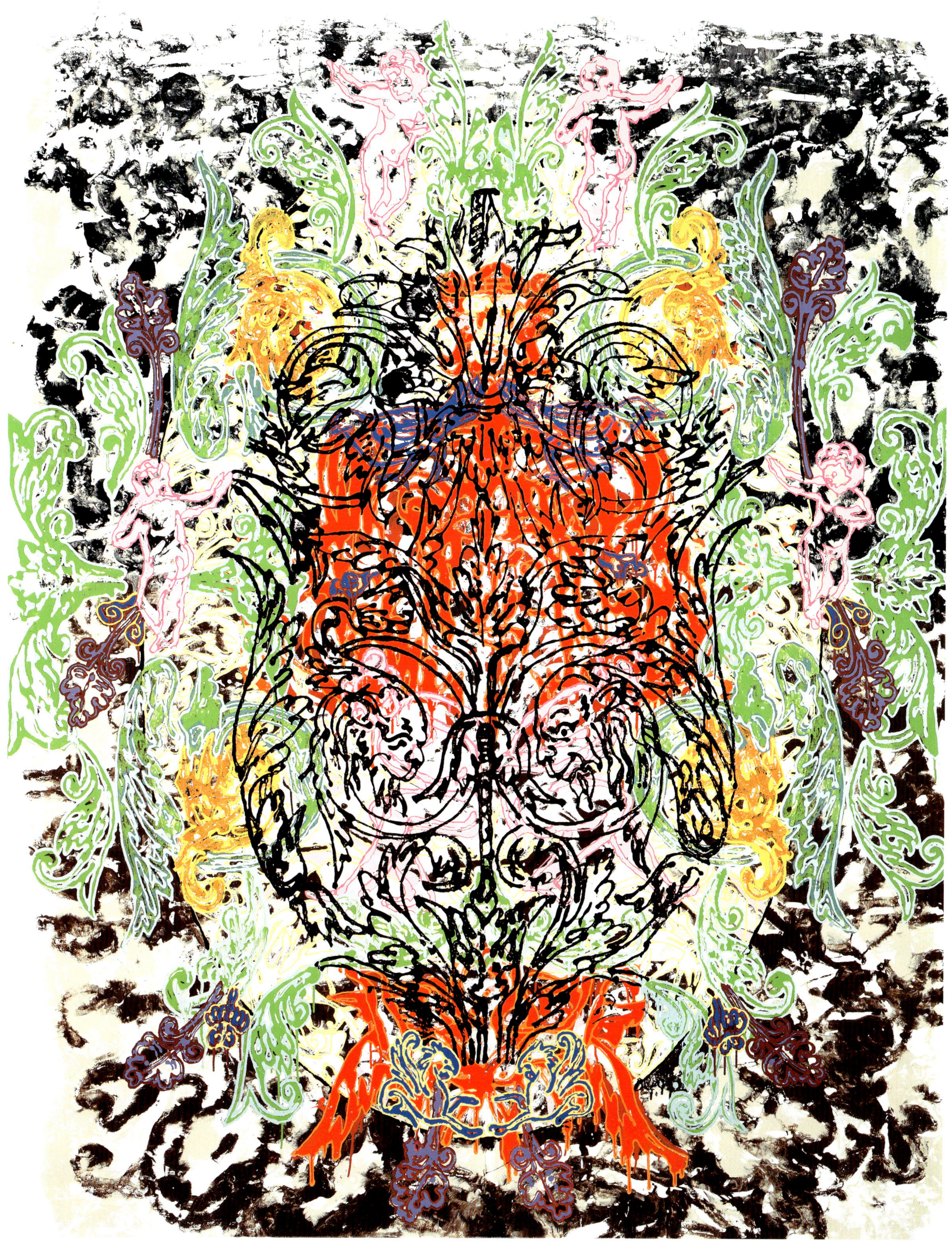

grotesk

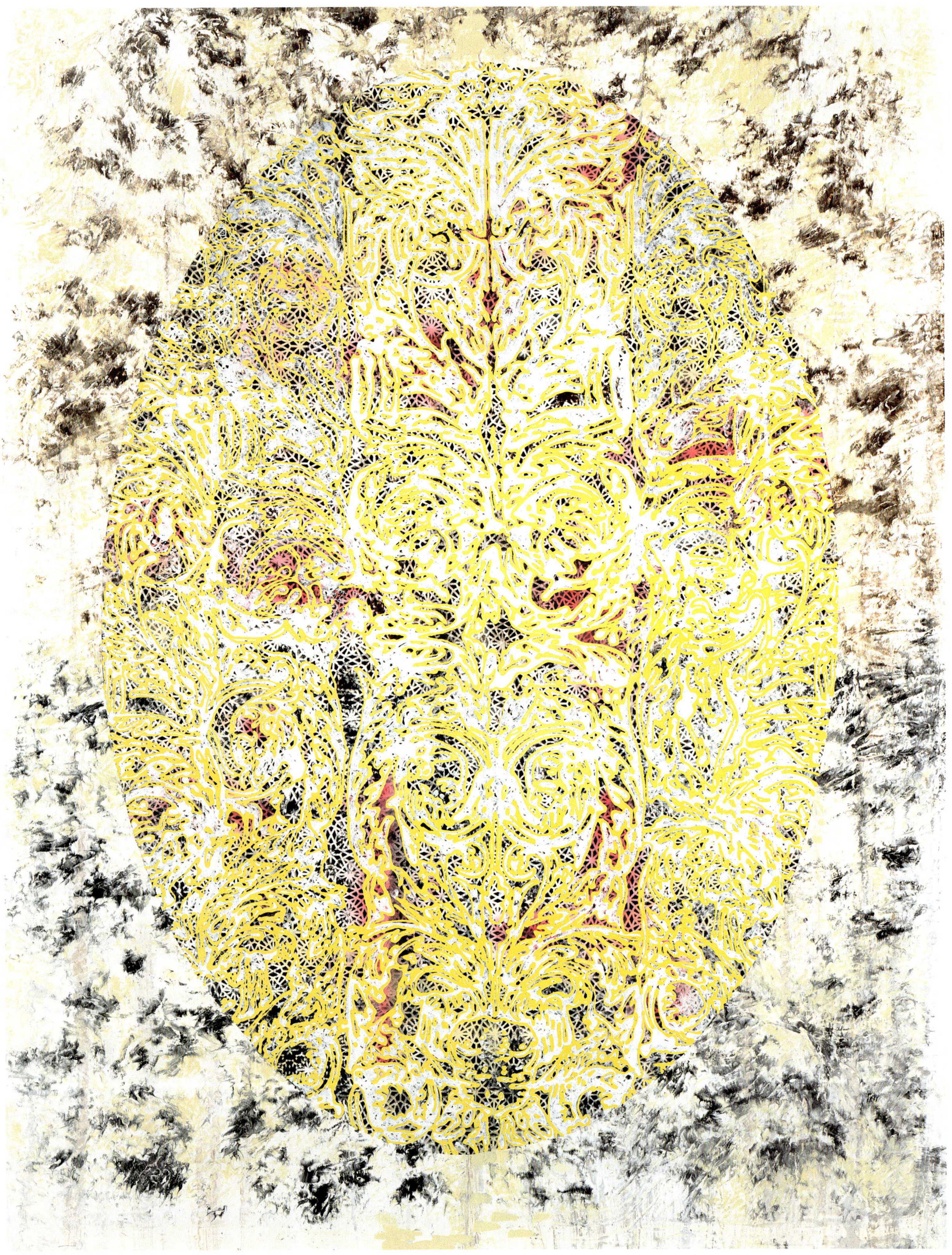

peeling

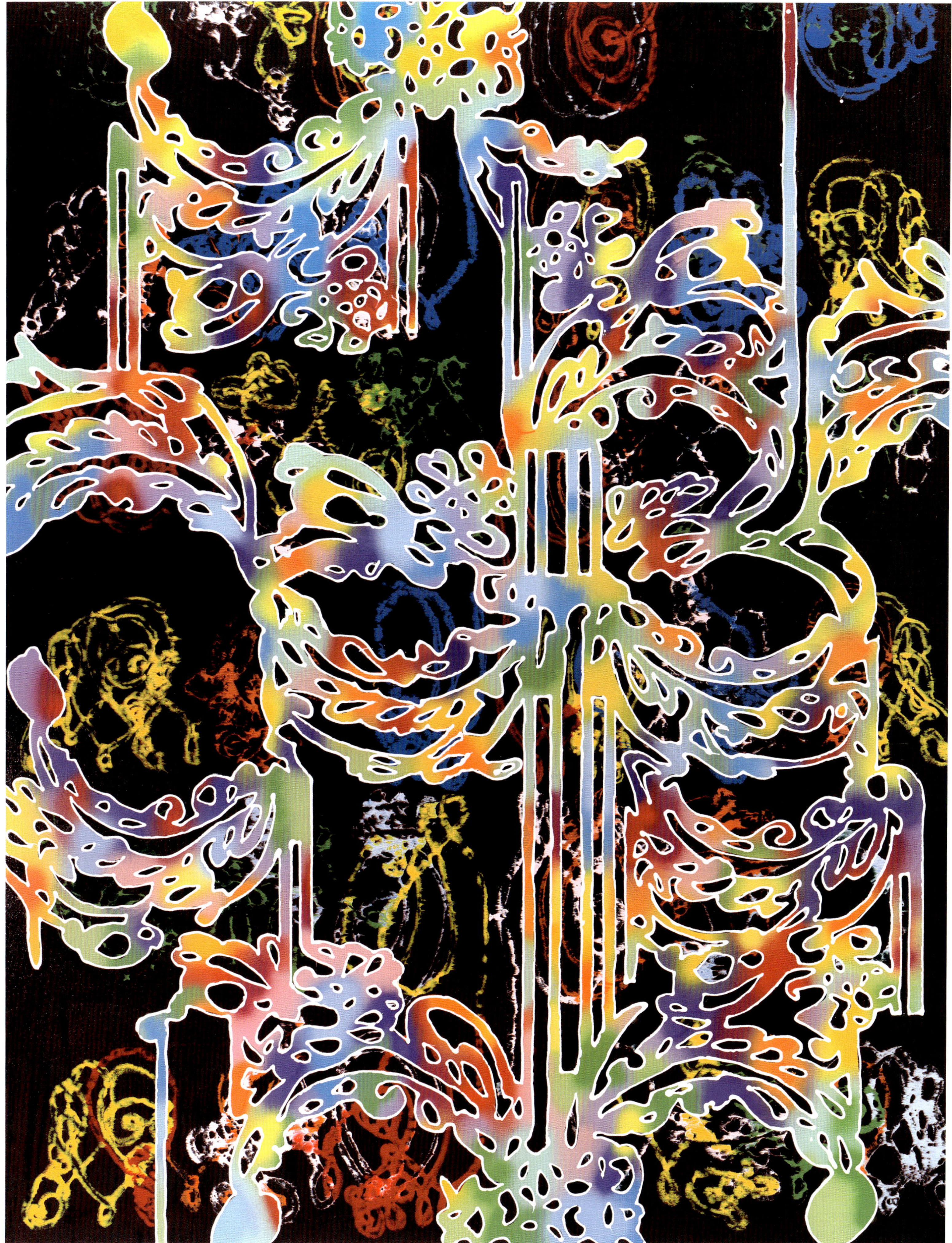

j´ai besoin de

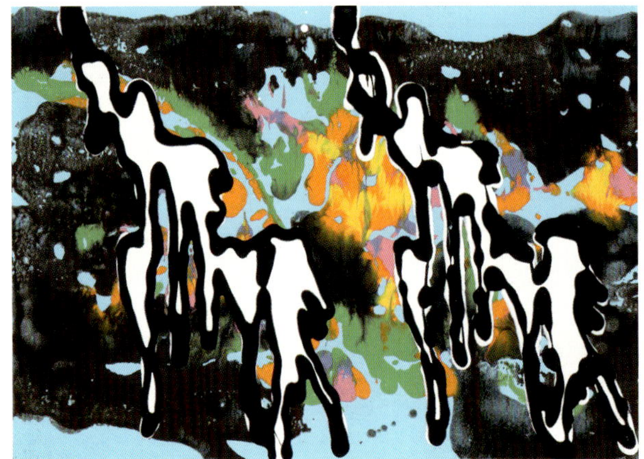

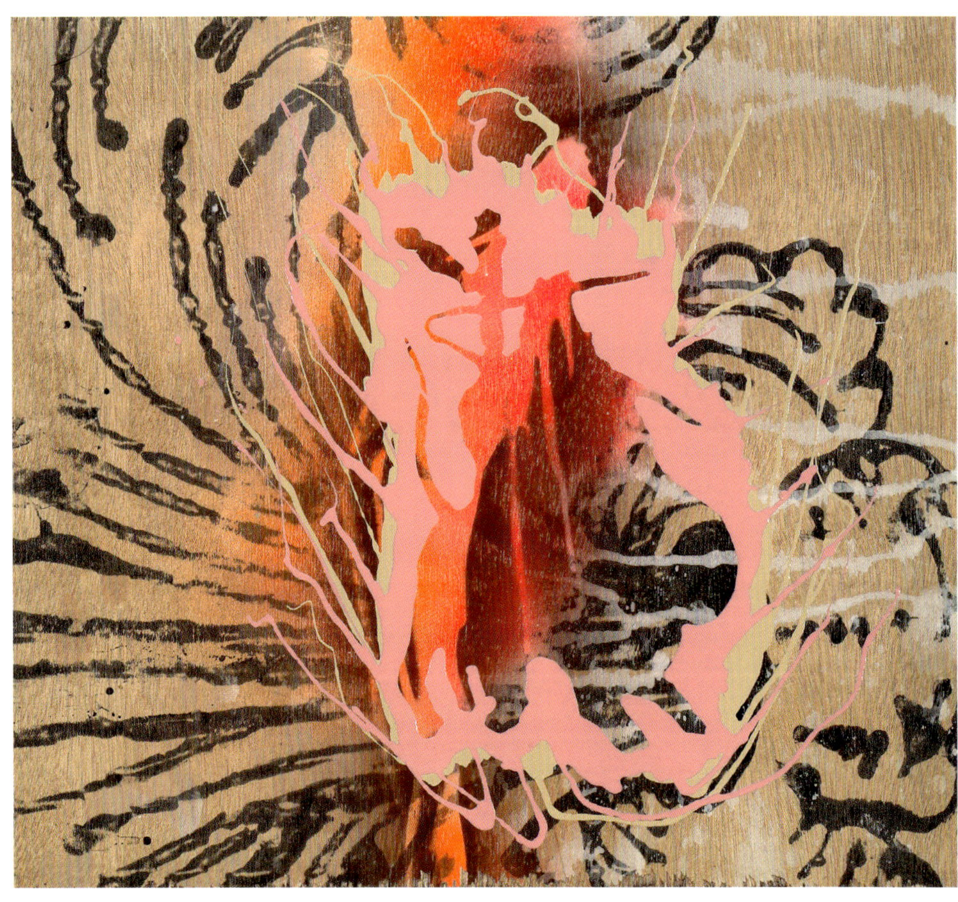

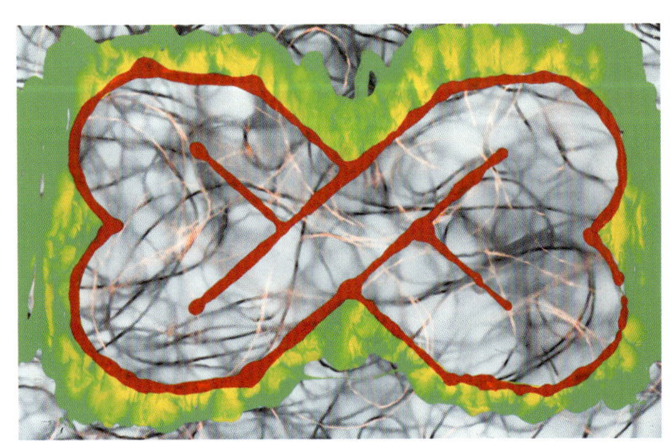

> automatische Scheibenwischer
< domestic 1
> einsamer Reiter
< nein, nie

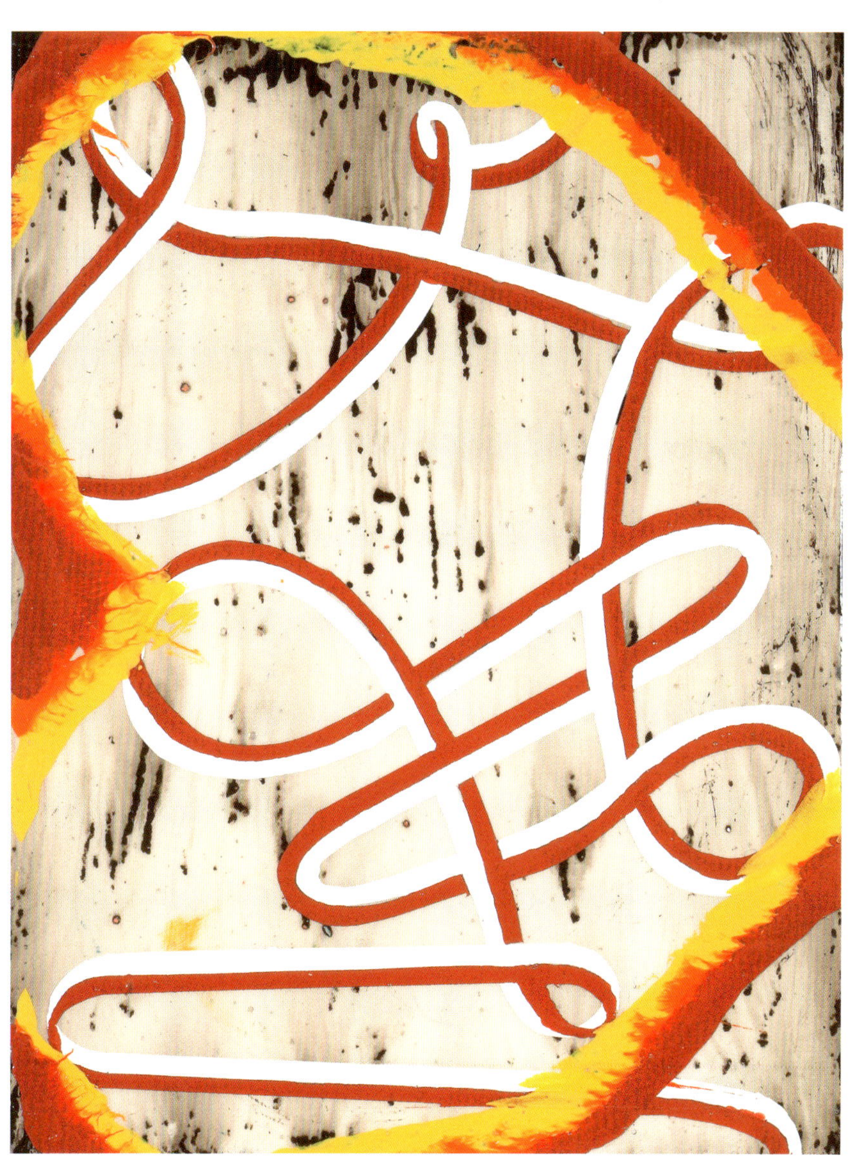

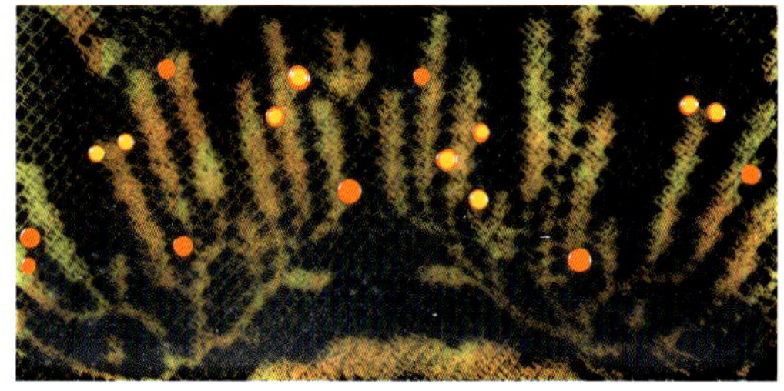

> Herzblut
< Nachtschattengewächs 1

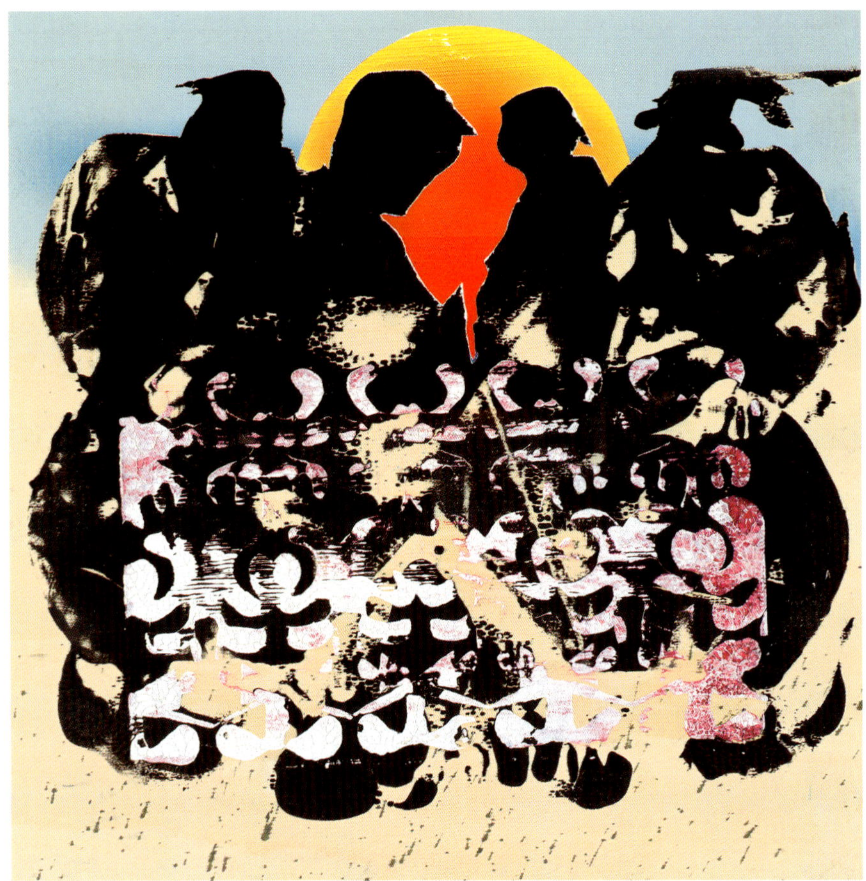

Romanze *war eines der ersten kleineren Bilder, das Christine in den Ateliers Höherweg 271 in Düsseldorf malte, und es hing dort während ihres Gastaufenthaltes an der Wand. Nach ihren eigenen Worten war es ein »Begleiter« dieser Zeit.*

Das Bild setzt sich aus verschiedenen Farbmaterialien auf einem ungrundierten, quadratischen Stück Sperrholz zusammen, das ein Fundstück ist. Zentral ist auf den Bildträger in braunem Lack ein Abdruck einer selbstentworfenen Schablone gesetzt. Dieser ist sowohl Idee als auch Ursprung der weiteren Malerei. In diesem Akt liegt ein Zufall, der bildbestimmend wird. Ausgehend von dem Abdruck in der Mitte, ist in der oberen Hälfte ein Sonnenuntergang dargestellt, vor dem zwei Figuren als Silhouetten erscheinen. Aufgrund ihrer unterschiedlichen Größe wirken diese räumlich voneinander entfernt, somit isoliert und gehören doch zusammen. Während die Malerei in der oberen Hälfte in einer Darstellung mündet, bleibt sie unten fragmentarisch und überzieht die Oberfläche mit Spritzern, die in das Sperrholz eingezogen sind. Bedeckt wird die untere Hälfte zusätzlich von einem rosa-weißen Abdruck in Öl, der wie eine Arabeske erscheint.

Demgegenüber deckt die Darstellung oben den Bildträger ab: braune Silhouetten in Lack vor einer strahlend gelb-orangefarbenen Sonne in Acryl und Spraylack, in einem blauen Himmel in Acryl. Die Sonnenuntergangsszene spielt mit dem Kitsch, mit einem gängigen bildlichen Klischee einer Romanze und dem ihr inhärenten Sehnsuchtsmotiv. Das Bild ist gekennzeichnet von einer Spannung zwischen Darstellung und Abstraktion, zwischen malerischer Illusion und malerischer Präsenz. Es hat das Atelier verlassen und ist nun mein »Begleiter« geworden.

Deniz Pekerman

Romanze *was one of the first smaller paintings which Christine produced during her guest sojourn in the Düsseldorf studios on Höherweg 271, where she hung it on the wall. As she said herself, in those days the painting was her "companion".*

The painting consists of different colour materials on an ungrounded square piece of plywood which she found. In the centre of this she positioned a brown enamel print using a stencil which she designed herself. This print is both the idea and the origin of the rest of the painting. The act involved an element of change that determined the painting. Starting with the print in the centre, she then went on to paint, in the upper half of the work, a sunset in front of which are the silhouettes of two figures. Although they seem, given their different sizes, to be spatially separated and thus isolated, they still belong together. Whereas the painting in the upper part of the work is representational, it remains fragmentary in the lower part; the surface is covered with splashes that have seeped into the plywood. The lower part is also covered with a pinkish-white oil print similar to an arabesque.

By contrast, the representation above covers the whole carrier: brown silhouettes in front of a glowing yellowish-orange sun painted in acrylic and spray paint in a blue acrylic sky. This sunset scene plays on the traditional kitschy cliché of a romance with its inherent motif of longing. The painting comprises a manifest tension between representation and abstraction, between painterly illusion and painterly presence. It left the studio and has now become my "companion".

Deniz Pekerman

Translation: Pauline Cumbers

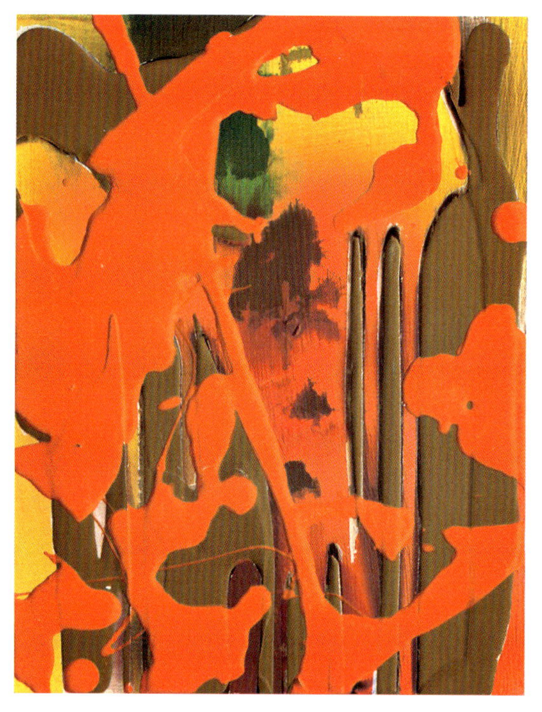

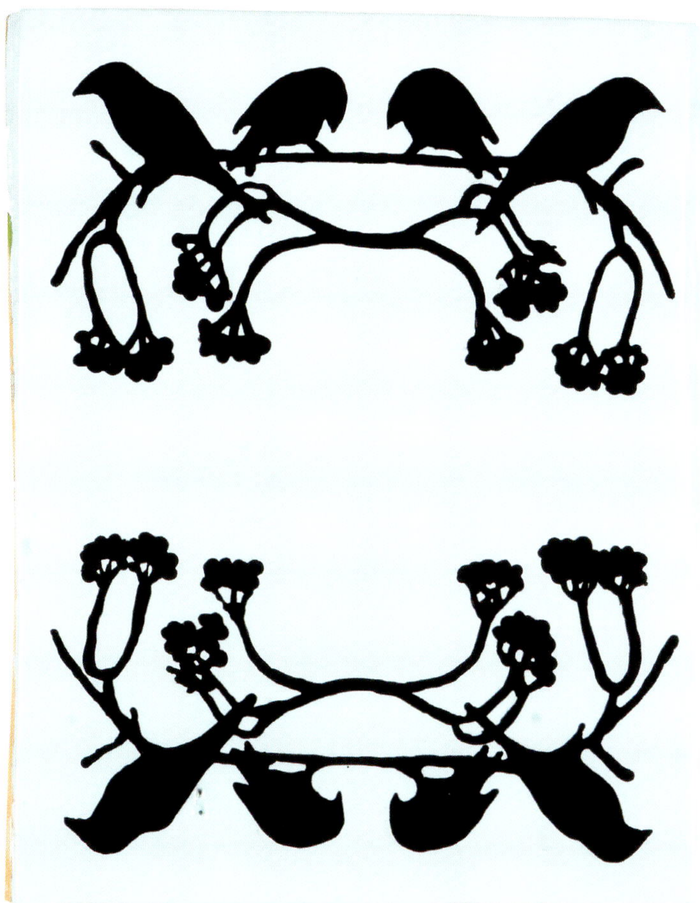

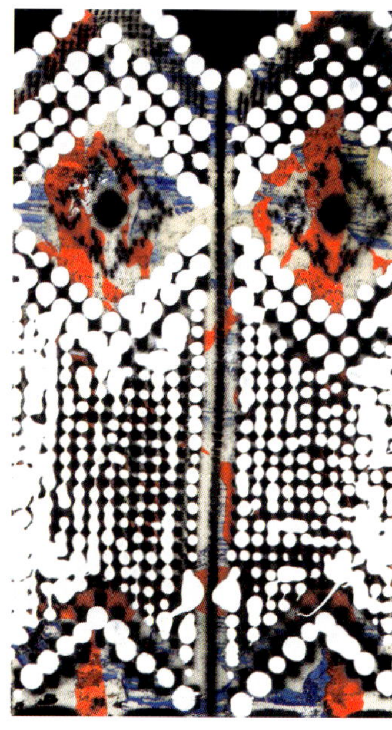

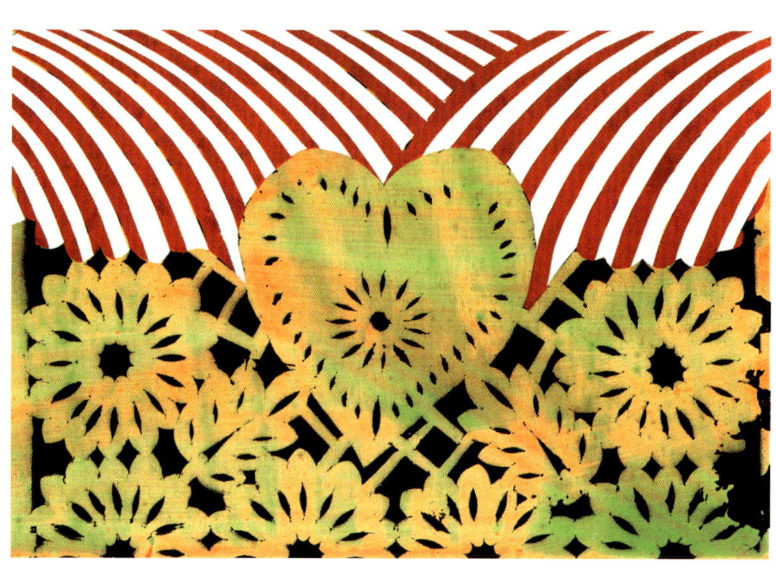

> sunset
< Tollkirschen
> northface
< Herzchen

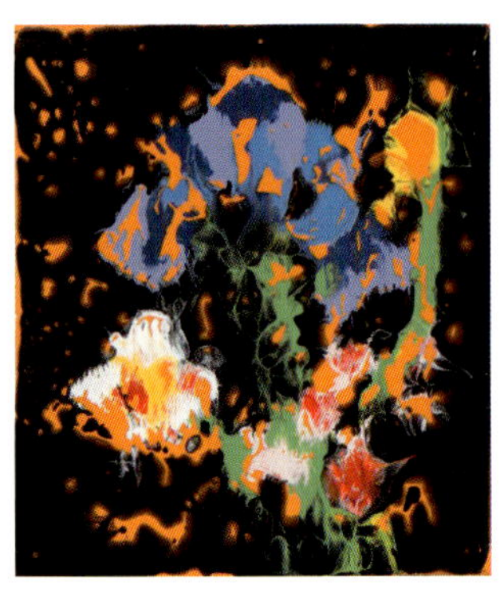

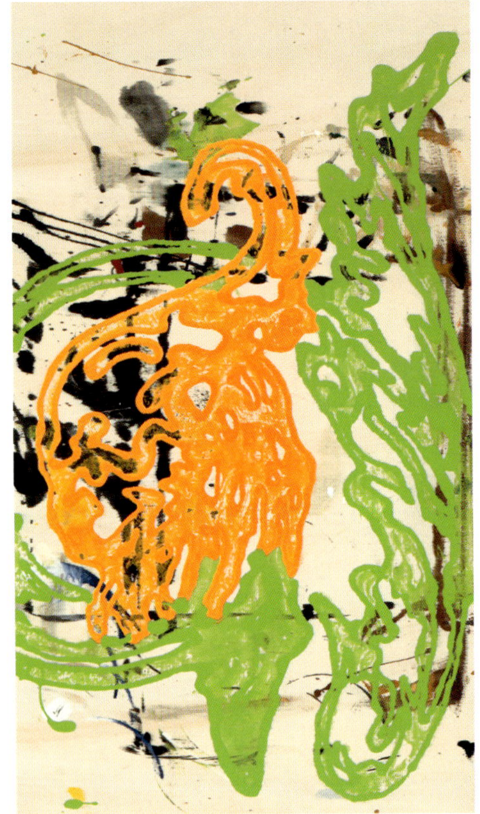

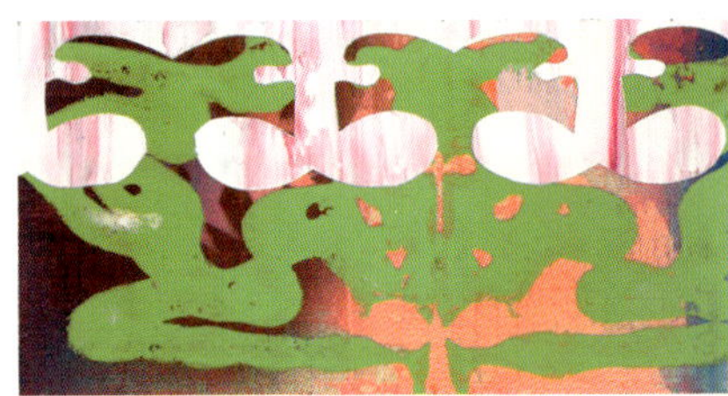

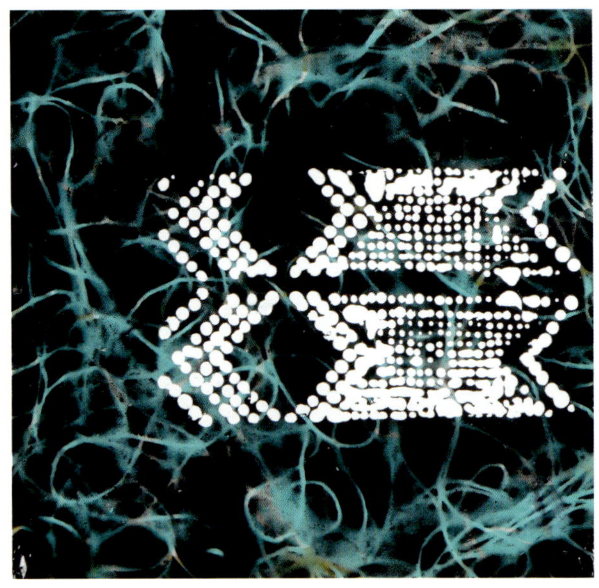

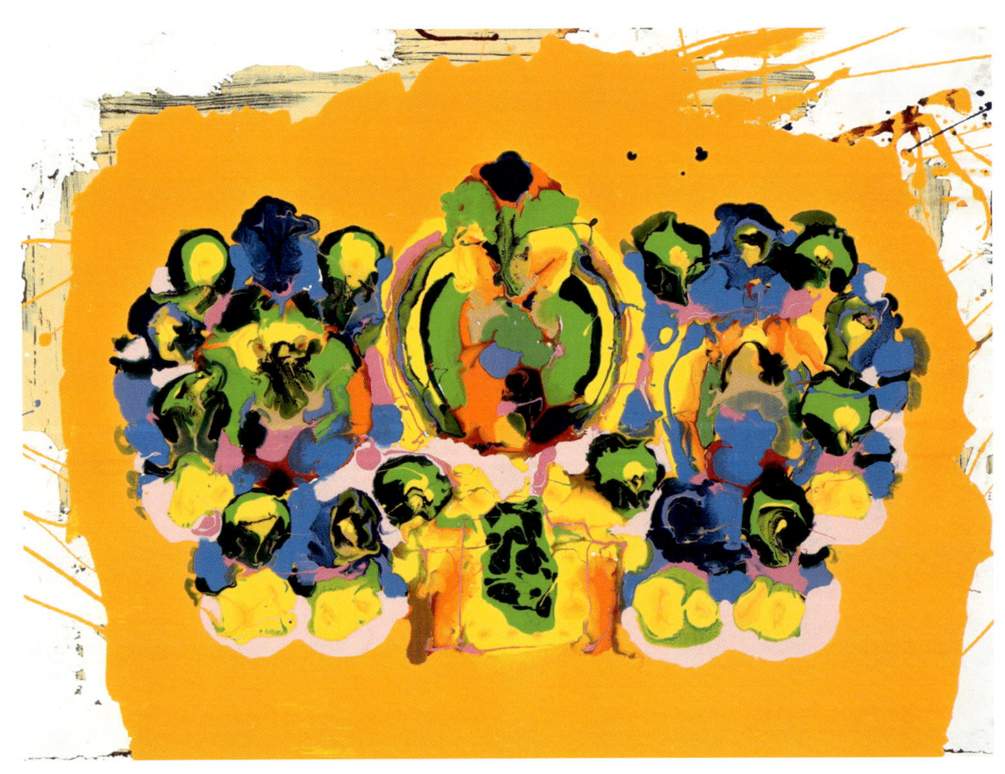

> Feuerfarbige 2
< Leo 1
< Flora und Fauna
> Skuo
< Hummel

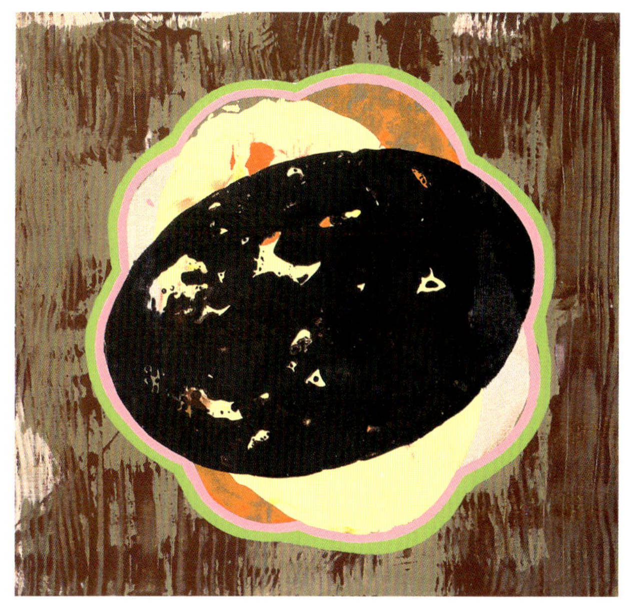

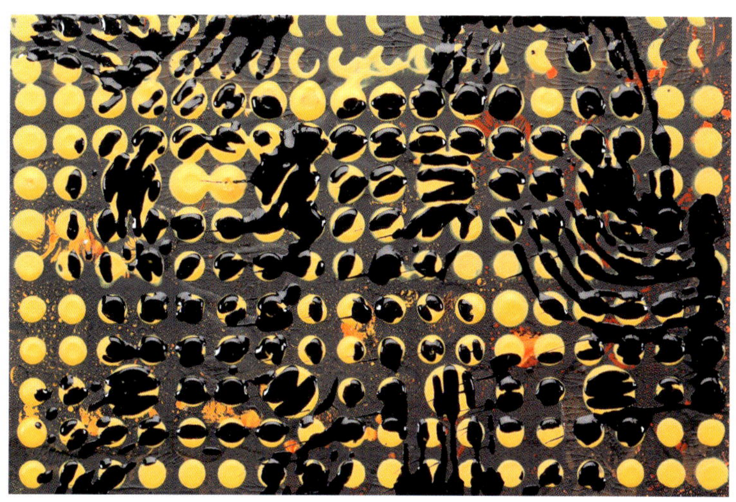

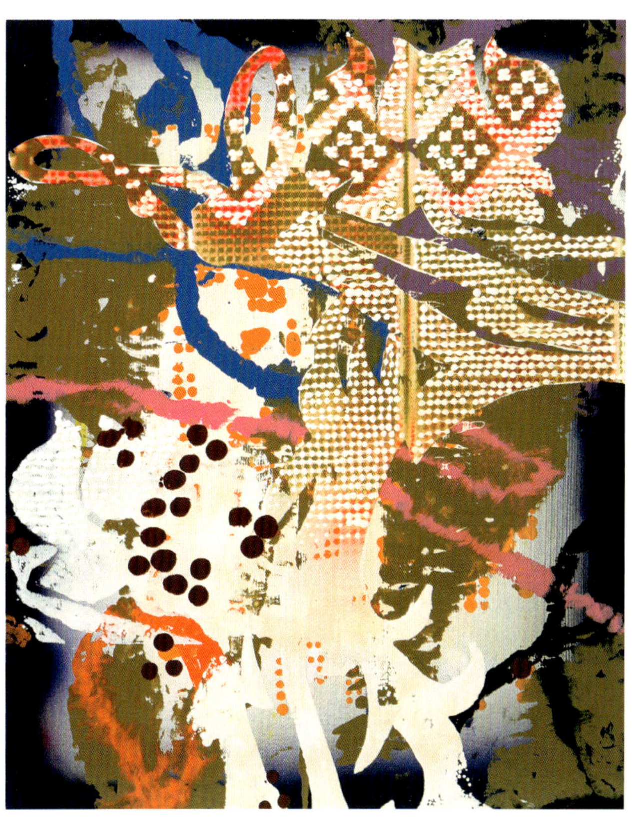

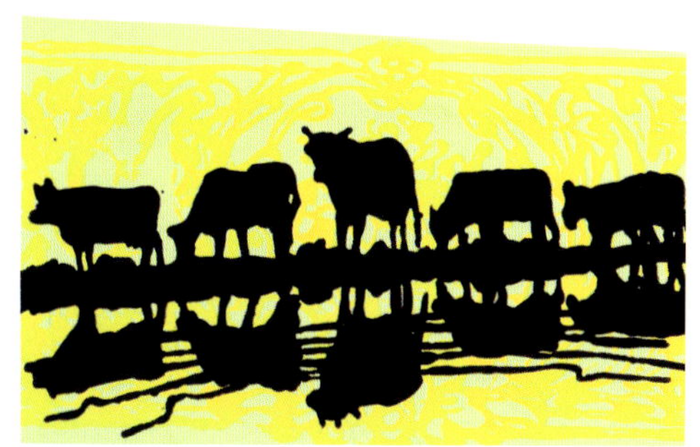

< 1 Mondjahr
> nonstopraining
< Taucher
> Dämmerung

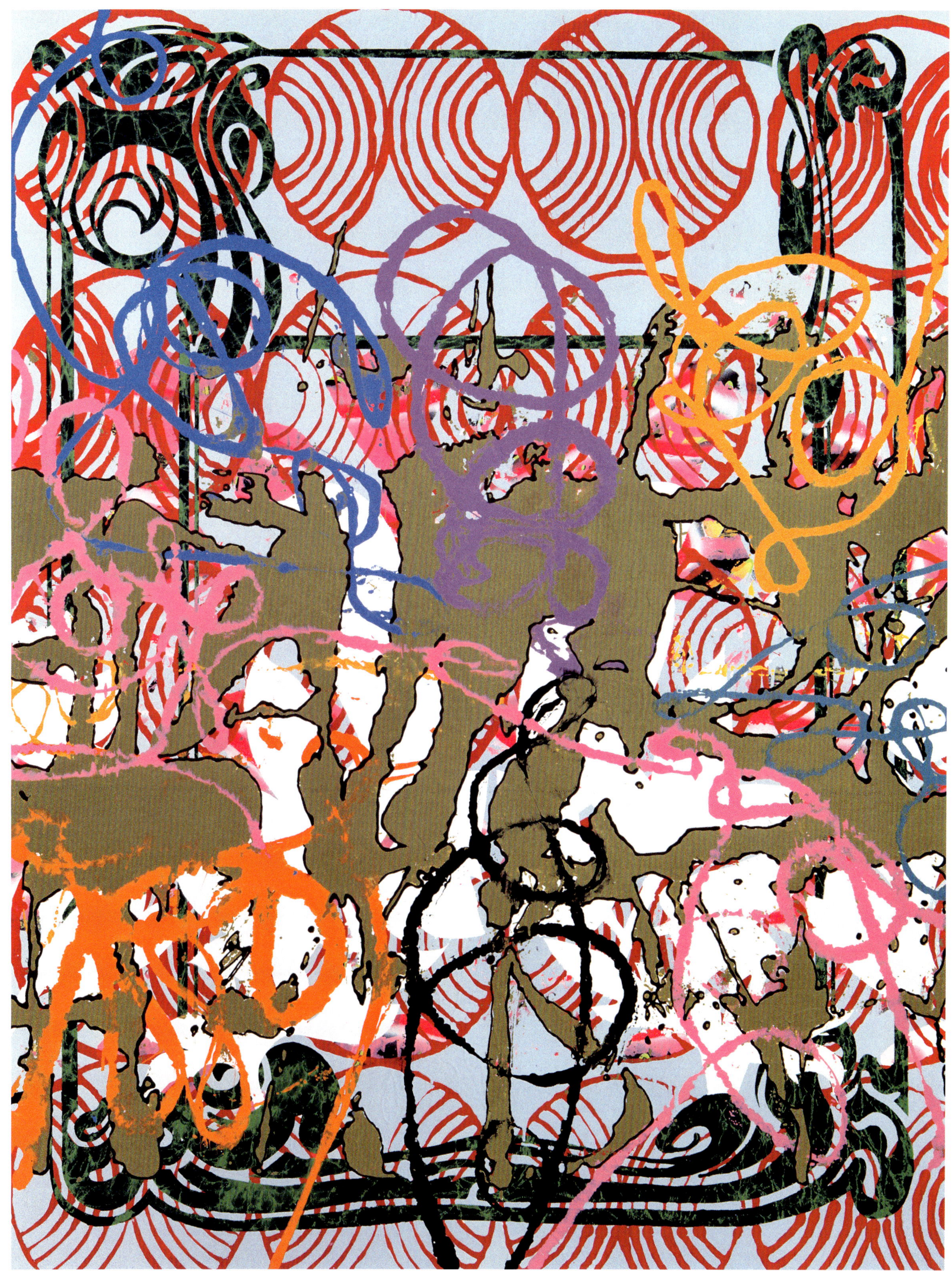

make me change my mind

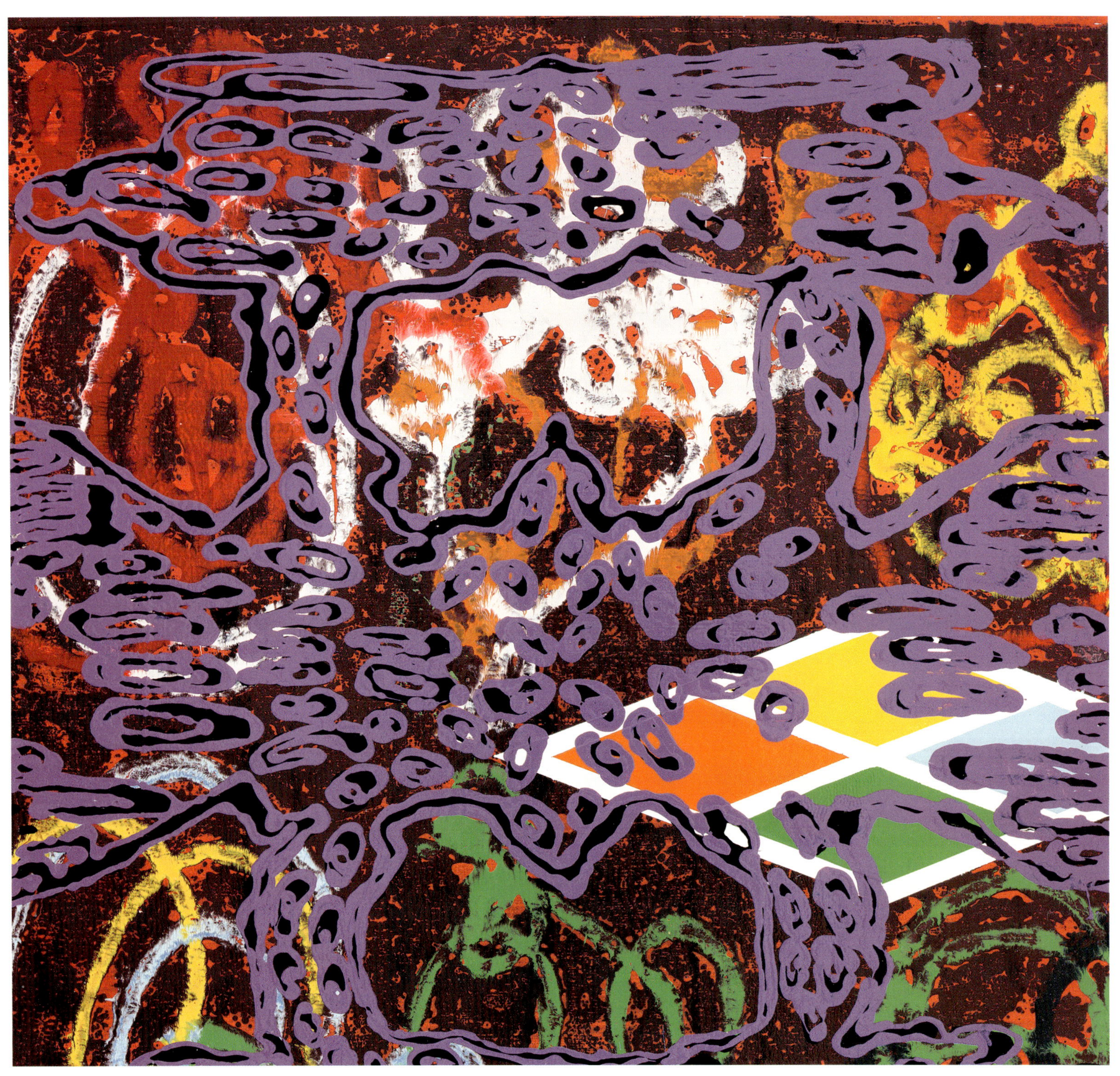

shelter

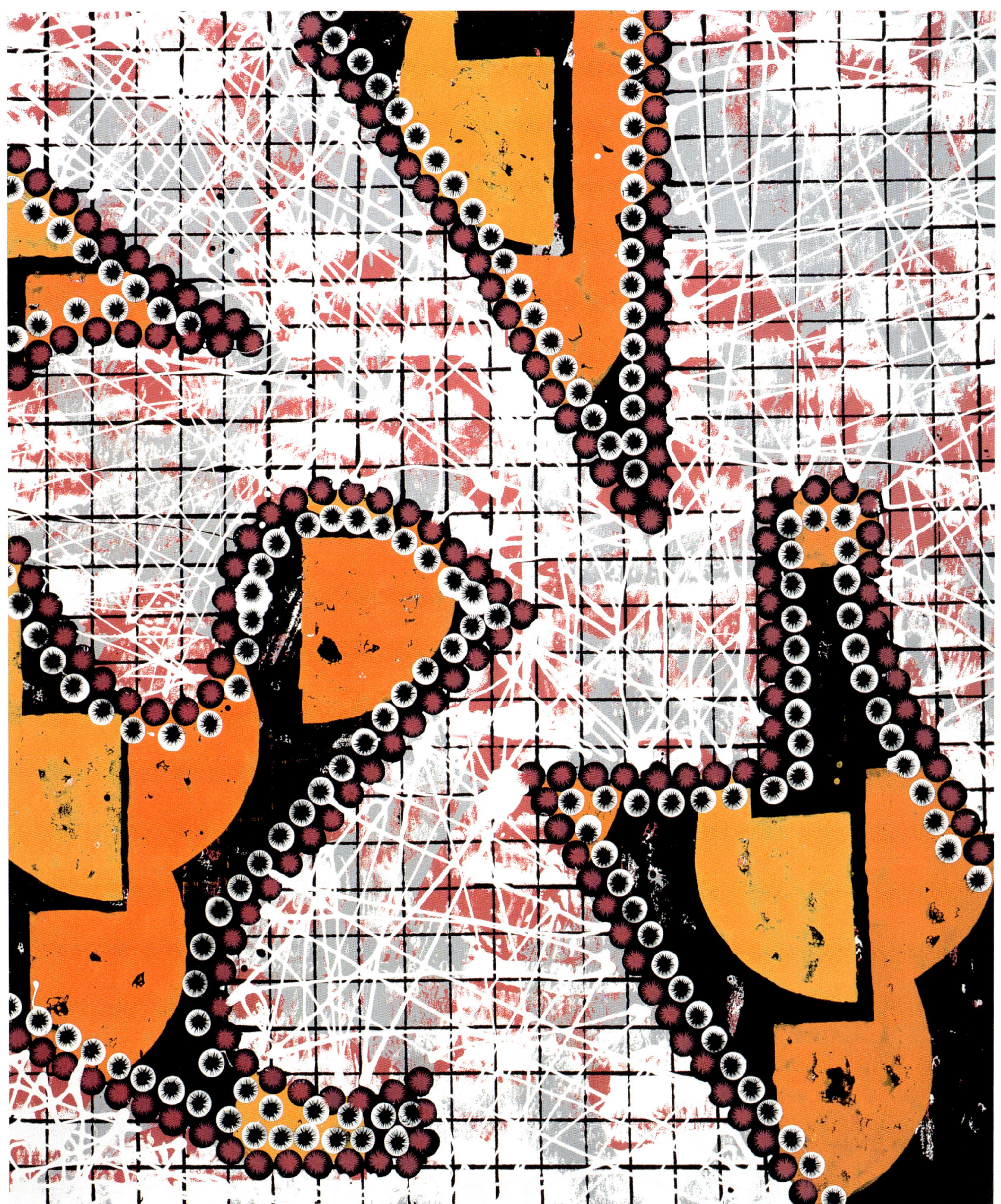

frozen for now

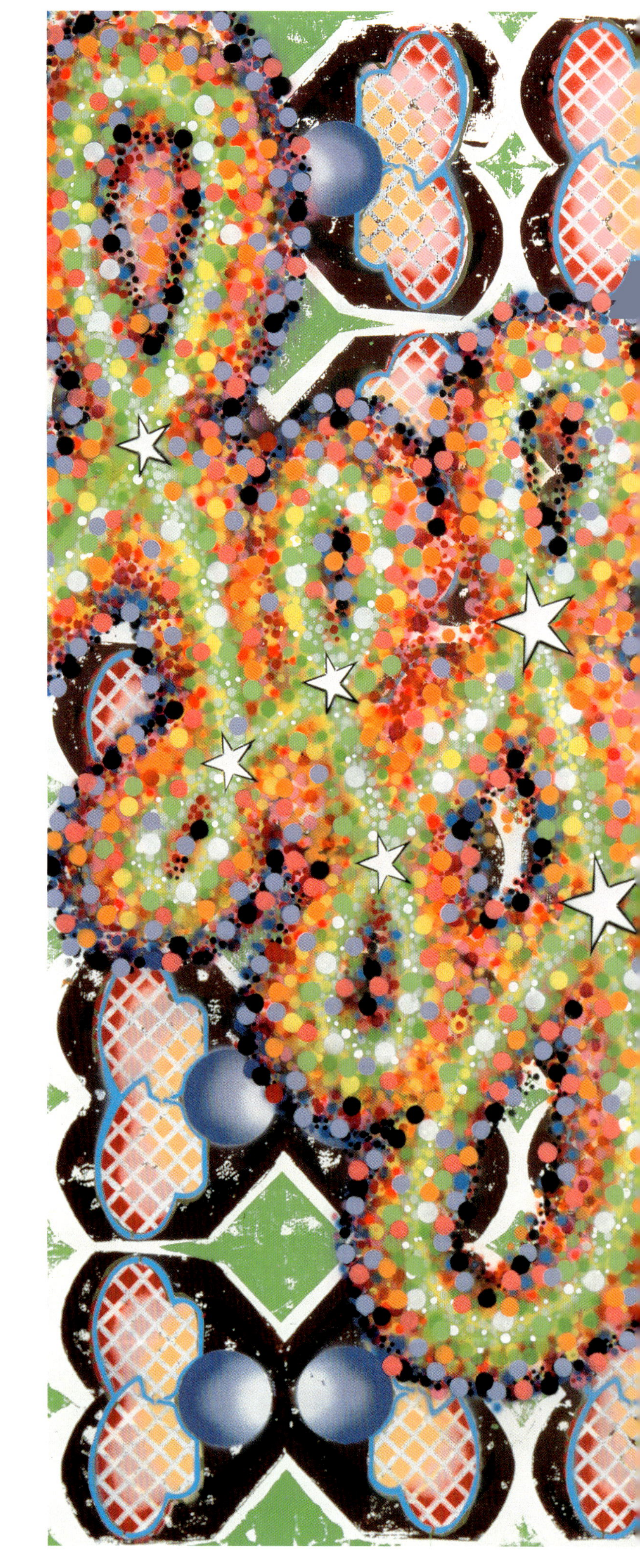

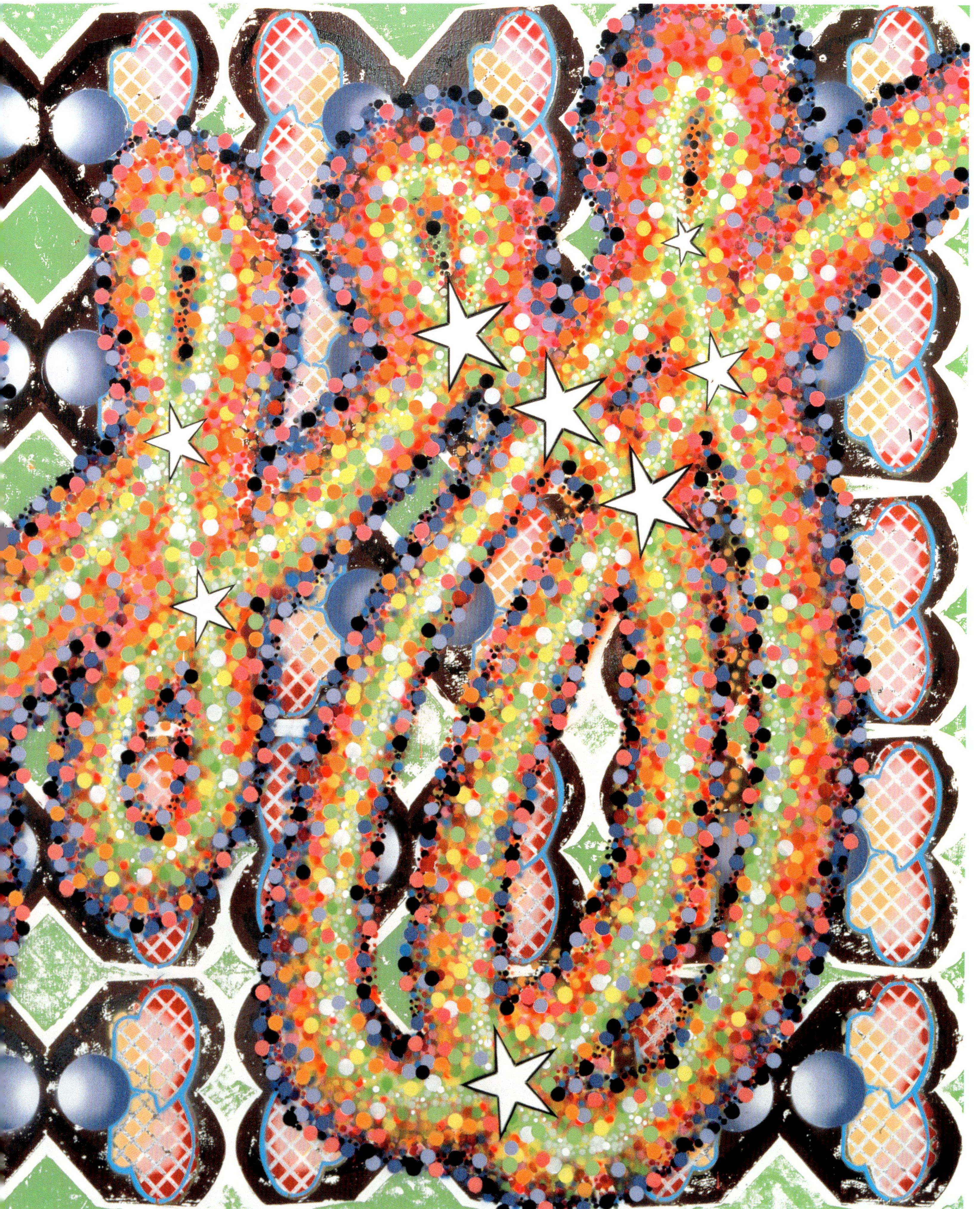

Falter

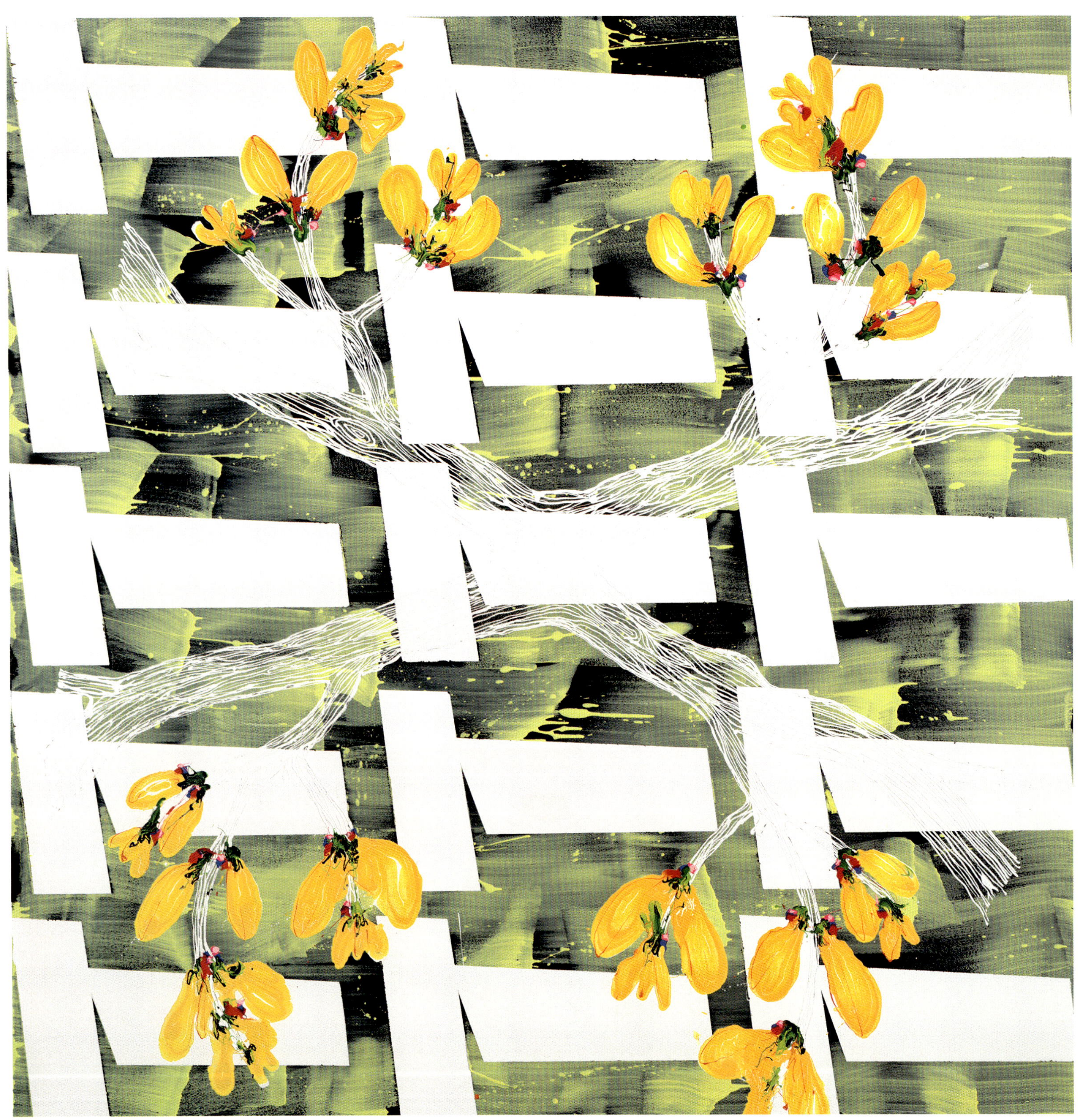

Zitterlein

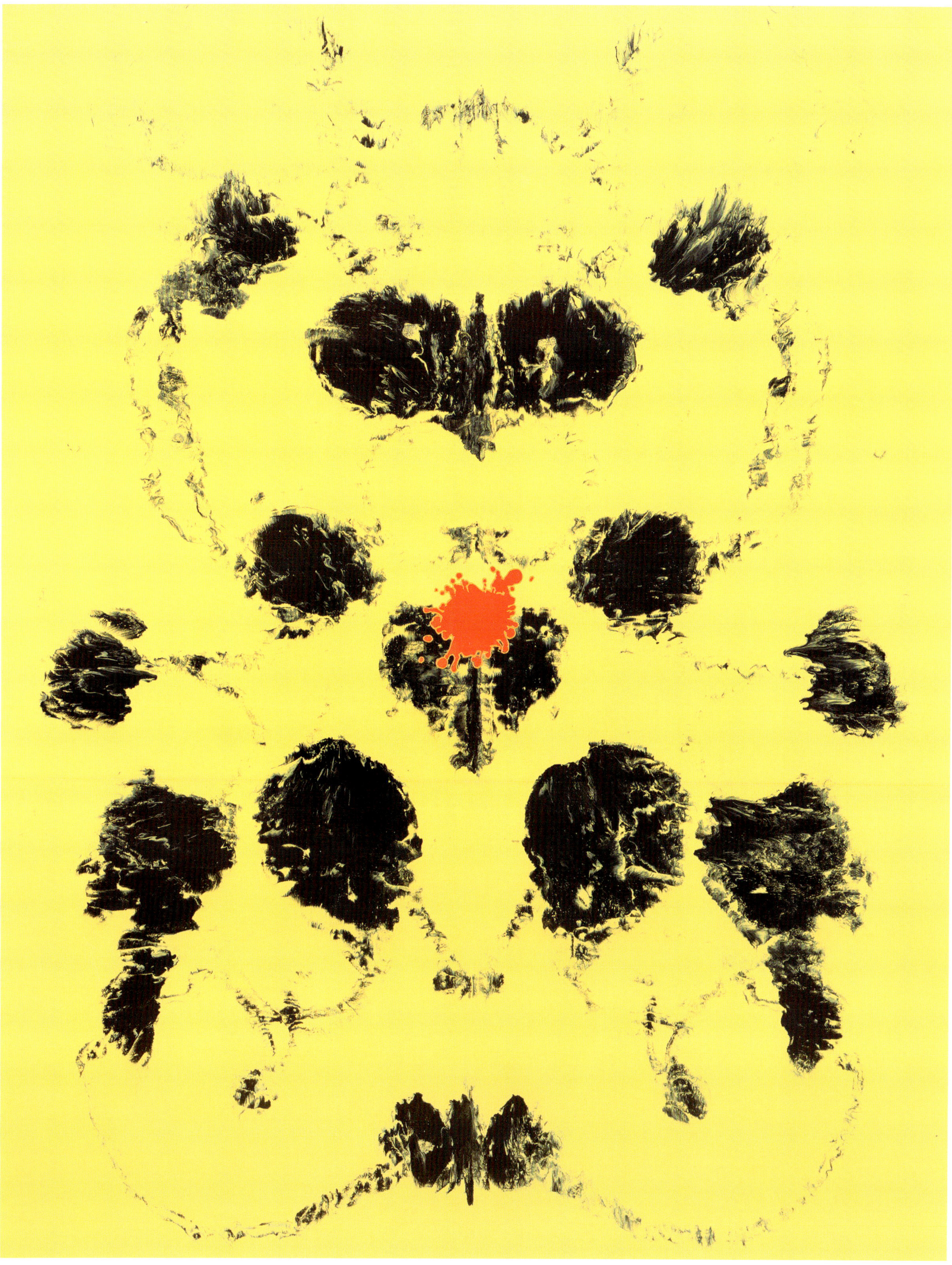

Bär

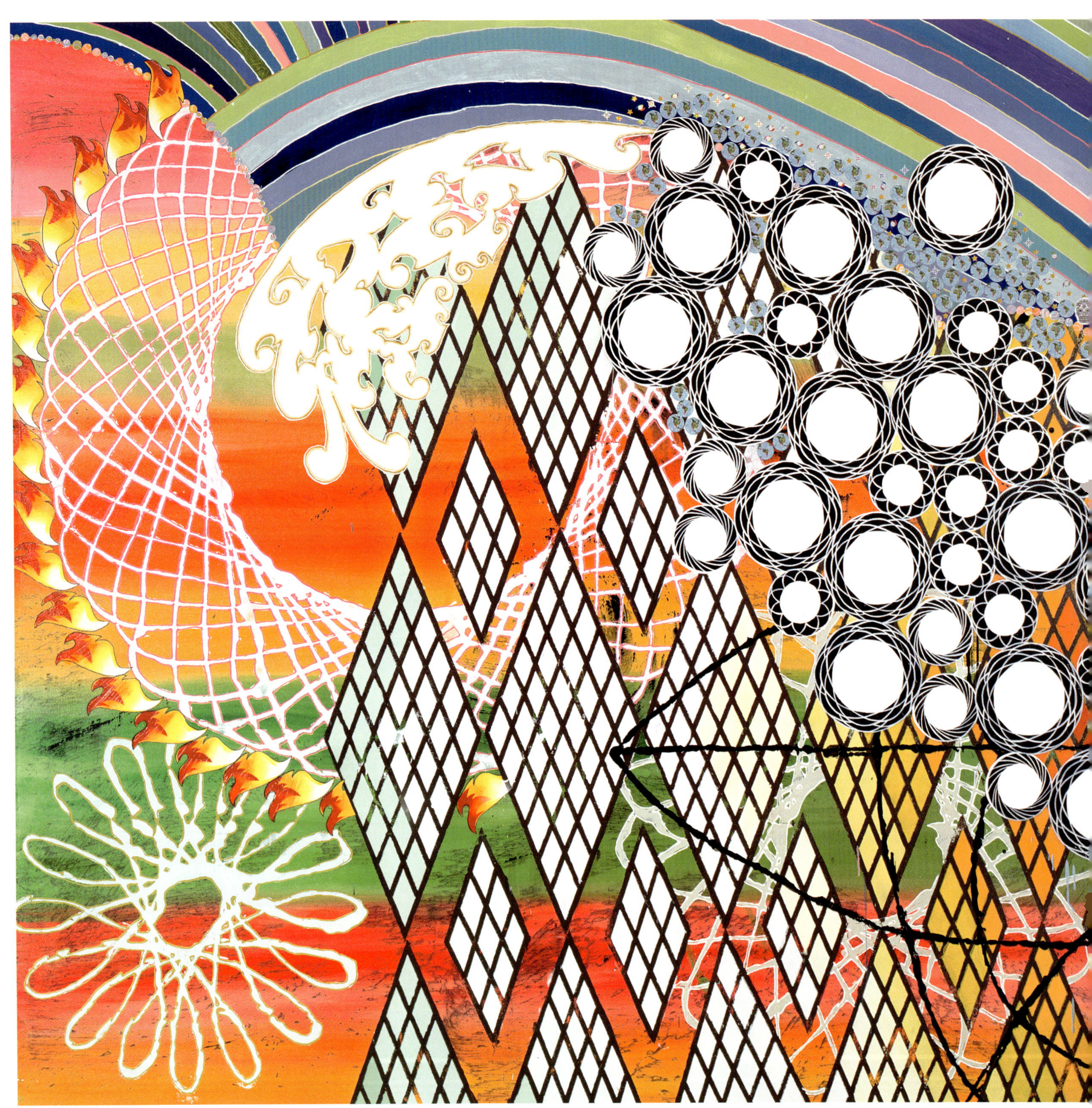

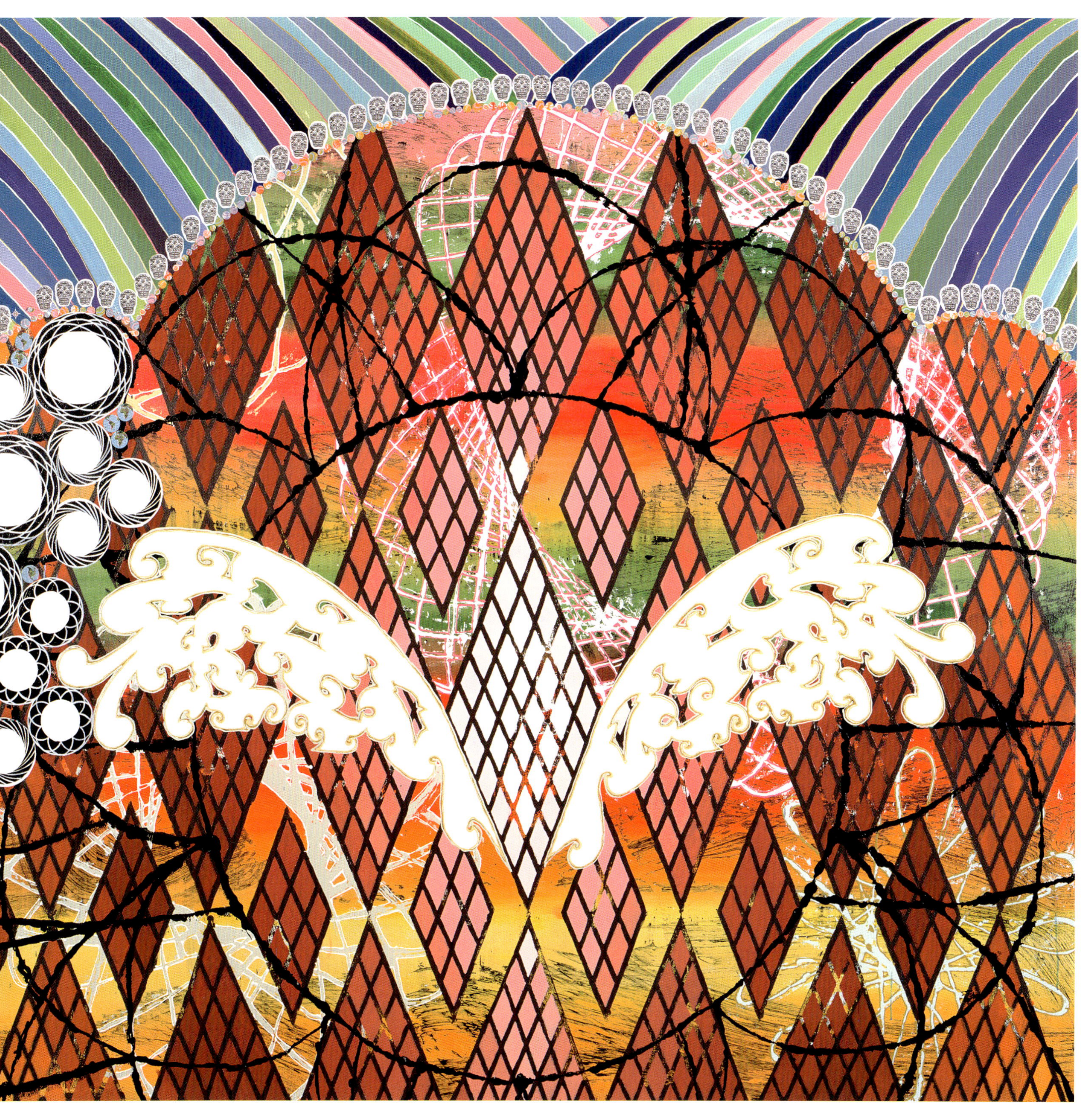

horizon takes me 2

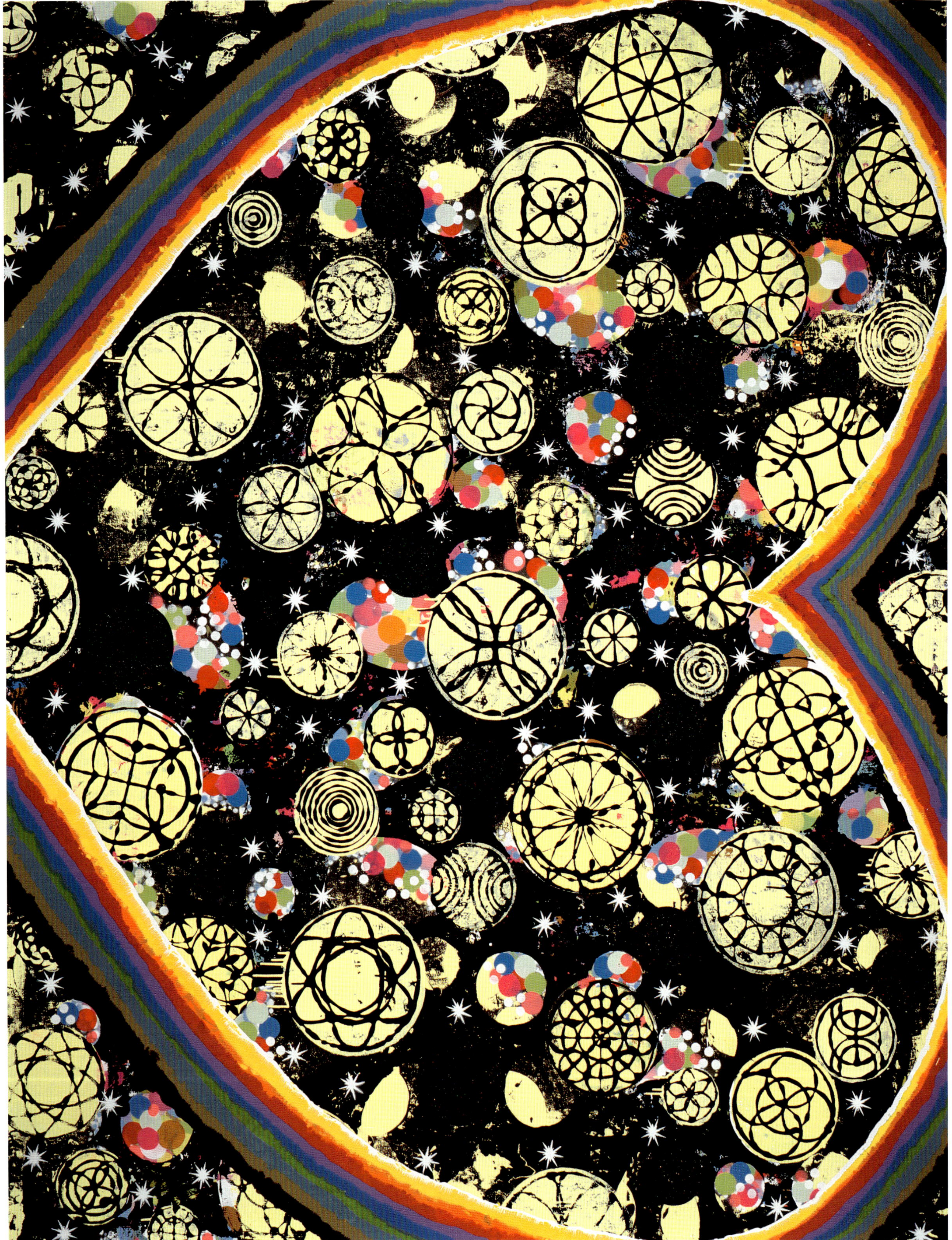

dicht dran

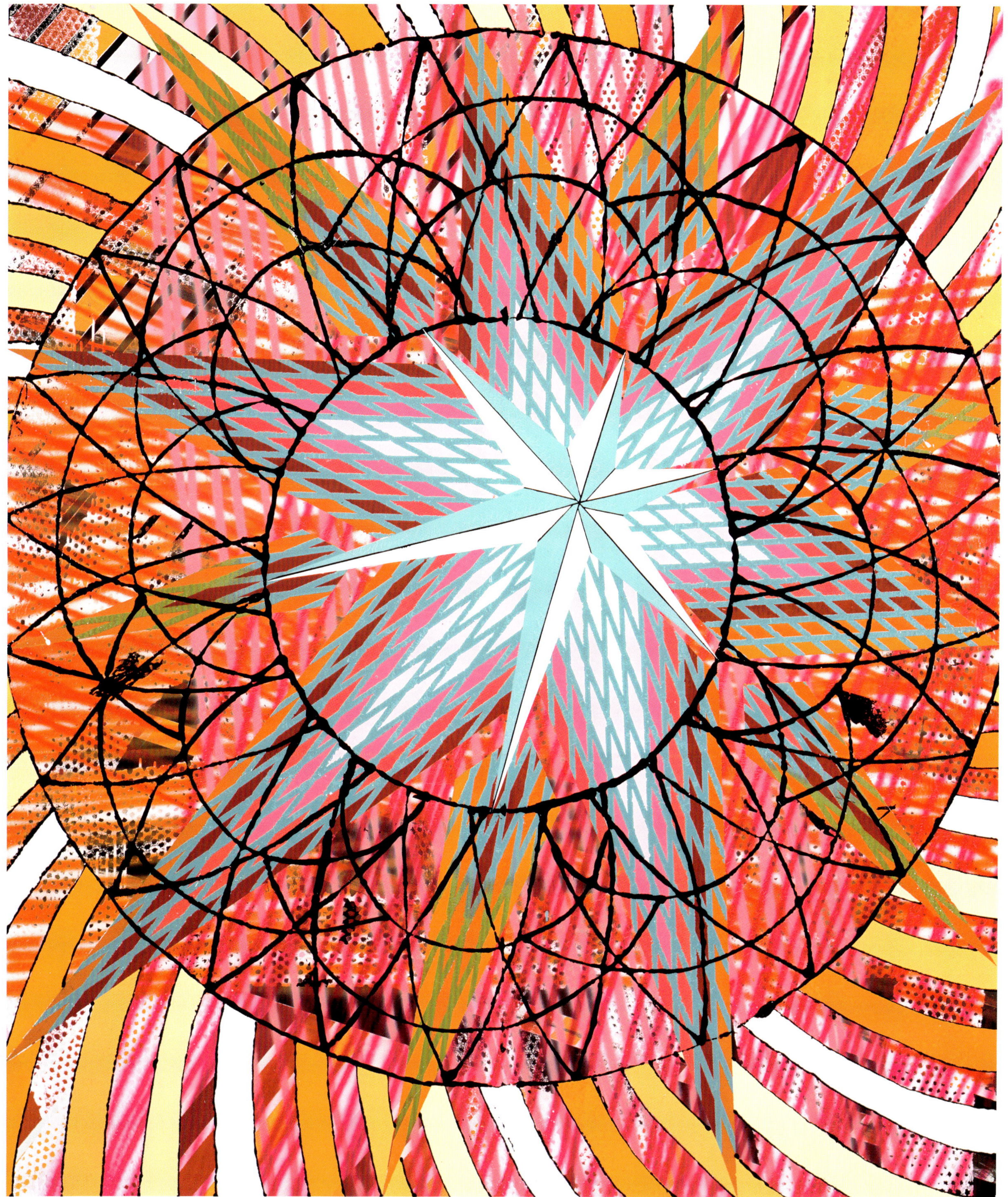

Alpha